AF555997

EFFECTIVE IMPLEMENTATION IN BUSINESS DEAL MAKING

EFFECTIVE IMPLEMENTATION IN BUSINESS DEAL MAKING

Dr. Chandrama Singh

RANDOM PUBLICATIONS

NEW DELHI - 110 002 (INDIA)

Effective Implementation in Business Deal Making

ISBN 978-93-51117-14-8

Published in 2015 in India by

RANDOM PUBLICATIONS

4376-A/4B, Gali Murari Lal, Ansari Road
New Delhi-110 002
Phone: +9111-43580356, 23289044
E-mail: randomexports@gmail.com; sales@randompublications.com; info@randompublications.com

Reprinted 2025

Type Setting by: Friends Media, Delhi-110089
Printed at : Replika Press Pvt. Ltd.

Preface

The most important external variable to the success of your business is whether or not you had great parents. But you can't do anything about that. Having the right deals in place, at the right times. No one has the team, the resources and the reach to succeed by themselves. Well-constructed partnerships, carefully-structured joint ventures, and timely endorsements help a start-up build its brand, credibility, momentum and customer base. Mergers & Acquisitions (M&A) is undergoing a profound transformation. From start to finish, the deal-making process is changing as a new wave of disruptive technologies—social media and advanced analytic tools—infuse themselves into both our business and our personal lives. How technology may be used is not normally clear, but what is clear is that it is here to stay. No business executive can afford to ignore the question of how to leverage these technologies to create competitive advantage.

People hear the words "business deal" and tend to think of some scene where a guy gets into a Rolls Royce, exchanges a few words with another guy in dark suit, and then hops out at his mansion and carries on with his business. The truth is, a business deal isn't always that pretty. In fact, it can be quite costly and harmful to your business if you fail to go about it correctly. Here are a few insights that you may find useful when setting up a business deal. Right off the bat – choose your partners wisely. This is essential if you want to give your business a fighting chance. Business is human and humans can make or break your business. When you go to make a business deal with potential partners, make sure you put in the time to do a little background research on them first. New technologies are proliferating, and deal professionals are taking note. Many are using cutting-edge tools to gain visibility into acquisition targets, negotiate deal terms, and smooth the integration process. While there's no substitute for on-the-ground due diligence and live meetings, it's becoming increasingly imperative for deal professionals to think creatively about how these emerging concepts could enhance their evaluation and pricing of a target and give them an edge. Getting deals done efficiently yet prudently is an elusive goal for many corporate development teams. One-third of respondents indicate that six or more executives or committees must approve a transaction before it is completed; 15% must pass it by 10 or more. Unfortunately, bottlenecks and back-channel dealings can still paralyze the process. To avoid a "Keystone Cops" situation, it is advisable to specifically define the deal process and to align decision-making with the process. One success factor that is often overlooked is the role that qualitative aspects like culture and judgement play in M&A decisions. It is essential to make sure that "org charts" are not driving the process, but rather that the people involved—from the most junior to the most senior—are truly equipped for the tasks that are set before them. Roughly two-thirds of executives feel that these investment vehicles provide a competitive advantage, with access to new technology and new product innovation rising to the top of the list of benefits. About half expect to see more of these funds launched within their industries, particularly as this style of investing pushes beyond the traditional spaces of technology and life sciences and into new industries such as consumer products and basic manufacturing. While financial return is important, corporate development professionals are in a good position to lead the charge and make sure that venture investments align with corporate strategy and are consistent with other types of inorganic growth.

This book is primarily a textbook targeted to students taking negotiation courses. It is designed to introduce the students to the multiple dimensions of deal making.

I thank all members of my team who have helped in the preparation of the book. My special thanks go to "Random Publications" who have published the book.

— *Dr. Chandrama Singh*

Contents

Chapter 1

Mergers and Acquisition

Introduction

An entrepreneur may grow its business either by internal expansion or by external expansion. In the case of internal expansion, a firm grows gradually over time in the normal course of the business, through acquisition of new assets, replacement of the technologically obsolete equipments and the establishment of new lines of products. But in external expansion, a firm acquires a running business and grows overnight through corporate combinations.

These combinations are in the form of mergers, acquisitions, amalgamations and takeovers and have now become important features of corporate restructuring. They have been playing an important role in the external growth of a number of leading companies the world over. They have become popular because of the enhanced competition, breaking of trade barriers, free flow of capital across countries and globalisation of businesses. In the wake of economic reforms, Indian industries have also started restructuring their operations around their core business activities through acquisition and takeovers because of their increasing exposure to competition both domestically and internationally.

Mergers and acquisitions are strategic decisions taken for maximisation of a company's growth by enhancing its production and marketing operations. They are being used in a wide array of fields such as information technology, telecommunications, and business process outsourcing as well as in traditional businesses in order to gain strength, expand the customer base, cut competition or enter into a new market or product segment.

Mergers or Amalgamations

A merger is a combination of two or more businesses into one business. Laws in India use the term 'amalgamation' for merger. The Income Tax Act,1961 [Section 2(1A)] defines amalgamation as the merger of one or more companies with another or the merger of two or more companies to form a new company, in such a way that all assets and liabilities of the amalgamating companies become assets and liabilities of the amalgamated company and shareholders not less than nine-tenths in value of the shares in the amalgamating company or companies become shareholders of the amalgamated company.

Thus, mergers or amalgamations may take two forms:-

- Merger through Absorption:- An absorption is a combination of two or more companies into an 'existing company'. All companies except one lose their identity in such a merger. For example, absorption of Tata Fertilizers Ltd (TFL) by Tata Chemicals Ltd. (TCL). TCL, an acquiring company (a buyer), survived after merger while TFL, an acquired company (a seller), ceased to exist. TFL transferred its assets, liabilities and shares to TCL.
- Merger through Consolidation:- A consolidation is a combination of two or more companies into a 'new company'. In this form of merger, all companies are legally dissolved and a new entity is created. Here, the acquired company transfers its assets, liabilities and shares to the acquiring company for cash or exchange of shares. For example, merger of Hindustan Computers Ltd, Hindustan Instruments Ltd, Indian Software Company Ltd and Indian Reprographics Ltd into an entirely new company called HCL Ltd.

A fundamental characteristic of merger (either through absorption or consolidation) is that the acquiring company (existing or new) takes over the ownership of other companies and combines their operations with its own operations.

Besides, there are three major types of mergers:-

- Horizontal merger:- is a combination of two or more firms in the same area of business. For example, combining of two book publishers or two luggage manufacturing companies to gain dominant market share.
- Vertical merger:- is a combination of two or more firms involved in different stages of production or distribution of the same product. For example, joining of a TV manufacturing (assembling) company and a TV marketing company or joining

of a spinning company and a weaving company. Vertical merger may take the form of forward or backward merger. When a company combines with the supplier of material, it is called backward merger and when it combines with the customer, it is known as forward merger.

- Conglomerate merger:- is a combination of firms engaged in unrelated lines of business activity. For example, merging of different businesses like manufacturing of cement products, fertilizer products, electronic products, insurance investment and advertising agencies. L&T and Voltas Ltd are examples of such mergers.

Acquisitions and Takeovers

An acquisition may be defined as an act of acquiring effective control by one company over assets or management of another company without any combination of companies.

Thus, in an acquisition two or more companies may remain independent, separate legal entities, but there may be a change in control of the companies. When an acquisition is 'forced' or 'unwilling', it is called a takeover. In an unwilling acquisition, the management of 'target' company would oppose a move of being taken over. But, when managements of acquiring and target companies mutually and willingly agree for the takeover, it is called acquisition or friendly takeover.

Under the Monopolies and Restrictive Practices Act, takeover meant acquisition of not less than 25 percent of the voting power in a company. While in the Companies Act (Section 372), a company's investment in the shares of another company in excess of 10 percent of the subscribed capital can result in takeovers. An acquisition or takeover does not necessarily entail full legal control. A company can also have effective control over another company by holding a minority ownership.

History of Mergers

History of Mergers and Acquisitions

Tracing back to history, merger and acquisitions have evolved in five stages and each of these are discussed here. As seen from past experience mergers and acquisitions are triggered by economic factors. The macroeconomic environment, which includes the growth in GDP, interest rates and monetary policies play a key role in designing the process of mergers or acquisitions between companies or organisations.

First Wave Mergers

The first wave mergers commenced from 1897 to 1904. During this phase merger occurred between companies, which enjoyed monopoly over their lines of production like railroads, electricity etc. the first wave mergers that occurred during the aforesaid time period were mostly horizontal mergers that took place between heavy manufacturing industries.

End of 1st Wave Merger

Majority of the mergers that were conceived during the 1st phase ended in failure since they could not achieve the desired efficiency. The failure was fuelled by the slowdown of the economy in 1903 followed by the stock market crash of 1904. The legal framework was not supportive either. The Supreme Court passed the mandate that the anticompetitive mergers could be halted using the Sherman Act.

Second Wave Mergers

The second wave mergers that took place from 1916 to 1929 focused on the mergers between oligopolies, rather than monopolies as in the previous phase. The economic boom that followed the post world war I gave rise to these mergers.

Technological developments like the development of railroads and transportation by motor vehicles provided the necessary infrastructure for such mergers or acquisitions to take place. The government policy encouraged firms to work in unison. This policy was implemented in the 1920s.

The 2nd wave mergers that took place were mainly horizontal or conglomerate in nature. Te industries that went for merger during this phase were producers of primary metals, food products, petroleum products, transportation equipments and chemicals. The investments banks played a pivotal role in facilitating the mergers and acquisitions.

End of 2nd Wave Mergers

The 2nd wave mergers ended with the stock market crash in 1929 and the great depression. The tax relief that was provided inspired mergers in the 1940s.

Third Wave Mergers

The mergers that took place during this period (1965-69) were mainly conglomerate mergers. Mergers were inspired by high stock prices, interest rates and strict enforcement of antitrust laws. The bidder firms in the 3rd wave merger were smaller than the Target

Firm. Mergers were financed from equities; the investment banks no longer played an important role.

End Of The 3rd Wave Merger

The 3rd wave merger ended with the plan of the Attorney General to split conglomerates in 1968. It was also due to the poor performance of the conglomerates. Some mergers in the 1970s have set precedence. The most prominent ones were the INCO-ESB merger; United Technologies and OTIS Elevator Merger are the merger between Colt Industries and Garlock Industries.

Fourth Wave Merger

The 4th wave merger that started from 1981 and ended by 1989 was characterized by acquisition targets that wren much larger in size as compared to the 3rd wave mergers. Mergers took place between the oil and gas industries, pharmaceutical industries, banking and airline industries. Foreign takeovers became common with most of them being hostile takeovers. The 4th Wave mergers ended with anti takeover laws, Financial Institutions Reform and the Gulf War.

Fifth Wave Merger

The 5th Wave Merger (1992-2000) was inspired by globalization, stock market boom and deregulation. The 5th Wave Merger took place mainly in the banking and telecommunications industries. They were mostly equity financed rather than debt financed. The mergers were driven long term rather than short term profit motives. The 5th Wave Merger ended with the burst in the stock market bubble.

Hence we may conclude that the evolution of mergers and acquisitions has been long drawn. Many economic factors have contributed its development. There are several other factors that have impeded their growth. As long as economic units of production exist mergers and acquisitions would continue for an ever-expanding economy.

Mergers and Acquisitions History

Most of the mergers and acquisitions are an outcome of the favourable economic factors like the macroeconomic setting, escalation in the GDP, higher interest rates and fiscal policies. These factors not only trigger the M & A process but also play an active role in laying the mergers and acquisition strategies between bidding and target firms.

The history of mergers and acquisitions can be traced back to the 19th century which has evolved in different phases mentioned as under:

From 1897 – 1904

During this period merger took place between the firms which were anti-competition and enjoyed their dominance in the market according to their productivity in sectors like electricity, railways, etc. Most of the mergers during this period were horizontal in nature and occurred between the steel, metal and construction industries.

From 1903 – 1905

Most of the mergers which took place during the first phase were considered as unsuccessful for not being efficient enough to attain the required competence. The crash was stimulated by the decelerating of the world's financial system in 1903, which was followed by a stock market collapse in 1904. During this phase the authorized structure was not encouraging either. Later the apex judiciary body issued its directive on the anti-competitive mergers stating that they could be de-merged by implementing the Sherman Act.

From 1916 – 1940

Unlike the preceding phase, this period concentrated on mergers between oligopolies, rather between anti-competitive firms. The mergers and acquisitions process was triggered by the financial boom which was seen after the World War I. The expansion further lead to developments in the fields of science and technology and the emergence of infrastructure firms which provided services for required growth in railroads and transportation by automobiles.

The government strategies laid in 1920s made the corporate ambiance supportive enough for firms to work in harmony. Financial institutions like government and private banks also played a significant part in aiding the mergers and acquisitions process.The mergers which occurred during 1916-1929 were horizontal or multinational in nature. Most of these industries were the manufacturers of metals, automobile tools, food commodities, chemicals, etc.

This phase ended in 1929 with a massive decline in stock market followed by great depression. However, the tax exemptions in 1940s encouraged the conglomerates to involve themselves in M & A activities.

From 1965 – 1970

Most of the mergers from 1965-70 were horizontal mergers and were triggered by elevating stock and interest rates, and stern implementation of anti-trust rules and regulations. During this phase the bidding companies were small in size and fiscal strength than the target companies.

These kinds of mergers were sponsored by equities, thereby eliminating the roles of banks which they actively played in investment activities earlier.

In 1968, the Attorney General decided to break the multinationals which resulted in the end of merging activities after than. The decision was triggered by the inefficient performance of the multinationals. But 1970s saw the emergence of mergers which made their mark by performing effectively. Some of them were INCO merging with ESB, OTIS Elevator with United Technologies and Colt Industries with Garlock Industries.

From 1981 – 1989

This phase saw the acquisition of the companies which were much bigger in size as compared to the firms in previous phases. Industries like oil and gas, pharmaceuticals, banking, aviation combined their business with their national and international counterparts. Cross border buyouts became regular with most of them being unfriendly in nature. This phase came to an end with the introduction of anti acquisition laws, restructuring of fiscal organisations and the Gulf War.

From 1992 till Present

This period was stimulated by globalization, upsurge in stock market boom and deregulation policies. Major mergers were seen taking place between telecom and banking giants out of which most were sponsored by equities.

There was a change in the attitude of the industrialists, who opted for mergers and acquisitions for long term profitability rather than short lived benefits. Promising economic trends, investments by corporate and revised government policies motivated the participation of many conglomerates to contribute in the acquisition trend.

Therefore, we can conclude that as long as business entities exist and the economic factors are favourable, the trend of mergers and acquisitions will continue.

Valuation for Mergers and Acquisitions: An Overview

Why Companies Merge or Acquire: A Historical Perspective

Companies grow in two main ways: either organically or by merging with or acquiring other companies. Although the number and volume of M&As broke records in the first decade of the 21st century, these transactions are not a recent phenomenon. We begin our journey by identifying the periods that were characterized by a high level of M&A activity and then summarize the major reasons companies make acquisitions.

Mergers and Acquisitions Waves

M&As come in "waves." Martynova and Renneboog (2008) reviewed a century of transactions and identified six major waves of M&As: 1890–1903, 1910–1929, 1950–1973, 1981–1989, 1993–2001, and 2003–2007. Their research shows that the end of a wave typically coincides with a crisis or a recession—for example, the most recent wave ended with the subprime debt crisis in 2007. What triggers the start of a wave varies across time, but three factors have clearly driven M&A activity since the end of the 19th century: industrial and technological shocks, regulatory changes, and credit availability.

The 1890s and early 1900s witnessed what is considered the first wave of M&As. Companies in the United States tried to build monopolies in their respective industries by forming trusts—in essence, an extreme form of horizontal integration. Examples include the creation of Standard Oil Company of New Jersey in 1899, United States Steel Corporation in 1901, and International Harvester Corporation in 1902. After the government enacted laws prohibiting anticompetitive behaviour, acquisition-oriented companies turned their attention to vertical integration as a means of growth.

Vertical integration is perhaps best illustrated by the oil and gas industry; companies that began as pure oil exploration businesses eventually moved into refining, transportation, and, ultimately, retailing of oil and gas products.

Most of the M&As that took place during the second wave in the 1920s involved small U.S. companies that were left outside the monopolies created during the previous wave. Those companies merged with or acquired one another to gain economies of scale and to be able to compete with the dominant player in their industry. The 1929 crisis and the depression that followed put an end to this second wave of M&As. Because of World War II, M&A activity remained low until the 1950s.

The 1950s, 1960s, and early 1970s witnessed a third wave of M&As, during which companies tried to diversify their revenue streams and, in doing so, reduce their perceived riskiness. This trend led to the creation of conglomerates and holding companies composed of many unrelated businesses. General Electric Company is a typical example of this trend. However, today's capital markets no longer place a premium on highly diversified companies. In fact, the share prices of most highly diversified companies are subject to a conglomerate discount because equity markets struggle to see the benefits of these complex enterprises. In essence, equity markets now prefer "pure plays"—that is, companies that operate in a single industry—to highly diversified companies, in large part because understanding and valuing pure plays is easier than conglomerates. This third wave of M&As peaked in 1968 and collapsed with the oil crisis in 1973.

The late 1970s and early 1980s were characterized by relatively high inflation rates and, consequently, high borrowing costs. To remain profitable, many companies sought ways to reduce both operating and financing costs. Reaching a critical size was often viewed as *the* way to survive the industry "shake-outs" that inevitably characterize such economic periods, giving rise to the fourth wave of M&As. Many companies merged with or acquire one another to take advantage of the economies of scale associated with larger-volume producers. Moreover, some companies saw M&As as a means to reduce their riskiness and lower their financing costs, which reached as high as 25 to 30 percent in some instances in the late 1970s and early 1980s.

The 1980s were also marked by deregulation and the creation and development of new instruments and markets. One such example is the "junk" bond market, or the market for bonds issued by companies with poor credit quality. The availability of credit to finance highly risky companies and transactions fuelled an increase in leveraged buyouts (LBOs) and leveraged recapitalizations. Some companies that had bought unrelated businesses during the previous wave took advantage of the booming M&A market to sell their poorly performing divisions and refocus on their core business. The stock market crash of 1987 and the collapse of several highly leveraged companies put an end to this fourth wave of M&As.

The 1990s saw new justifications for acquisitions emerge, paving the way for a fifth wave of M&As. Some companies made acquisitions to gain access to knowledge-based assets, particularly in the late 1990s, when the "first mover" advantage became highly prized. The 1990s also witnessed an increase in the number and volume of cross-border acquisitions. With the evolution of the global economy, many companies saw M&As as the quickest and least expensive means of acquiring a presence in a foreign country and preserving their place in the global economy. This latter trend was largely driven by the formation of multination trade zones such as the European Union (E.U.), Mercosur, and the North Atlantic Free Trade Agreement (NAFTA).

In addition, some companies viewed M&As as an opportunity to consolidate industries characterized by excess market participants and, hence, low profitability. These "consolidators" recognised that not every participant could survive such economic conditions and fostered a mentality of "Acquire or be acquired." Examples of industries affected by this global trend include the oil and gas industry (consider the mergers of British Petroleum [BP] and Amoco, and of Exxon and Mobil), the pharmaceutical industry (for example, the creations of Pharmacia, the result of the merger of Pharmacia & Upjohn with Monsanto, and of GlaxoSmithKline, the result of the merger of SmithKline Beecham and Glaxo Wellcome), and the automobile industry (think of the merger of Daimler and Chrysler, and the acquisition of Volvo by Ford). The burst of the dotcom bubble in 2000 and the recession that followed marked the end of this fifth wave of M&As.

M&A activity soon recovered, with a sixth wave starting in 2003. This wave saw the continuation of the two trends initiated in the 1990s: cross-border acquisitions and industry consolidations. But it was also reminiscent of the 1980s, in that leveraged transactions made a comeback. The low-interest environment coupled with the seemingly endless credit availability fuelled an increase in LBOs, many sponsored by private equity firms. Investors went in search of diversification benefits and higher yields. As they poured money into new asset classes such as private equity, large amounts of funds became available to take companies private and purchase divisions for sale. This sixth wave of M&As came to an abrupt end following the subprime debt crisis of 2007.

As of this writing, M&A activity is picking up, and some market participants are suggesting that a new wave of M&As could be underway. However, it is too early to tell.

Motivations for Mergers and Acquisitions

Companies make acquisitions for a long list of reasons. Some of these reasons are good, in that the motivation for the transaction is to maximize shareholder value. Unfortunately, other reasons are bad, or at least questionable.

Theoretically, companies should pursue an acquisition *only* if it creates value—that is, if the value of the acquirer and the target is greater if they operate as a single entity than as separate ones. Put another way, a merger or acquisition is justified if synergies are associated with the transaction. Synergies can take three forms: operating, financial, or managerial.

Operating synergies arise from the combination of the acquirer and target's operations. A first type of operating synergies is revenue enhancement. It includes gaining pricing power in a particular market or being able to increase sales volume by accessing new markets—for example, by leveraging one company's sales force or distribution network, or by selling one company's products to the other company's customers. A second type of operating synergies is cost reduction.

As mentioned earlier, many companies view M&As as a way to reach a critical size and, consequently, be able to benefit from economies of scale with lower production costs. An acquisition might also generate cost savings in advertising, marketing, or research and development. Revenue enhancement and cost reduction are more likely in cases of horizontal integration and can also play a role in vertical integration.

Financial synergies come from lower financing costs. Big companies usually have access to a wider and cheaper pool of funds than small companies. One rationale for the third wave of M&As was that diversifying into unrelated businesses enabled companies to reduce risk and, therefore, increase their debt capacity and lower their before-tax cost of financing. The risk reduction benefit is compounded by the beneficial tax treatment of debt relative to equity. Thus, the more debt a company has in its capital structure, the lower its cost of financing, net of taxes. History has shown, however, that companies tend to overestimate the risk reduction and tax benefits associated with M&As. Although financial synergies are a source of value, particularly in the case of leveraged transactions such as LBOs, they should not be the only motivation for a merger or acquisition.

Managerial synergies arise when a high-performing management team replaces a poor-performing one. One advantage of acquisitions is that they give the acquirer the opportunity to remove incompetent managers, which could improve the target's performance.

Unfortunately, not all M&As are motivated by the goal of creating shareholder value. Research has shown that some managers look after their own self-interest instead of shareholders'. They might use M&As to build empires and diversify their human capital, even if little or no value is associated with the merger or the acquisition. Managers also sometimes suffer from hubris; they are overconfident in their ability to negotiate a good deal for their shareholders and then run the combined entity.

Thus, they tend to overpay for their acquisitions. Last, some managers go through an acquisition spree to deliver growth and earnings targets, even if the acquisitions are not strategically sound or have a negative effect on the company's profitability and ability to create shareholder value.

Do Mergers and Acquisitions Create Shareholder Value?

Although evidence clearly indicates that the shareholders of a target profit from a merger or acquisition, the same cannot be said for the shareholders of the acquirer. An abundance of studies show that the share price of almost all targets increases around the announcement of a merger or an acquisition. However, the share price of acquirers rarely follows the same trend; the average share price performance of acquirers around the announcement of a merger or an acquisition is slightly negative, and acquirers commonly experience a significant decrease in share price after announcing their intention to merge with or acquire another company. Kengelbach and Roos, from the Boston Consulting Group (BCG) (2011), studied approximately 26,000 transactions completed between 1988 and 2010. They showed that the average share price performance over a seven-day window centred on the announcement date was 15.5 percent for the target but –1.0 percent for the acquirer.

The study revealed that acquirers perform better if they purchase a foreign target instead of a domestic one, if they pay in cash rather than in securities or a mix of cash and securities, if they make only one acquisition, and if the acquisition takes place during a downturn rather than an upturn. A follow-up study by Kengelbach, Kemmer, and Roos (2012) also indicated that some sectors fare better than others. For instance, the share price performance for an average acquirer was 1.9 percent in the manufacturing sector but –2.2 percent in the telecommunication sector.

This evidence suggests, among other things, that equity markets are skeptical about the ability of acquirers to create shareholder value. Whether offer prices are seen as excessive, the proposed synergies are thought unlikely to materialize, or current management is perceived as incapable of successfully merging two different cultures, equity markets doubt the value associated with most transactions. Sadly, equity markets are correct: Few transactions achieve their anticipated gains. KPMG (2011) analyzed a large sample of M&As completed between January 2007 and July 2009 and showed that, in 44 percent of the transactions, the acquirer achieved either none or very little of the anticipated synergies. Moreover, Kengelbach, et al. (2012), observed that, in 2011, divestitures made up 45 percent of the number of M&As.

As mentioned in the vignette at the beginning of this chapter, it is not unusual for companies to end up selling their poorly performing acquisitions.

To help understand why many M&As fail to create shareholder value, it is instructive to consider data on the premiums paid in these transactions. We turn to that topic now.

Merger and Acquisition Premiums

The premium in a merger or acquisition is defined as the difference between the offer price and the market price of the target before the announcement of the transaction. A substantial body of evidence indicates that M&A premiums average 20 to 30 percent above a target's preacquisition share price.

For example, Kengelbach and Roos (2011) found that the average premium was 36 percent during the period 1990–2010. As conventional wisdom suggests, acquirers perform better when they pay a premium that is below average rather than above average. As mentioned earlier, a high premium is a sure path to overpaying and reducing the likelihood of making the acquisition a success.

M&A premiums are sometimes referred to as control premiums. In general, the target's shareholders demand them as compensation for transferring controlling interest in the target to the acquirer. Majority control in a company conveys many valuable rights and benefits, including control over all operating policies and decisions, the selection of management and the board of directors, and the distribution of cash to shareholders.

M&A premiums can also represent compensation for other economic benefits, such as the expected synergies associated with the transaction. They can reflect capital market pricing inefficiencies as well, wherein a target is undervalued because the company or its industry is out of favour with investors.

If M&As yield these valuable economic rights and benefits, why do so many of them destroy value?

The reasons are many, but the five principal explanations for value destruction appear to be the following:

- Overestimation of the target's value, primarily caused by an overestimation of the growth and/or market potential (a forecasting error problem).
- Overestimation of the expected synergies (another forecasting error problem).

- Overbidding and overpayment, which is often a consequence of management's hubris. The risk of overbidding and overpayment increases when several bidders are competing for the target because this heightened competition gives the target more bargaining power to negotiate a higher offer price and, thus, premium.
- Failure to undertake a thorough due diligence of the target.
- Failure to successfully integrate the target after the merger or the acquisition.

In essence, in about every other transaction, the acquirer's management commits some type of critical error—in the due diligence investigation, in the bidding process, or in the postacquisition integration of the target.

How to avoid each of these pitfalls is beyond the scope of this book; instead, we focus on the process of assessing the target's value—namely, the specific accounting, finance, and taxation issues that the analyst must successfully deal with to estimate the value associated with a merger or acquisition.

Valuation Process

Analysts frequently refer to five types of value: book value, break-up value, liquidation value, fundamental value, and market value.

- Book value refers to the accounting value of a company—that is, the value reported in the balance sheet. The book value of equity, also referred to as the company's net worth, is equal to its total assets minus its total liabilities. It represents a company's residual value, assuming that assets can be sold for their reported values and that the proceeds are used to satisfy all liabilities at their recorded values.
- Break-up value refers to the amount that could be realised if a company were split into saleable units that could be disposed of in a negotiated transaction. This concept is especially relevant for companies composed of a variety of individual business units, divisions, or segments.
- Liquidation value refers to the amount that could be realised if a company were liquidated in a distress sale. A company's liquidation value is usually lower than its book and break-up values because assets that must be disposed of quickly are usually sold at a discount.

- Fundamental value, also called intrinsic value, refers to the value based on the after-tax cash flows that the company is expected to generate in the future, discounted at an appropriate rate that reflects the riskiness of those cash flows. It is a forward-looking concept and requires an assessment of a company's potential future cash flows.
- Market value refers to the value established in an orderly marketplace such as a securities market.

  For example, the market value of equity, also called the market capitalization, is equal to the share price multiplied by the number of shares outstanding.

Although all five types of value can be used for valuing a company, this book deals primarily with the assessment of *fundamental value* because it represents the "ongoing" value of a company.

Thus, the value of a company is defined herein with reference to the future cash flows that a company is expected to generate.

The process of valuing a company usually involves five steps:

1. Identify and screen potential target candidates thoroughly to ensure that the proposed transaction is appropriate from a *strategic* standpoint.
2. Analyze the historical performance of the target to ensure that it is an appropriate partner from a *financial* standpoint, as well as to gain a thorough understanding of the target's business model, operations, and capital structure.
3. Forecast the future performance of the target by preparing pro forma financial statements. Nothing is more important in assessing a target's value than a complete and accurate modelling of the company's operations.

   This critical step requires a fine-grained understanding of the target's environment, its business model (including its revenue and cost drivers) and realistic assumptions about the target's future operations and, potentially, capital structure.
4. Apply one or several valuation methods to get an estimate or estimates of the target's value.
5. Assess the sensitivity of the key pro forma and valuation assumptions on the target's value.

Step 4 requires the analyst to select one or several valuation methods. In the next section, we present the most widely used valuation methods and give an overview of their main characteristics and uses.

Valuation Methods: An Overview

Several valuation methods are available, depending on a company's industry, its characteristics (for example, whether it is a start-up or a mature company), and the analyst's preference and expertise. In this chapter and the rest of the book, we focus on the mainstream valuation methods. These methods are classified into four categories, based on two dimensions. The first dimension distinguishes between direct (or absolute) valuation methods and indirect (or relative) valuation methods; the second dimension separates models that rely on cash flows from models that rely on another financial variable, such as sales (revenues), earnings, or book value.

Table: *Exhibit : Overview of Valuation Methods*

	Direct (or Absolute) Valuation Methods	***Relative (or Indirect) Valuation Methods***
Valuation methods that rely on cash flows	*Discounted cash flow models:* Free cash flow to the firm model Free cash flow to equity model Adjusted present value model *Option-pricing models:* Real option analysis	*Price multiples:* Price-to-cash-flow ratio
Valuation methods that rely on a financial variable other than cash flows	*Economic income models:* Economic value analysis	*Price multiples**: Price-to-earnings ratios (P/E ratio, P/EBIT ratio, and P/EBITDA ratio) Price-to-sales ratio Price-to-book ratio *Enterprise value multiples:* EV/EBITDA multiple EV/Sales multiple
* E stands for earnings; EBIT for earnings before interest and taxes; EBITDA to earnings before interest, taxes, depreciation, and amortization; and EV for enterprise value.		

Provides an overview of the mainstream valuation methods.

As their name indicates, direct valuation methods provide a direct estimate of a company's fundamental value. In the case of public companies, the analyst can then compare the company's fundamental value obtained from that valuation analysis to the company's market value. The company appears fairly valued if its market value is equal to its fundamental value, undervalued if its market value is lower than its fundamental value, and overvalued if its market value is higher than its fundamental value.

In contrast, relative valuation methods do *not* provide a direct estimate of a company's fundamental value: They do not indicate whether a company is fairly priced; they indicate only whether it is fairly priced *relative* to some benchmark or peer group. Because valuing a company using an indirect valuation method requires identifying a group of comparable companies, this approach to valuation is also called the comparables approach.

Academicians and practitioners are in relative agreement on what drives a company's fundamental value: its future cash flows. However, no consensus has settled on what drives a company's share price. In today's global economic environment, it would be naïve to suggest that any single factor drives share prices. Indeed, the proliferation of valuation methods partly reflects the financial community's inability to agree on exactly which factors the primary drivers of share are prices—cash flows, sales, accounting earnings, book value, or economic income. The dominant viewpoint is that changes in share prices are most closely related to changes in future cash flows, with all else being equal. This is the viewpoint this book endorses.

Relative Valuation Methods

The notion that "time is money" or, stated alternatively, that "time is an expensive and limited commodity" is one of the principal reasons for relative valuation methods. Other reasons are that they are simple to apply and easy to understand. In essence, relative valuation methods give corporate executives and analysts a "quick and dirty" way to estimate the value of a company.

Relative valuation methods rely on the use of multiples. A multiple is a ratio between two financial variables. In most cases, the numerator of the multiple is either the company's market price (in the case of price multiples) or its enterprise value (in the case of enterprise value multiples). The enterprise value of a company is typically defined as the market value of its capital (debt and equity), net of cash. The denominator of the multiple is an accounting metric, such as the company's earnings, sales, or book value. Multiples can be calculated from per-share amounts (market price per share, earnings per share, sales per share, or book value per share) or total amounts.

Note that whether the analyst uses per-share amounts or total amounts does not affect the multiple, as long as the same basis is used in both the numerator and the denominator.

Price Multiples

The most popular price multiples are earnings multiples. The price-to-earnings (P/E) ratio, which is equal to a company's market price per share divided by its earnings per share (EPS), is the most widely used earnings multiple. It provides an indication of how much investors are willing to pay for a company's earnings. For example, a company whose P/E ratio is 15 is said to be selling for 15 times earnings; put another way, investors are willing to pay $15 for each $1 of current or future earnings. Companies with high earnings growth prospects usually carry high P/E ratios because these companies are expected to be able to reward investors with a quicker and larger return on their investment in the form of dividends, increase in share price, or both.

Because the earnings of a company are influenced to varying degrees by how the company is financed (with debt or with equity) and where it pays income taxes, some analysts have turned to a variant of the P/E ratio that removes the effect of a company's capital structure and income taxes on its earnings. This variant is the price-to-earnings before interest and taxes (P/EBIT) ratio. Still other analysts, worried about the distortive effect on earnings of accounting policies with respect to the depreciation of tangible assets and the amortization of intangible assets, prefer to use the price-to-earnings before interest, taxes, depreciation, and amortization (P/EBITDA) ratio. The P/EBITDA ratio is also popular because of the close relationship between a company's EBITDA and its cash flow from operations.

The P/E, P/EBIT, and P/EBITDA ratios all require positive accounting earnings. But not all companies are profitable—particularly young ones. For companies that are operating at a loss, analysts must find an alternative to accounting earnings. The most popular alternative is sales, which leads to the price-to-sales (P/Sales) ratio. The P/Sales ratio is useful in the early stages of a company's life cycle, when marketplace acceptance and growth in market share are considered to be the two best indicators of the company's likely future operating earnings and cash flows.

Another price multiple is the price-to-book (P/Book) ratio. It indicates the relative premium that investors are willing to pay over the book value of their equity investment in a company. Unfortunately, a company's book value is highly sensitive to accounting standards and management's accounting decisions. For this reason, the P/B ratio is used selectively; realistically, it is neither a valid nor viable valuation method for most companies, except perhaps for financial institutions and insurance companies.

These companies have highly liquid assets and liabilities on their balance sheets, which makes book values more realistic proxies for market values.

In contrast to the previous five multiples, the last one is based on cash flows. Because cash flows are less sensitive than earnings to accounting choices and potential accounting manipulations, some analysts prefer to base their valuation on the price-to-cash-flow (P/CF) ratio than on the P/E, P/EBIT, or even P/EBITDA ratios. This approach is also consistent with the viewpoint that value is primarily driven by cash flows.

Enterprise Value Multiples

Price multiples are popular with buy-side and sell-side analysts interested in valuing a company's price per share—that is, the company's equity value per share. In the context of M&As, however, corporate executives and analysts are often interested in assessing a target's total value, reflecting both debt and equity. In this case, the enterprise value is a better basis for the valuation, hence the reason enterprise value multiples are widely used when valuing an acquisition target.

The most popular enterprise value multiple is the EV/EBITDA multiple, although the EV/Sales multiple can be used for unprofitable companies. For example, an EV/EBITDA multiple of 8 indicates that the acquirer is willing to pay eight times the target's current or future EBITDA.

Many analysts often check that the EV/EBITDA multiple offered to acquire a target is in line with the EV/EBITDA multiples paid in previous acquisitions. Offering an EV/EBITDA multiple that is substantially higher than the average EV/EBITDA multiple for comparable transactions is usually an indication that the acquirer is overpaying for the target.

Direct Valuation Methods

Unlike the relative valuation methods, direct valuation methods give investors an explicit equity value per share or share price objective. Preeminent among the group of direct valuation methods are the discounted cash flow (DCF) models.

Discounted Cash Flow Models

DCF models are premised on one of the most fundamental tenets of corporate finance: The value of a company today is equal to the present value of the future (but uncertain) cash flows to be generated by the company's operations, discounted at a rate that reflects the riskiness (or uncertainty) of those cash flows.

The most widely used version of the DCF model is sometimes referred to as the free cash flow to the firm model, or weighted average cost of capital model. It provides an estimation of the company's total value, based on its free cash flows (FCFs) to the firm discounted at the weighted average cost of capital (WACC). The FCFs of the firm are the cash flows from operations available to all capital providers, net of the required capital investments necessary to maintain the company as a going concern.

The WACC reflects the hurdle rate that providers of capital require, based on the risk they face from investing in the company. The equity value per share—that is, the value accruing to the common (or voting) shareholders—is given by the operating value of the company minus the value of any claims on the company's cash flows by debt holders, preferred shareholders, noncontrolling (minority) interest shareholders, and any contingent claimants.

A variant is the free cash flow to equity model, which provides a direct estimate of a company's equity value per share. Instead of relying on the FCFs available to all capital providers, it considers the FCFs available to equity holders: the FCFs to the firm minus all the cash flows owed to claimants other than common shareholders. Because the focus is on equity holders, the discount rate is the cost of equity, or the hurdle rate for common shareholders.

The FCF to the firm and FCF to equity models are highly effective valuation methods, particularly when the capital structure of a target is expected to remain stable over time. Some acquisitions, however, are predicated on material changes in capital structure, as in the case of an LBO. In these situations, the adjusted present value (APV) model is easier to implement than the other DCF models. Under the APV model, the value of a target is decomposed into two components: the value of the company assuming that it is financed entirely with equity, and the value of the tax shield (benefits) provided by a company's actual (or expected) debt financing. Because interest is tax deductible, using financial leverage increases a company's value by reducing its cash outflow for income taxes. As a company's capital structure changes over time, the first component (the unleveraged, or unlevered, value) is unaffected; the change in financial leverage affects only the second component (the interest tax shield), which is relatively straightforward to estimate.

Non Discounted Cash Flow Models

Real option analysis is another valuation method that relies on cash flows, although it is grounded in option-pricing models instead of DCF models. Analysts rarely use real option analysis to value an entire company. However, this valuation method proves useful when a company has investment opportunities that have option-like features; these features are usually difficult, if not impossible, to capture using DCF models. For example, a company might have rights (but not obligations) to delay investments, expand into new markets, redeploy resources between projects, or exit investments. These rights are valuable options, particularly in an uncertain environment. Real option analysis, which applies to real assets some of the techniques used for valuing financial options, enables analysts to value the wide range of rights a company has.

Economic income models, also called residual income models, differ from DCF models and real option analysis, in that they rely not on cash flows, but on earnings to estimate a company's fundamental value. However, in contrast with price and enterprise value multiples that are based on accounting earnings, economic income models rely on economic income. Economic income is usually defined as net income minus a charge for using equity—one of the issues with accounting earnings such as net income is that they include a charge for using debt (interest expense), but not for using equity. The principle behind economic income models is that a company that produces positive economic income creates shareholder value. Consequently, it should be rewarded with a higher share price. The most popular economic income model is economic value analysis, although other versions are also available.

Academicians agree that, in theory, the FCF to the firm, FCF to equity, APV, and economic income models are equivalent, provided, of course, that the models use the same assumptions. In practice, however, differences arise, primarily because of implementation issues. Thus, as we review the different valuation methods, "Traditional Valuation Methods," and 4, "Alternative Valuation Methods," we address the major issues an analyst faces when using relative and direct valuation methods.

The Use of Valuation Methods

Imam, Barker, and Clubb (2008) conducted semi-structured interviews with sell-side and buy-side analysts in the United Kingdom to determine which valuation methods analysts used, why they used them, and how they used them. Their results showed that

- The two most widely used valuation methods are the P/E ratio and the FCF to the firm model. In contrast, few analysts used economic value analysis, multiples based on book values (whether price or enterprise value multiples), or the P/Sales ratio.
- Approximately 60 percent of the analysts expressed a strong preference for cash flow–based valuation methods, particularly buy-side analysts. However, most analysts admit that they often complement their cash flow–based analysis with a multiples-based analysis.
- Some valuation methods are sector specific. For example, the P/B ratio and EV/Sales ratios are rarely used, except to value financial institutions and retailers, respectively.

The results of this survey are consistent with our own experience. This is the reason we have classified the FCF to the firm model and the P/E ratio as "traditional" valuation methods in this book, and we cover. Although other valuation methods are less often used, they are part of the analyst toolbox.

History

Mergers and Acquisitions

History can effectively help in gathering information about the significant mergers and acquisitions of the world.

Mergers and Acquisitions History often surprises us as we come to know that the concepts of Mergers and Acquisitions are not new, on the contrary they are continuing from the early years of history.

Mergers and Acquisitions History helps us to understand the evolution of the concepts of Mergers and Acquisitions in the world. If we involve in the detailed analysis of the History of Merger of Acquisitions, we will find that Mergers and Acquisitions started to take place in the world from very early years.

US Mergers and Acquisitions History

In USA, mergers and acquisitions started in twentieth century. After that Mergers and Acquisitions continued to occur in cycle. These cycles of Mergers and Acquisitions, took place in USA in 1929, in the last half of 1960s, in the first half of 1980s and again in the last half of 1990s. Here, it should be mentioned that, by cycle we are referring to the period, in which the maximum number of mergers took place.

Among the mergers and acquisitions cycles cited above, the most significant mergers of USA took place in the last half of 1990s. The reason of this was that, the stock market was quite strong in US in that period and this strong stock market supported the high incidence of mergers and acquisitions. The mergers and acquisitions of this period involved big brands and huge amount of dollars.

Significant Mergers and Acquisitions of the History

- In 1987, an Australian Company named Stephen Jaques Stone James, which was a partnership company with 79 partners, merged with the company named Mallesons. After the Merger, the new joint company was known as Mallesons Stephen Jaques. This Merger contributed significantly to the telecommunication sector development in Australia.
- In 1988, Tower Federal Savings Bank of Indiana acquired two financial institutions of Michigan. Then in 1991, the Standard Federal Bank strengthened their position in Ohio by acquiring a financial institution of Toledo. These two acquisitions had great impact on the banking Sector of USA.
- In 2001, a merger between Association of European Universities and the Confederation of European Union Rectors' Conference took place in Spain. This merger provided more power to the University community of Europe.

Anti-takeover Measures

Measures taken on a continual or sporadic basis by a firm's management in order to prevent or deter unwanted takeovers.

An anti-takeover measure is a precautionary strategy used by companies to avoid being bought by another company.

How it Works/Example: For a myriad of reasons, a company may not want to be taken over. Thus, if management believes a takeover bid is likely to occur, there are a number of strategies or obstacles it may use to avoid being bought.

One such measure, known as the macaroni strategy, is when the company issues bonds that must be called at a high premium in the event the company is taken over. This can make the company prohibitively expensive to purchase. Another strategy, known as the Pac-Man strategy, would be for the takeover-threatened company to make a reactionary takeover bid against the purchasing company.

Why it Matters: For companies being purchased, the futures for management, employees, and investors can be in doubt as control of the company is relinquished to another authority (i.e. the purchasing company). In this respect, *anti-takeover measures* protect a company's autonomy and market competitiveness.

Vopak´s principal defence against a hostile takeover is the company´s ability to issue cumulative preference shares ('protective preference shares´) to Stichting Vopak. Such defencive preference shares will be issued, should Stichting Vopak exercise its option right. On 18 October 1999, the AGM decided to grant Stichting Vopak the right to take up protective preference shares up to a maximum nominal amount equal to 100% of the share capital issued at that time to third parties in the form of ordinary and financing preference shares, less one ordinary share. Vopak and Stichting Vopak further formalized their relationship with regard to the option right in an option agreement of 1 November 1999. This agreement was amended on 5 May 2004, whereby the original put option granted to Vopak was cancelled.

In light of a possible future introduction of other classes of shares, at the EGM of 17 September 2013, the general meeting resolved to increase the right of Stichting Vopak to acquire protective preference shares in such way that the right to acquire protective preference shares is not only related to the share capital issued to third parties in the form of ordinary and financing preference shares at the time Stichting Vopak exercises its right to acquire protective preference shares, but to all shares in the share capital of Vopak issued to third parties at such time, less one ordinary share.

On 17 September 2013 the option agreement with Stichting Vopak was amended as to reflect the increase of the option right of Stichting Vopak.

Exercise by Stichting Vopak of its option right in part does not affect the right of Stichting Vopak to acquire the remaining protective preference shares under the option granted to Stichting Vopak. The option agreement provides that in the event that Stichting Vopak has exercised its option right and the results thereof have been fully or partially cancelled (for instance as a result of the cancellation of the protective preference shares issued), Stichting Vopak will continue to be able to exercise its option right.

The granting of the call option to Stichting Vopak has been entered in the Company Registry and is disclosed in this Annual Report. The objective of Stichting Vopak is to promote the interests of Vopak and companies affiliated to the Vopak group, in such a way that safeguards the interests of Vopak and all stakeholders to the greatest possible extent and, to the best of its ability, to resist influences which, opposing those interests, could impair the independence and/or continuity and/or the identity of Vopak and to undertake all actions relating to or conducive to the above objectives. The board of Stichting Vopak therefore determines whether and when it is necessary to issue the protective preference shares.

These measures can be taken in the event of a takeover, for example, if it is in the interest of Vopak to establish its position in respect of the hostile party and its plans, and to create opportunities to seek scenarios. Vopak reviews its anti-takeover measures as necessary against implementation acts enacted from time to time pursuant to EU directives.

Anti-takeover Protections: Raise the Gates, the Hostiles are Coming

With Proxy Season underway and hostile activity on the rise, we at Westlaw Business are taking a detailed look at rising adoption of anti-takeover protections and other defencive measures. This is part of a two-part series on changes in anti-takeover protection and the disclosures of companies who adopt such standards. Part two will focus on Poison Pills.

Can hostile acquirors take advantage of depressed equity prices to buy coveted companies on the cheap? Can activist shareholders shake up disappointing boards with impunity? They may want to, but today's boards seem to be one step ahead and have recently increased their adoption of protective measures. In particular, boards are turning to several tools to protect themselves: staggered boards, golden parachutes, supermajority voting provisions, and of course poison pills. Milder forms of protective action are being taken as well: tightened advance notice requirements for special shareholder meetings among them. What they're putting in place and how they're disclosing is of great interest as we move into a new year filled with M&A promise.

Both hostile transactions and shareholder activism are on the rise – alarming some boards and causing them to react. The Yahoo/Microsoft battle was one well-publicized example, but other companies have also seen attempted board exchanges from what usually appears to be well-meaning stakeholders. Ramius, a hedge fund, has been battling Orthofix International over its board, and the two aren't seeing eye to eye. Ramius has asked for a special meeting to elect four new board members. Activist investor Ron Burkle, who recently took a significant stake in Whole Foods, has publicly stated his interest in the "substantial opportunities for the Company to improve operations."

Companies are putting in place various protective measures in order to fend-off potential takeovers. Anti-takeover protections of choice include staggered boards and golden parachutes, along with the ever-popular poison pill – often discussed (including by Legal Currents, as you'll see in Related Resources) and to be the subject of Part 2 of this series. Other forms of "shark repellant" being put in place include supermajority votes and standstill provisions. Reminiscent of Soviet/ U.S. Cold War counter-measures, shareholders are jumping in the mix as well – with counter-point initiatives like declassification, golden parachute removal and supermajority removal.

Boards are disclosing anti-takeover measures in various ways. Take Synovus Financial Corp.'s recent proxy statement in which the company details its strategies that make it a "less attractive target for an acquisition who lacks the support of Synovus' Board." Amerisourcebergen, meanwhile, asks shareholders to vote against a proposal to eliminate its poison pill because it feels the plan is "an important tool for preserving and maximizing the company's value for all stockholders."

Poison pills are the most commonly used mechanism to protect a company from potential unsolicited bids or hostile takeover attempts. These are usually adopted through the issuance of rights that would convert to shares, upon a trigger event. Hardee's franchisor CKE Restaurants just implemented a poison pill plan, joining other notable names including retailer Saks & Co. and Six Flags.

Staggered boards, in which a company's directors are classed and elected at different stages, have also been implemented by some companies. Consider, for example, Noble Corp.'s structure of three classes of board members, allowing one class of directors to be elected each year. Similarly, Interstate Data USA Inc. recently implemented a classified board system after amending its bylaws. The board structure was divided into three classes, with the directors serving terms based on their classification. Staggered boards are desired by some, as they lend a patina of stability. They also complicate, or completely confound, the conduct of a shareholder takeover. This distinction (between confounding and merely complicating) is driven by the document embedding the board's structure: Charter or by-laws, as by-laws are amendable by boards. An interesting nuance: Some staggered board structures allow shareholders to take back their directors should activity incite the majority to give in to hostile pressures.

Yet another mechanism used is the golden parachute. This effectively confounds a potential bidder, requiring giant piles of cash or tax burdens to be paid to executives, should a change in control occur. Agilent Technologies, for example, has provisions in place that would cancel any tax deductions on golden parachute compensation. Similarly, chemical manufacturer Cabot Corp. asks shareholders to approve terms of a golden parachute in its executive long-term incentive plan. Such terms would confound a potential bidder due to the change in control provisions – potentially forcing a 20% non-deductible tax burden on the company.

As an alternative mechanism, boards are also tightening rules for shareholder access to proxy statements and meetings. Crane Co. recently amended its bylaws relating to the election and nomination of its directors. Instead of a simple plurality vote, which the company had in place, Crane went two steps further in clarifying its bylaws. The industrial products manufacturer's amendments ask that shareholders give the Secretary advance notice and not withdraw any proposals prior to two weeks before the mailing of the shareholder meeting notice.

On the flip side, shareholders are demanding less of these same measures, as part of good governance. For example, Sonus Networks presented its plans to declassify its board as a move to strengthen its governance policies. However, it's not as simple as that — the company's shareholders must approve the plan to consolidate its board. Along the same lines, Hospitality Properties Trust received a shareholder proposal from CalPERS asking the company to restructure its board into one classification. The company sought to exclude this proposal from its next proxy statement.

Notably, along the same lines, a particularly large shareholder (aka the U.S. government) has insisted golden parachutes be removed for any recipient of TARP funds. Though hidden in an exhibit, Morgan Stanley's latest 10-K notes its CEO's acknowledgement of the possibility that significant modifications may be made to compensation agreements, including golden parachutes – this is similar to that of many other banks and even former non-banks, like American Express, talking shelter under the Fed's umbrella .

In this era of market turmoil, staggered boards, golden parachutes, supermajority voting provisions, and poison pills are ever more popular defence mechanisms. As proxy season heats up, filers are urged to maintain their levels of disclosure on any takeover defences – both proposed or potentially removed.

Proposes to Modernise its Anti-takeover Measures

Wereldhave has evaluated its anti-takeover measures and after a stakeholder consultation, proposes changes to the articles of association to modernise and simplify the anti-takeover measures. The number of protective measures will be reduced to one, the issue of protective preference shares. The priority shares will be abolished. The option to issue preference shares can only be used as a temporary protective measure that enables a careful weighing of the interests of all stakeholders. If needed, it also offers time for a good and balanced reaction, for instance in case of a (public or non-public) offer or the announcement of the intention to make an offer.

The cancellation of all priority shares is proposed, whilst maintaining the possibility to issue protective (preference) shares to a maximum of 50% of the issued share capital, calculated after issue.

The current put option for the Foundation for the holding of preference and priority shares B will be converted to a call option. Upon exercise of the full call-option, it will not automatically revive. A new call-option will in that case be requested. The change from a put to a call option improves the independency of the Foundation, putting the decision to use a protective device outside the Company.

Advantages of Mergers and Acquisitions

The most common motives and advantages of mergers and acquisitions are:-

- Accelerating a company's growth, particularly when its internal growth is constrained due to paucity of resources. Internal growth requires that a company should develop its operating facilities- manufacturing, research, marketing, etc. But, lack or inadequacy of resources and time needed for internal development may constrain a company's pace of growth. Hence, a company can acquire production facilities as well as other resources from outside through mergers and acquisitions. Specially, for entering in new products/markets, the company may lack technical skills and may require special marketing skills and a wide distribution network to access different segments of markets. The company can acquire existing company or companies with requisite infrastructure and skills and grow quickly.

- Enhancing profitability because a combination of two or more companies may result in more than average profitability due to cost reduction and efficient utilisation of resources. This may happen because of:-
- Economies of scale:- arise when increase in the volume of production leads to a reduction in the cost of production per unit. This is because, with merger, fixed costs are distributed over a large volume of production causing the unit cost of production to decline. Economies of scale may also arise from other indivisibilities such as production facilities, management functions and management resources and systems. This is because a given function, facility or resource is utilised for a large scale of operations by the combined firm.
- Operating economies:- arise because, a combination of two or more firms may result in cost reduction due to operating economies. In other words, a combined firm may avoid or reduce over-lapping functions and consolidate its management functions such as manufacturing, marketing, R&D and thus reduce operating costs. For example, a combined firm may eliminate duplicate channels of distribution, or crate a centralized training centre, or introduce an integrated planning and control system.
- Synergy:- implies a situation where the combined firm is more valuable than the sum of the individual combining firms. It refers to benefits other than those related to economies of scale. Operating economies are one form of synergy benefits. But apart from operating economies, synergy may also arise from enhanced managerial capabilities, creativity, innovativeness, R&D and market coverage capacity due to the complementarity of resources and skills and a widened horizon of opportunities.
- Diversifying the risks of the company, particularly when it acquires those businesses whose income streams are not correlated. Diversification implies growth through the combination of firms in unrelated businesses. It results in reduction of total risks through substantial reduction of cyclicality of operations. The combination of management and other systems strengthen the capacity of the combined firm to withstand the severity of the unforeseen economic factors which

could otherwise endanger the survival of the individual companies.

- A merger may result in financial synergy and benefits for the firm in many ways:-
- By eliminating financial constraints
- By enhancing debt capacity. This is because a merger of two companies can bring stability of cash flows which in turn reduces the risk of insolvency and enhances the capacity of the new entity to service a larger amount of debt
- By lowering the financial costs. This is because due to financial stability, the merged firm is able to borrow at a lower rate of interest.
- Limiting the severity of competition by increasing the company's market power. A merger can increase the market share of the merged firm. This improves the profitability of the firm due to economies of scale. The bargaining power of the firm vis-à-vis labour, suppliers and buyers is also enhanced. The merged firm can exploit technological breakthroughs against obsolescence and price wars.

Procedure for Evaluating the Decision for Mergers and Acquisitions

The three important steps involved in the analysis of mergers and acquisitions are:-

- Planning:- of acquisition will require the analysis of industry-specific and firm-specific information. The acquiring firm should review its objective of acquisition in the context of its strengths and weaknesses and corporate goals. It will need industry data on market growth, nature of competition, ease of entry, capital and labour intensity, degree of regulation, etc. This will help in indicating the product-market strategies that are appropriate for the company. It will also help the firm in identifying the business units that should be dropped or added. On the other hand, the target firm will need information about quality of management, market share and size, capital structure, profitability, production and marketing capabilities, etc.
- Search and Screening:- Search focuses on how and where to look for suitable candidates for acquisition. Screening process short-lists a few candidates from many available and obtains detailed information about each of them.

- Financial Evaluation:- of a merger is needed to determine the earnings and cash flows, areas of risk, the maximum price payable to the target company and the best way to finance the merger. In a competitive market situation, the current market value is the correct and fair value of the share of the target firm. The target firm will not accept any offer below the current market value of its share.

  The target firm may, in fact, expect the offer price to be more than the current market value of its share since it may expect that merger benefits will accrue to the acquiring firm.

A merger is said to be at a premium when the offer price is higher than the target firm's pre-merger market value. The acquiring firm may have to pay premium as an incentive to target firm's shareholders to induce them to sell their shares so that it (acquiring firm) is able to obtain the control of the target firm.

Regulations for Mergers and Acquisitions

Mergers and acquisitions are regulated under various laws in India. The objective of the laws is to make these deals transparent and protect the interest of all shareholders. They are regulated through the provisions of :-

The Companies Act, 1956

The Act lays down the legal procedures for mergers or acquisitions:

- Permission for merger:- Two or more companies can amalgamate only when the amalgamation is permitted under their memorandum of association. Also, the acquiring company should have the permission in its object clause to carry on the business of the acquired company. In the absence of these provisions in the memorandum of association, it is necessary to seek the permission of the shareholders, board of directors and the Company Law Board before affecting the merger.
- Information to the stock exchange:- The acquiring and the acquired companies should inform the stock exchanges (where they are listed) about the merger.
- Approval of board of directors:- The board of directors of the individual companies should approve the draft proposal for amalgamation and authorise the managements of the companies to further pursue the proposal.

- Application in the High Court:- An application for approving the draft amalgamation proposal duly approved by the board of directors of the individual companies should be made to the High Court.
- Shareholders' and creators' meetings:- The individual companies should hold separate meetings of their shareholders and creditors for approving the amalgamation scheme. At least, 75 percent of shareholders and creditors in separate meeting, voting in person or by proxy, must accord their approval to the scheme.
- Sanction by the High Court:- After the approval of the shareholders and creditors, on the petitions of the companies, the High Court will pass an order, sanctioning the amalgamation scheme after it is satisfied that the scheme is fair and reasonable. The date of the court's hearing will be published in two newspapers, and also, the regional director of the Company Law Board will be intimated.
- Filing of the Court order:- After the Court order, its certified true copies will be filed with the Registrar of Companies.
- Transfer of assets and liabilities:- The assets and liabilities of the acquired company will be transferred to the acquiring company in accordance with the approved scheme, with effect from the specified date.
- Payment by cash or securities:- As per the proposal, the acquiring company will exchange shares and debentures and/ or cash for the shares and debentures of the acquired company. These securities will be listed on the stock exchange.

The Competition Act, 2002

The Act regulates the various forms of business combinations through Competition Commission of India. Under the Act, no person or enterprise shall enter into a combination, in the form of an acquisition, merger or amalgamation, which causes or is likely to cause an appreciable adverse effect on competition in the relevant market and such a combination shall be void. Enterprises intending to enter into a combination may give notice to the Commission, but this notification is voluntary. But, all combinations do not call for scrutiny unless the resulting combination exceeds the threshold limits in terms of assets or turnover as specified by the Competition Commission of India. The Commission while regulating a 'combination' shall consider the following factors :

- Actual and potential competition through imports;
- Extent of entry barriers into the market;
- Level of combination in the market;
- Degree of countervailing power in the market;
- Possibility of the combination to significantly and substantially increase prices or profits;
- Extent of effective competition likely to sustain in a market;
- Availability of substitutes before and after the combination;
- Market share of the parties to the combination individually and as a combination;
- Possibility of the combination to remove the vigorous and effective competitor or competition in the market;
- Nature and extent of vertical integration in the market;
- Nature and extent of innovation;
- Whether the benefits of the combinations outweigh the adverse impact of the combination.

Thus, the Competition Act does not seek to eliminate combinations and only aims to eliminate their harmful effects.

- The other regulations are provided in the:- The Foreign Exchange Management Act, 1999 and the Income Tax Act,1961. Besides, the Securities and Exchange Board of India (SEBI) has issued guidelines to regulate mergers and acquisitions. The SEBI (Substantial Acquisition of Shares and Take-overs) Regulations,1997 and its subsequent amendments aim at making the take-over process transparent, and also protect the interests of minority shareholders.

Types of Mergers and Acquisitions

There are many types of mergers and acquisitions that redefine the business world with new strategic alliances and improved corporate philosophies. From the business structure perspective, some of the most common and significant types of mergers and acquisitions are listed below:

Horizontal Merger

This kind of merger exists between two companies who compete in the same industry segment. The two companies combine their operations and gains strength in terms of improved performance, increased capital, and enhanced profits. This kind substantially reduces the number of competitors in the segment and gives a higher edge over competition.

Vertical Merger

Vertical merger is a kind in which two or more companies in the same industry but in different fields combine together in business. In this form, the companies in merger decide to combine all the operations and productions under one shelter. It is like encompassing all the requirements and products of a single industry segment.

Co-Generic Merger

Co-generic merger is a kind in which two or more companies in association are some way or the other related to the production processes, business markets, or basic required technologies. It includes the extension of the product line or acquiring components that are all the way required in the daily operations. This kind offers great opportunities to businesses as it opens a hue gateway to diversify around a common set of resources and strategic requirements.

Conglomerate Merger

Conglomerate merger is a kind of venture in which two or more companies belonging to different industrial sectors combine their operations. All the merged companies are no way related to their kind of business and product line rather their operations overlap that of each other. This is just a unification of businesses from different verticals under one flagship enterprise or firm.

Merger Arbitrage

Merger arbitrage is the business of stock trading in companies that are known to acquire takeovers or undergo mergers. The process involves buying a stock at a defined price for immediate sale at a higher price.

There is mainly a hedge fund where all the stocks and shares of merging companies are brought and sold simultaneously to ensure a risk-free profit. A merger arbitrageur who takes care of the stock trading often takes advantage of this process because stock prices often come down during the merger. Later on when the merger is complete the prices increases and the arbitrageur always take profit of this thin line discrepancy of stock prices.

It is a fairly simple concept with which the offer and the target price often come into action. During the announcement of the merger, the stocks either decreases slightly or the stock of the acquirer jumps significantly. The jump is mainly based on the offer price that is between two extremes: an all cash offer or a pure stock offer. Merger transactions can gives an option of all cash offer or an all stock offer. In certain cases it can also come up as a combination of the two that also includes the existence of debts and bonds in the process.

In this process of price variation and option selection, merger arbitrage is possible. This is because the stock of the target firm is usually de-listed because of its possibility of not reaching the offer price until the deal is finalized. The best way to conduct a merger arbitrage is to purchase the stock after the announcement of the merger and sell it after the deal finalization when the stock reaches the offer price.

Merger and Acquisition Valuation

The number as well as the average size of merger and acquisition deals is increasing in India. During post liberalization, increase in domestic competition and competition against cheaper imports have made organisations merge themselves to reap the benefits of a large-sized company. The merger and acquisition valuation is the building block of a proposed deal. It is a technical concept that needs to be estimated carefully.

M&A valuation involves determining the maximum price that a buyer is willing to pay to buy the target company. From the seller's point of view, it means estimating the minimum price he wants to take against his business. If there are many buyers, then each one bids a purchase price based on his valuation. Finally, the seller will give the business to the highest bidder.

The use of different valuation techniques and principles has made valuation a subjective process. A conflict in the choice of technique is the main reason for the failure of many mergers. For instance, the asset value can be determined both at the market price and the cost price. Therefore, it is important that the merging parties should first discuss and agree upon the methods of valuation.

Calculating the swap ratio is at the core of the valuation process. It is the ratio at which the shares of the acquiring company will be exchanged with the shares of the acquired company. For instance, a swap ratio of 1:2 means that the acquiring company will provide its one share for every two shares of the other company.

Strategies of Merger and Acquisition

Strategies play an integral role when it comes to merger and acquisition. A sound strategic decision and procedure is very important to ensure success and fulfilling of expected desires. Every company has different cultures and follows different strategies to define their merger. Some take experience from the past associations, some take lessons from the associations of their known businesses, and some hear their own voice and move ahead without wise evaluation and examination.

Following are some of the most essential strategies of merger and acquisition that can work wonders in the process:

- The first and foremost thing is to determine business plan drivers. It is very important to convert business strategies to set of drivers or a source of motivation to help the merger succeed in all possible ways.
- There should be a strong understanding of the intended business market, market share, and the technological requirements and geographic location of the business. The company should also understand and evaluate all the risks involved and the relative impact on the business.
- Then there is an important need to assess the market by deciding the growth factors through future market opportunities, recent trends, and customer's feedback.
- The integration process should be taken in line with consent of the management from both the companies venturing into the merger.
- Restructuring plans and future parameters should be decided with exchange of information and knowledge from both ends. This involves considering the work culture, employee selection, and the working environment as well.
- At the end, ensure that all those involved in the merger including management of the merger companies, stakeholders, board members, and investors agree on the defined strategies. Once approved, the merger can be taken forward to finalizing a deal.

Mergers and Acquisitions: Valuation Matters

Investors in a company that are aiming to take over another one must determine whether the purchase will be beneficial to them. In order to do so, they must ask themselves how much the company being acquired is really worth.

Naturally, both sides of an M&A deal will have different ideas about the worth of a target company: its seller will tend to value the company at as high of a price as possible, while the buyer will try to get the lowest price that he can.

There are, however, many legitimate ways to value companies. The most common method is to look at comparable companies in an industry, but deal makers employ a variety of other methods and tools when assessing a target company. Here are just a few of them:

1. Comparative Ratios - The following are two examples of the many comparative metrics on which acquiring companies may base their offers:
    - Price-Earnings Ratio (P/E Ratio) - With the use of this ratio, an acquiring company makes an offer that is a multiple of the earnings of the target company. Looking at the P/E for all the stocks within the same industry group will give the acquiring company good guidance for what the target's P/E multiple should be.
    - Enterprise-Value-to-Sales Ratio (EV/Sales) - With this ratio, the acquiring company makes an offer as a multiple of the revenues, again, while being aware of the price-to-sales ratio of other companies in the industry.
2. Replacement Cost - In a few cases, acquisitions are based on the cost of replacing the target company. For simplicity's sake, suppose the value of a company is simply the sum of all its equipment and staffing costs. The acquiring company can literally order the target to sell at that price, or it will create a competitor for the same cost. Naturally, it takes a long time to assemble good management, acquire property and get the right equipment. This method of establishing a price certainly wouldn't make much sense in a service industry where the key assets - people and ideas - are hard to value and develop.
3. Discounted Cash Flow (DCF) - A key valuation tool in M&A, discounted cash flow analysis determines a company's current value according to its estimated future cash flows. Forecasted free cash flows (net income + depreciation/amortization - capital expenditures - change in working capital) are discounted to a present value using the company's weighted average costs of capital (WACC). Admittedly, DCF is tricky to get right, but few tools can rival this valuation method.

Synergy: The Premium for Potential Success

For the most part, acquiring companies nearly always pay a substantial premium on the stock market value of the companies they buy. The justification for doing so nearly always boils down to the notion of synergy; a merger benefits shareholders when a company's post-merger share price increases by the value of potential synergy.

Let's face it, it would be highly unlikely for rational owners to sell if they would benefit more by not selling.

That means buyers will need to pay a premium if they hope to acquire the company, regardless of what pre-merger valuation tells them.

For sellers, that premium represents their company's future prospects. For buyers, the premium represents part of the post-merger synergy they expect can be achieved. The following equation offers a good way to think about synergy and how to determine whether a deal makes sense.

The equation solves for the minimum required synergy:

$$\frac{\text{Pre} - \text{Merger Value of Both Firms} + \text{Synergy}}{\text{Post} - \text{Merger Number of Shares}} = \text{Pre} - \text{Merger Stock Price}$$

In other words, the success of a merger is measured by whether the value of the buyer is enhanced by the action. However, the practical constraints of mergers, which we discuss in part five, often prevent the expected benefits from being fully achieved. Alas, the synergy promised by deal makers might just fall short.

What to Look for

It's hard for investors to know when a deal is worthwhile. The burden of proof should fall on the acquiring company.

To find mergers that have a chance of success, investors should start by looking for some of these simple criteria:

- Price-Earnings Ratio (P/E Ratio) - With the use of this ratio, an acquiring company makes an offer that is a multiple of the earnings of the target company. Looking at the P/E for all the stocks within the same industry group will give the acquiring company good guidance for what the target's P/E multiple should be.
- Enterprise-Value-to-Sales Ratio (EV/Sales) - With this ratio, the acquiring company makes an offer as a multiple of the revenues, again, while being aware of the price-to-sales ratio of other companies in the industry.

Mergers are awfully hard to get right, so investors should look for acquiring companies with a healthy grasp of reality.

Mergers and Acquisitions: Doing the Deal

Start with an Offer

When the CEO and top managers of a company decide that they want to do a merger or acquisition, they start with a tender offer. The process typically begins with the acquiring company carefully and discreetly buying up shares in the target company, or building a position. Once the acquiring company starts to purchase shares in the open market, it is restricted to buying 5% of the total outstanding shares before it must file with the SEC. In the filing, the company must formally declare how many shares it owns and whether it intends to buy the company or keep the shares purely as an investment.

Working with financial advisors and investment bankers, the acquiring company will arrive at an overall price that it's willing to pay for its target in cash, shares or both. The tender offer is then frequently advertised in the business press, stating the offer price and the deadline by which the shareholders in the target company must accept (or reject) it.

The Target's Response

Once the tender offer has been made, the target company can do one of several things:

- Accept the Terms of the Offer - If the target firm's top managers and shareholders are happy with the terms of the transaction, they will go ahead with the deal.
- Attempt to Negotiate - The tender offer price may not be high enough for the target company's shareholders to accept, or the specific terms of the deal may not be attractive. In a merger, there may be much at stake for the management of the target - their jobs, in particular. If they're not satisfied with the terms laid out in the tender offer, the target's management may try to work out more agreeable terms that let them keep their jobs or, even better, send them off with a nice, big compensation package.

Not surprisingly, highly sought-after target companies that are the object of several bidders will have greater latitude for negotiation. Furthermore, managers have more negotiating power if they can show that they are crucial to the merger's future success.

- Execute a Poison Pill or Some Other Hostile Takeover Defence – A poison pill scheme can be triggered by a target company when a hostile suitor acquires a predetermined percentage of company stock. To execute its defence, the target company grants all shareholders - except the acquiring company - options to buy additional stock at a dramatic discount. This dilutes the acquiring company's share and intercepts its control of the company.

- Find a White Knight - As an alternative, the target company's management may seek out a friendlier potential acquiring company, or white knight. If a white knight is found, it will offer an equal or higher price for the shares than the hostile bidder.

Mergers and acquisitions can face scrutiny from regulatory bodies. For example, if the two biggest long-distance companies in the U.S., AT&T and Sprint, wanted to merge, the deal would require approval from the Federal Communications Commission (FCC). The FCC would probably regard a merger of the two giants as the creation of a monopoly or, at the very least, a threat to competition in the industry.

Closing the Deal

Finally, once the target company agrees to the tender offer and regulatory requirements are met, the merger deal will be executed by means of some transaction. In a merger in which one company buys another, the acquiring company will pay for the target company's shares with cash, stock or both.

A cash-for-stock transaction is fairly straightforward: target company shareholders receive a cash payment for each share purchased. This transaction is treated as a taxable sale of the shares of the target company.

If the transaction is made with stock instead of cash, then it's not taxable. There is simply an exchange of share certificates. The desire to steer clear of the tax man explains why so many M&A deals are carried out as stock-for-stock transactions.

When a company is purchased with stock, new shares from the acquiring company's stock are issued directly to the target company's shareholders, or the new shares are sent to a broker who manages them for target company shareholders. The shareholders of the target company are only taxed when they sell their new shares.

When the deal is closed, investors usually receive a new stock in their portfolios - the acquiring company's expanded stock. Sometimes investors will get new stock identifying a new corporate entity that is created by the M&A deal.

Mergers and Acquisitions: Why They Can Fail

It's no secret that plenty of mergers don't work. Those who advocate mergers will argue that the merger will cut costs or boost revenues by more than enough to justify the price premium. It can sound so simple: just combine computer systems, merge a few departments, use sheer size to force down the price of supplies and the merged giant should be more profitable than its parts. In theory, 1+1 = 3 sounds great, but in practice, things can go awry.

Historical trends show that roughly two thirds of big mergers will disappoint on their own terms, which means they will lose value on the stock market. The motivations that drive mergers can be flawed and efficiencies from economies of scale may prove elusive. In many cases, the problems associated with trying to make merged companies work are all too concrete.

Flawed Intentions

For starters, a booming stock market encourages mergers, which can spell trouble. Deals done with highly rated stock as currency are easy and cheap, but the strategic thinking behind them may be easy and cheap too. Also, mergers are often attempt to imitate: somebody else has done a big merger, which prompts other top executives to follow suit.

A merger may often have more to do with glory-seeking than business strategy. The executive ego, which is boosted by buying the competition, is a major force in M&A, especially when combined with the influences from the bankers, lawyers and other assorted advisers who can earn big fees from clients engaged in mergers. Most CEOs get to where they are because they want to be the biggest and the best, and many top executives get a big bonus for merger deals, no matter what happens to the share price later.

On the other side of the coin, mergers can be driven by generalized fear. Globalization, the arrival of new technological developments or a fast-changing economic landscape that makes the outlook uncertain are all factors that can create a strong incentive for defencive mergers. Sometimes the management team feels they have no choice and must acquire a rival before being acquired. The idea is that only big players will survive a more competitive world.

The Obstacles to Making it Work

Coping with a merger can make top managers spread their time too thinly and neglect their core business, spelling doom. Too often, potential difficulties seem trivial to managers caught up in the thrill of the big deal.

The chances for success are further hampered if the corporate cultures of the companies are very different. When a company is acquired, the decision is typically based on product or market synergies, but cultural differences are often ignored. It's a mistake to assume that personnel issues are easily overcome. For example, employees at a target company might be accustomed to easy access to top management, flexible work schedules or even a relaxed dress code. These aspects of a working environment may not seem significant, but if new management removes them, the result can be resentment and shrinking productivity.

More insight into the failure of mergers is found in the highly acclaimed study from McKinsey, a global consultancy. The study concludes that companies often focus too intently on cutting costs following mergers, while revenues, and ultimately, profits, suffer. Merging companies can focus on integration and cost-cutting so much that they neglect day-to-day business, thereby prompting nervous customers to flee. This loss of revenue momentum is one reason so many mergers fail to create value for shareholders.

But remember, not all mergers fail. Size and global reach can be advantageous, and strong managers can often squeeze greater efficiency out of badly run rivals. Nevertheless, the promises made by deal makers demand the careful scrutiny of investors. The success of mergers depends on how realistic the deal makers are and how well they can integrate two companies while maintaining day-to-day operations.

Mergers & Acquisitions Benefit from the Greater Efficiency and Competitive Strength

A merger is a pivotal event for the companies involved. Both parties hope to benefit from the greater efficiency and competitive strength found in the combined company. Strategies are altered and as a result product lines are broadened, strengthened, or refocused; management systems and personnel are changed; and levels and growth rates of profits are shifted.

In many instances, however, one side or the other (or both) lose substantial sums of money. Merger costs, including the direct costs of attorneys, accountants, investment bankers, and consultants, are substantial even though they are not a large percentage of the value of the merger. There is also substantial cost in terms of time required by key employees to evaluate, complete, and implement the merger. Perhaps half of all mergers and acquisitions fail or do not achieve the desired results. Many mergers fail because projected synergies do not materialize, often due to human obstacles.

If a merger is not well received by the employees of the new entity, then its chances of success are greatly diminished. It is critical that the parties involved in a merger become skilled in managing change. Sometimes acquisitions fail for the acquiring company simply because it pays too much for the acquired company. An understanding of pre- and post-merger valuation analysis is required to avoid this pitfall.

Because an entire company is acquired in a merger, determining the advisability of a potential merger requires a much broader analysis of the factors involved than most other areas of financial management. In addition to the usual tax, legal, cash flow, and cash outlay considerations, competitive positions and strategies are important.

The occurrence of a merger often raises concerns in antitrust circles. Devices such as the Herfindahl index can analyze the impact of a merger on a market and what, if any, action could prevent it. Regulatory bodies such as the European Commission and the United States Department of Justice may investigate anti-trust cases for monopolies dangers, and have the power to block mergers.

The remainder of this article will discuss several topics important to understanding the basic nature of and issues surrounding mergers and acquisitions. These include methods of business combinations, motives for mergers and acquisitions, accounting for mergers, and before-and-after financial analysis.

Methods of Business Combination

There are several methods for achieving a business combination. It is useful to have an understanding of these different methods. Hereafter, the term acquisitions will be used to refer to any type of business combination.

Acquisition

An acquisition usually refers to the purchase of the assets of a company. However, in the remainder of this course, the term will be used in a much broader sense to indicate the purchase of shares, assets, or companies in the merger process. Thus, the narrow, distinct meaning of the term will not be used. An acquisition can take the form of a purchase of the stock or other equity interests of the target entity, or the acquisition of all or a substantial amount of its assets.

- Share purchases - in a share purchase the buyer buys the shares of the target company from the shareholders of the target company. The buyer will take on the company with all its assets and liabilities.
- Asset purchases - in an asset purchase the buyer buys the assets of the target company from the target company. In simplest form this leaves the target company as an empty shell, and the cash it receives from the acquisition is then paid back to its shareholders by dividend or through liquidation.

  However, one of the advantages of an asset purchase for the buyer is that it can "cherry-pick" the assets that it wants and leave the assets - and liabilities - that it does not.

Merger

In a merger, two separate companies combine and only one of them survives. In other words, the merged (acquired) company goes out of existence, leaving its assets and liabilities to the acquiring company. Usually when two companies of significantly different sizes merge, the smaller company will merge into the larger one, leaving the larger company intact.

Consolidation

A consolidation is a combination of two or more companies in which an entirely new corporation is formed and all merging companies cease to exist. Shares of the new company are exchanged for shares of the merging ones.

Two similarly sized companies usually consolidate rather than merge. Although the distinction between merger and consolidation is important, the terms are often used interchangeably, with either used to refer generally to a joining of the assets and liabilities of two companies.

Leveraged Buyout

A leveraged buyout (LBO) is a type of acquisition that occurs when a group of investors, sometimes led by the management of a company (management buyout or MBO), borrows funds to purchase the company. The assets and future earnings of the company are used to secure the financing required to purchase the company.

Sometimes employees are allowed to participate through an employee stock ownership plan, which may provide tax advantages and improve employee productivity by giving employees an equity stake in the company.

Holding Company

A holding company is a company that owns sufficient voting stock to have a controlling interest in one or more companies called subsidiaries. Effective working control or substantial influence can be gained through ownership of as little as 5 percent to as much as 51 percent of the outstanding shares, depending on how widely the shares are distributed. A holding company that engages in the management of the subsidiaries is called a parent company.

Divestitures

While divestitures do not represent a business combination, they are a means of facilitating the acquisition of part of a company. Sometimes divestitures are used by companies as a means to improve earnings and shareholder value, or as a means of raising capital. A divestiture involves the sale of a portion of a company. Two popular means of divestiture are spin-offs and equity carve-outs.

In a spin-off, a company distributes all of its shares in a subsidiary to the company's shareholders as a tax-free exchange. The reorganisation of AT&T is an example of a spin-off. AT&T was reorganised into three separate publicly traded corporations, and a fourth business was sold. What remained was AT&T, comprised of long distance and wireless phone businesses, a credit card business, and two other companies that were formed and spun off to shareholders by giving them stock in the two companies. One of these companies, now Lucent Technologies, was an equipment producer and research company. It was spun-off to avoid conflicts with customers of other AT&T products. The other company was NCR, a computer company. This was spun-off to remove the effects of a poor-performing business from AT&T's results. An equity carve-out is similar to a spin-off. It occurs when a company sells some of its shares in a subsidiary to the public. This raises additional capital for the company.

Hostile versus Friendly Combinations

Acquisitions may be hostile or friendly. In a hostile acquisition, the acquiring, or bidder, company makes an offer to purchase the acquired or target company, but the management of the target company resists the offer. At that point, the bidder often tries to take control of the target through a tender offer, whereby the bidder offers to purchase a majority of the target's stock at a predetermined price, set sufficiently higher than the current market price to attract the shareholders' attention. Hostile acquisitions are typically more expensive for both parties since they involve more time and negotiations, fees to experts such as attorneys and investment bankers, and may result in a bidding war where multiple bidders enter the contest for control. The large number of hostile acquisitions in the 1980s led to the coining of the term "market for corporate control." This terminology reflects the view that acquisitions are really market-based contests whereby corporate managers bid to control corporate assets, with the highest bidder receiving control.

Even though hostile acquisitions receive much of the media attention surrounding acquisitions, the great majority of acquisitions are; friendly. In a friendly acquisition, the management of both companies come to an agreement over the terms of the acquisition. Many acquisitions that begin as hostile end up being completed on a friendly basis.

Motives for Acquisitions

The overriding motive for any acquisition should be to maximize shareholder value. There has been increasing emphasis on maximizing shareholder value and managers are under more and more pressure to do so. The threat of a hostile takeover places pressure on all corporate managers to manage their companies to maximize value, or risk being taken over and restructured by another management. Increasingly competitive global capital markets, active institutional investors, active and independent boards of directors, and better informed market participants have all led to an increased focus by shareholders on shareholder value, and have placed increased pressure on corporate managers to maximize shareholder value.

Acquisitions are a means of creating shareholder value by exploiting synergies, increasing growth, replacing inefficient managers, gaining market power, and extracting benefits from financial and operational restructuring. However, for value to be created, the benefits of these motives must exceed the costs.

These motives are considered to *add shareholder value*:

- Economies of scale: This refers to the fact that the combined company can often reduce duplicate departments or operations, lowering the costs of the company relative to theoretically the same revenue stream, thus increasing profit.
- Increased revenue/Increased Market Share: This motive assumes that the company will be absorbing a major competitor and dtjdf its power (by capturing increased market share) to set prices.

- Cross selling: For example, a bank buying a stock broker could then sell its banking products to the stock broker's customers, while the broker can sign up the bank's customers for brokerage accounts. Or, a manufacturer can acquire and sell complementary products.
- Synergy: Better use of complementary resources.
- Taxes: A profitable company can buy a loss maker to use the target's tax write-offs. In the United States and many other countries, rules are in place to limit the ability of profitable companies to "shop" for loss making companies, limiting the tax motive of an acquiring company.
- Geographical or other diversification: This is designed to smooth the earnings results of a company, which over the long term smoothens the stock price of a company, giving conservative investors more confidence in investing in the company. However, this does not always deliver value to shareholders .
- Resource transfer: resources are unevenly distributed across firms and the interaction of target and acquiring firm resources can create value through either overcoming information asymmetry or by combining scarce resources.
- Financial restructuring: a change in control can lead to a more cost-effective or safer capital structure, and more efficient use of financial assets.
- Business mix restructuring: the acquirer may divest non-core businesses.

The following motives are considered to *not* add shareholder value:

- Diversification: While this may hedge a company against a downturn in an individual industry it fails to deliver value, since it is possible for individual shareholders to achieve the same hedge by diversifying their portfolios at a much lower cost than those associated with a merger.
- Overextension: Tend to make the organisation fuzzy and unmanageable.
- Manager's hubris: manager's overconfidence about expected synergies from M&A which results in overpayment for the target company.
- Empire Building: Managers have larger companies to manage and hence more power.

- Manager's Compensation: In the past, certain executive management teams had their payout based on the total amount of profit of the company, instead of the profit per share, which would give the team a perverse incentive to buy companies to increase the total profit while decreasing the profit per share (which hurts the owners of the company, the shareholders); although some empirical studies show that compensation is rather linked to profitability and not mere profits of the company.
- Bootstrapping: Example: how ITT executed its merger.
- Vertical integration: Companies acquire part of a supply chain and benefit from the resources.

Why Grow through Acquisitions?

There are numerous reasons for a company to want to grow. Growth is often considered vital to the health of a company. A stagnating company may have difficulty attracting high-quality management. Furthermore, larger companies may pay higher salaries to top management than smaller companies. In some industries, size itself may bring competitive advantages.

For example, marketing dominance may be strengthened through improved access to advertising. In addition, a large company may have significantly higher production or distribution efficiencies than a smaller one.

Sometimes growth is a means of survival. For example, companies in the telecommunications industry have grown through acquisition in an effort to compete to control phone lines, cable systems, and content. The merger of Viacom, Blockbuster, and Paramount created a conglomeration of television and movie production, video distribution and publishing, and cable channels in an industry where many companies are merging to compete to become comprehensive media powerhouses. Firms in the defence industry have merged to survive in a declining market. Finally, tax laws may encourage merger growth.

Despite these reasons to grow, growth by itself does not necessarily benefit either the stockholders or the managers of a company. Growth is not something that must be achieved regardless of its price. Throughout this course, emphasis will be placed on an acquisition's impact on value. Careful comparisons between benefits and costs will be made. A good acquisition will be defined as one that can be expected to increase the stock price (other things being equal) of the acquiring company.

Furthermore, a merger is not always the best way to grow. A company can achieve internal expansion through investment in projects generated within the company itself. By doing so, efficiency may be improved, existing activities may be expanded, and new products may be introduced.

External expansion takes place through an acquisition. Because of the similarities between the acquisition and the capital budgeting process, the same approval and review forms, control procedures, and post-audit examinations commonly used for analyzing capital expenditures can be applied to an acquisition analysis as well. In addition, consideration should be given at the highest levels of the business to how the proposed acquisition fits in with the needs and strategic thrust of the company. With a good fit, even at a relatively high price, the company being considered may be viewed as a good investment. Without a good fit, the acquisition may not be a good deal at almost any price.

Financial Analysis

An acquisition is essentially as an investment decision. An initial outlay is invested to obtain expected future benefits. A good acquisition will generate greater benefits, in present value terms, than its costs. The likely effect of a good acquisition will be to increase the stock value of the acquiring company.

To properly conduct this type of acquisition analysis, some strategic concepts and many valuation tools are required. The discipline of corporate finance shapes both the strategic and the financial analysis necessary to identify and evaluate acquisition candidates and assess the impact of acquisitions on company value.

Acquisitions are financial decisions that should be consistent with the company's goal of shareholder wealth maximization. Sound and thorough financial analysis should be a part of any acquisition. Many acquisitions that fail, in the sense that they do not add value to the acquiring company, do so because they were motivated by wishful thinking rather than sound and thorough financial analysis. This discipline starts with the methods for analyzing a company's financial statements. The next step is an understanding of lenders' and investors' required returns and corporate valuation analysis. Through this framework, the financial analyst will be better able to view the acquisition process as a competition with other stock purchasers, all of whom are looking for good buys.

Acquisitions are also strategic decisions that should be consistent with the mission of the acquiring company and fit into its overall strategic plan. The reasons for an acquisition must be understood in the context of a company's strategic analysis. Acquisitions can be justified in terms of the competitive advantages they produce (for example, marketing positions may be strengthened or production costs reduced). Other motives include improved management, tax benefits, or defencive maneuvers to prevent takeover by other companies. Finally, many acquisitions produce benefits purely from the financial and business restructuring that follows a change in control — as illustrated by the value increases following leveraged buyouts.

Accounting for Mergers

Two methods of accounting for acquisitions — purchase and pooling of interests — are often discussed. Financial statements that record the results of an acquisition must follow one of these two techniques. Financial managers must be aware of the accounting requirements as merger negotiations near completion.

Under the purchase method, the acquired company is treated by the acquiring company as an investment, analogous to a capital budgeting expenditure. A totally new ownership is assumed. Asset values are reappraised in light of estimates of their current market values, and the balance sheet is restated to the new levels. As a result of these adjustments, goodwill often results. Goodwill is the amount by which the price paid for a company exceeds the company's estimated net worth at market value. Goodwill must be written off against future net income over a reasonable period. Such deductions against income are not deductible for tax purposes in most countries.

Under the pooling of interests method, the assets and liabilities of the two combining companies are simply added together. Since only the book values of the assets and liabilities are considered, no goodwill results. In most countries, there are severe restrictions on a company's use of the pooling of interests method. As a result of these restrictions, the pooling of interests method is used much less today than it was in the past.

Merger Negotiation and Due Diligence

Negotiating the merger can be difficult. The simple answer to making it work is: hire the best advisors. Their job is to manage the negotiation process in such a way that it reaches a satisfactory conclusion — both parties must see a gain, and both parties must be protected — and it does not run a foul of legal and regulatory constraints. The goal is to reach an agreement that is embodied in the "sale and purchase agreement" — which includes all the key terms of the deal, such as price, payment method, adjustments, constraints on the seller, etc as well as accounting definitions, accounting and tax warranties and indemnities, etc.

Quite often, a proposed merger or acquisition gets canned or valued down following conflicts over intellectual property rights, personnel, accounting discrepancies or incompatibilities in integrating information technology systems. The process of researching, understanding and, in some cases, avoiding these risks is known as due diligence.

"Due diligence is going in and digging a hole in the ground and seeing if there's oil, instead of taking someone's word on it," says Joseph Bankoff, a lawyer. "If you don't do a sufficient amount of due diligence, you don't really know what questions to ask."

Due diligence for mergers and acquisitions requires broad and deep data analysis of assets and liabilities, including large balance sheet items such as accounts receivable, inventory, and accounts payable to establish fair market value. It also means analyzing

collections of receivables and inventory to identify doubtful accounts or obsolete stock, and analyzing cash receipts and billing files using historical trends to assess the reliability and adequacy of projected cash flows. The due diligence team must sift through press reports and regulatory filings to uncover any actual or potential legal, environmental, or other problems. In the case of a technology acquisition, a due diligence investigation should answer pertinent questions such as whether an application is too bulky to run on the mobile devices the marketing plan calls for or whether customers are right when they complain about a lack of scalability for a high-end system.

Due diligence entails taking all the "reasonable steps" to ensure that both buyer and seller get what they expect "and not a lot of other things that you did not count on or expect," Bankoff explains. The process involves everything from reading the fine print in corporate legal and financial documents such as equity vesting plans and patents to interviewing customers, corporate officers and key developers. It helps to identify potential risks and red flags.

Financing the Deal

Mergers are generally differentiated from acquisitions partly by the way in which they are financed and partly by the relative size of the companies. Various methods of financing an M&A deal exist:

A company acquiring another will frequently pay for the other company with cash. Such transactions are usually termed acquisitions rather than mergers because the shareholders of the target company are removed from the picture and the target comes under the (indirect) control of the bidder's shareholders alone.

An acquisition can involve a cash and debt combination, or a combination of cash and stock of the purchasing entity, or just stock.

A "merger" or "merger of equals" is often financed by an all stock deal (a stock swap), known in the UK as an all share deal. Such deals are considered a mergers rather than acquisitions because neither company pays money, and the shareholders of each company end up as the combined shareholders of the merged company. There are two methods of merging companies in this way:

- one company takes ownership of the other, issuing new shares in itself to the shareholders of the company being acquired as payment, or
- a third company is created which takes ownership of both companies (or their assets) in exchange for shares in itself issued to the shareholders of the two merging companies.

Where one company is notably larger than the other, people may nevertheless may be wary of calling the deal a merger, as the shareholders of the larger company will still dominate the merged company If cash is paid, the cash can be raised in a number of ways. The company may have sufficient cash available in its account, but this is unlikely. More often the cash will be borrowed from a bank, or raised by an issue of bonds, or of equity.

Acquisitions financed through debt are known as leveraged buyouts, and the debt will typically be moved down onto the balance sheet of the acquired company. Many leveraged acquisitions include a component of mezzanine debt, which falls between senior secured bank debt and equity.

Post-merger Integration

Some problems must inevitably occur when two companies combine; however, these problems can be anticipated and minimized. Managers of the acquired company will feel some loss of autonomy since their decisions must now be meshed with the policies of the merged company. Once-simple procedures become complicated by a new control system. Furthermore, the acquired company's managers are often concerned about personal recognition, advancement, and job security in the new company. Historically, many managers of acquired companies have lost their jobs following an acquisition.

Problems in the acquiring company will emerge as well. Its strengths and weaknesses and the skills and potential of its personnel will not be immediately apparent in the combined company. In addition, the staff of the acquiring company may lack the expertise to understand completely the production processes of the acquired company and may therefore be unable to make appropriate decisions about them. Disciplines, procedures, and controls that have been well established over time may not work as well in the new environment. There may be a clash of corporate cultures.

Solutions to these problems cover too broad an area for satisfactory coverage in this brief introduction. Several suggestions can be given. Immediate arrangements should be made for orientation of the new staff, for discussing procedures with operational personnel, and for making shifts in assignments where necessary. Teams who are responsible for preventing the imposition of inappropriate controls on the new division, and for educating top management about the characteristics of the unfamiliar company, can be appointed during the merger planning process. Furthermore, the increased opportunities for advancement in the larger, merged company can be communicated to lower-level employees. Finally, a special effort can be made to listen to what is happening during the initial period of difficulty.

Chapter 2

Corporate Restructuring

Definition of Corporate 'Restructuring'

A significant modification made to the debt, operations or structure of a company. This type of corporate action is usually made when there are significant problems in a company, which are causing some form of financial harm and putting the overall business in jeopardy. The hope is that through restructuring, a company can eliminate financial harm and improve the business.

Corporate restructuring is the process of redesigning one or more aspects of a company. The process of reorganising a company may be implemented due to a number of different factors, such as positioning the company to be more competitive, survive a currently adverse economic climate, or poise the corporation to move in an entirely new direction. Here are some examples of why corporate restructuring may take place and what it can mean for the company.

Restructuring a corporate entity is often a necessity when the company has grown to the point that the original structure can no longer efficiently manage the output and general interests of the company. For example, a corporate restructuring may call for spinning off some departments into subsidiaries as a means of creating a more effective management model as well as taking advantage of tax breaks that would allow the corporation to divert more revenue to the production process.

In this scenario, the restructuring is seen as a positive sign of growth of the company and is often welcome by those who wish to see the corporation gain a larger market share.

Valuations in Restructuring

In corporate restructuring, valuations are used as negotiating tools and more than third-party reviews designed for litigation avoidance. This distinction between negotiation and process is a difference between financial restructuring and corporate finance.

Restructuring in Europe

The "London Approach"

Historically, European banks handled non-investment grade lending and capital structures that were fairly straightforward. Nicknamed the "London Approach" in the UK, restructurings focused on avoiding debt write-offs rather than providing distressed companies with an appropriately sized balance sheet. This approach became impractical in the 1990s with private equity increasing demand for highly leveraged capital structures that created the market in high-yield and mezzanine debt. Increased volume of distressed debt drew in hedge funds and credit derivatives deepened the market—trends outside the control of both the regulator and the leading commercial banks.

Characteristics

- Cash management and cash generation during crisis
- Impaired Loan Advisory Services (ILAS)
- Retention of corporate management in the form of "stay bonus" payments or equity grants
- Sale of underutilised assets, such as patents or brands
- Outsourcing of operations such as payroll and technical support to a more efficient third party
- Moving of operations such as manufacturing to lower-cost locations
- Reorganisation of functions such as sales, marketing, and distribution
- Renegotiation of labour contracts to reduce overhead
- Refinancing of corporate debt to reduce interest payments
- A major public relations campaign to reposition the company with consumers
- Forfeiture of all or part of the ownership share by pre-restructuring stock holders (if the remainder represents only a fraction of the original firm, it is termed a stub)

- Improving the efficiency and productivity through new investments, R&D and business engineering.

Results

A company that has been restructured effectively will theoretically be leaner, more efficient, better organised, and better focused on its core business with a revised strategic and financial plan. If the restructured company was a leverage acquisition, the parent company will likely resell it at a profit if the restructuring has proven successful.

What is Corporate Restructuring?

In the current economic climate, many companies are facing a difficult operating environment. In some cases, this means that corporate restructuring may have to be undertaken for the business to remain viable.

What is corporate restructuring? Corporate restructuring can cover a whole range of activities, from cost-cutting and streamlining, re-branding, financial restructuring to the worst case scenario of winding down a business. Businesses can go through many forms of corporate restructuring to remain competitive and stay in business. Restructuring does not have to be something drastic, but can be a series of measures undertaken on a regular basis by the company's management.

Debt Restructuring

In the current economic climate, many businesses are having to go through corporate debt restructuring. Most businesses carry some form of debt, whether it is a simple business loan or corporate bonds. In certain situations, it makes sense for businesses to restructure their debt. For example, when interest rates are high, swapping high interest rate bank loans for other forms of debt can save money. In another scenario, if a business has made a big profit or has increased cash flow, it might make sense to pay down some of the debt, perhaps earlier than planned. In any scenario, debt restructuring, if done properly, can save businesses a lot of money in interest payments and fees.

The most extreme case of debt restructuring comes into play, when businesses cannot pay back creditors. In such cases, it is important to act earlier than later. Banks can help with consolidating your debt, if you have several loans, to help reduce interest payments or obtain a temporary freeze on interest payments, to help you cope until business rebounds. If you are unable to repay suppliers, speak directly to the suppliers and see if they can arrange a rolling credit or reduce prices. Sometimes suppliers will agree to some kind of repayment arrangement, if, for example, you agree to exclusively use them.

Streamlining Your Business

Another form of corporate restructuring is cost-cutting or streamlining a business. As businesses grow, it is easy for overheads to increase, employees numbers to swell or businesses to lose focus. It makes sense on an annual basis to review operations and figure out where the most costs are stemming from and try to streamline these areas of the business. Many businesses, as they grow, end up adding more and more functions and in some cases, may end up moving away from their core business.

For example, it may make sense to try to outsource certain aspects of the business, to cut costs. For example, for small businesses, it does not make financial sense to have their own payroll department or shipping department – these tasks can be outsourced, probably for much less than it would cost to hire people to undertake these tasks internally.

Getting Professional Help

Depending on the size of the business, it may make commercial sense to hire professional accountants or consultants to analyse your business and suggest corporate restructuring steps to be undertaken.

At Wilkins Kennedy we have a dedicated WK Restructuring and Recovery team who have helped revive many businesses in financial distress. Not only do we understand what you are going through but we also have a track record for providing realistic solutions. Contact our team today to see how we can best help your business.

Corporate Debt Restructuring (CDR) Meaning

Corporate Debt Restructuring ("CDR") mechanism is a voluntary non statutory mechanism under which financial institutions and banks come together to restructure the debt of companies facing financial difficulties due to internal or external factors, in order to provide timely support to such companies.

Corporate Debt Restructuring (CDR)

The intention behind the mechanism is to revive such companies and also safeguard the interests of the lending institutions and other stakeholders. The CDR mechanism is available to companies who enjoy credit facilities from more than one lending institution. The mechanism allows such institutions, to restructure the debt in a speedy and transparent manner for the benefit of all.

"To ensure timely and transparent mechanism for restructuring of corporate debts of viable entities facing problems, for the benefit of all concerned."

"To aim at preserving viable corporates that are affected by certain internal and external factors".

"To minimize the losses to creditors and other stakeholders through an orderly and co-ordinated restructuring programme".

The CDR Mechanism has a Three Tier Structure-

CDR standing Forum –The representative general body of banks and financial institutions participating in the CDR system. It is a self empowered body which lays down the policies and guidelines, such as the timeframe within which a unit shall become viable and the minimum level of promoter contribution. It also monitors the progress of corporate debt restructuring.

The Forum also provides a platform for borrowers and creditors to amicably evolve policies for working out debt restructuring plans in the interest of everyone. The CDR Standing Forum comprises of Chairman and Managing Director, Industrial Development Bank of India Ltd; Chairman, State Bank of India; Managing Director and CEO, ICICI Bank Limited; Chairman, Indian Banks' Association as well as Chairmen and Managing Directors of all banks and financial institutions participating as permanent members in the system. Most of the big financial institutions in India that lend money to companies are permanent participating members of the standing forum.

CDR Core Group – A CDR Core Group is carved out of the CDR Standing Forum to assist the Standing Forum in convening the meetings and taking decisions relating to policy, on behalf of the Standing Forum. The Core Group consists of Chief Executives of Industrial Development Bank of India Ltd., State Bank of India, ICICI Bank Ltd, Bank of Baroda, Bank of India, Punjab National Bank, Indian Banks' Association and Deputy Chairman of Indian Banks' Association representing foreign banks in India.

It lays down policies and guidelines to be followed by the CDR Empowered Group and CDR Cell for debt restructuring, including policies regarding the operational difficulties faced by the CDR Empowered Group. It also prescribes time frame, and modalities for the enforcement of time frame for cases that are referred for the CDR mechanism.

CDR Empowered Group- The individual cases of corporate debt restructuring are decided by the CDR Empowered Group. This group consists of Executive director level representatives of Industrial Development Bank of India Ltd., ICICI Bank Ltd. and State Bank of India as standing members, in addition to ED level representatives of financial institutions and banks who have an exposure to the concerned company. While standing members facilitate the conduct of the group's meetings, voting is in proportion to the exposure of the creditors only. The CDR Empowered Group considers the preliminary report of all cases of requests of restructuring, submitted to it by the CDR Cell. After the Empowered Group decides that restructuring of the company is prima-facie feasible and the enterprise is potentially viable in terms of the policies and guidelines evolved by the Standing Forum, the detailed restructuring package is worked out by the CDR Cell in conjunction with the Lead Institution, which is the institution which has the highest exposure in the concerned company.

The CDR Empowered Group examines the viability and rehabilitation potential of the company and approves the restructuring package within a specified time frame of 90 days, or at best within 180 days from the date on which it received the reference. The decision of the CDR Empowered Group is final and if it finds the restructuring package feasible and approves the scheme then the company is put on the restructuring mode. If restructuring is not found viable, the creditors are then free to take necessary steps for immediate recovery of dues and / or liquidation or winding up of the company, collectively or individually.

CDR Cell – The CDR Cell makes the initial scrutiny about the health of the company and the role of corporate governance, and scrutinizes the of the proposals received from borrowers / creditors, by calling for proposed rehabilitation plan and other information and puts up the matter before the CDR Empowered Group within one month to decide if rehabilitation is prima facie feasible. If found feasible, the CDR Cell will proceed to prepare detailed Rehabilitation Plan with the help of creditors and, if necessary with experts to be engaged from outside.

Reference to CDR System

Reference to the CDR Cell may be made by (i) one or more creditor who have minimum 20% share in either the working capital or term finance of the company in respect of which the reference is made, or (ii) by the concerned corporate if such corporate is supported by a bank or financial institution having 20% stake as above.

Legal Basis and the Case of Foreign Lenders

CDR is a non-statutory mechanism and a voluntary system which is based on debtor creditor agreement ("DCA") and inter-creditor agreement ("ICA"). The debtors accede to the DCA either at the time of the original loan documentation (for future cases) or at the time of reference to the CDR Cell. All participants in the CDR mechanism through their membership to the standing forum enter into a legally binding agreement, with necessary enforcement and penal clauses to operate the system through laid down policies and guidelines. The ICA signed by the creditors is valid for three years and renewed for a similar term thereafter.

The lenders in foreign currency outside the country are not part of the CDR mechanism. Such creditors and also creditors like GIC, LIC, UTI etc., who have not joined the CDR mechanism, could join the same for a particular companies debt restructuring by signing transaction to transaction ICA, wherever they have credit exposure.

As per section 9 of the ICA which deals with the participation of non members in the CDR mechanism;

> *"the Participating Financial Institutions and Banks agree that parties which are eligible and have not joined the CDR System may be permitted by the CDR Empowered Group to join in the Workout of Restructuring Scheme of an Eligible Borrower to whom they have provided Financial Assistance by signing/ executing letter of accession in the form provided in Part B of Schedule-II hereto on transaction–to-transaction basis, prior to the consideration of the preliminary Restructuring Scheme by the CDR Empowered Group. Upon admission by the CDR Empowered Group, such party shall be deemed to be a Participating Financial Institution or Bank, as the case may be, for the purposes of this Agreement and shall pay Rs. 2 lakh (Rupees Two Lakh) at the time of signing the Letter of Accession."*

Accordingly, a foreign lender may become party to an ICA agreement if permitted by the participating financial institution or bank, on a case by case basis. When a foreign lender who has extended credit to a company wants to be a party to the CDR mechanism it is up to the existing participating banks and financial institutions to allow or refuse such an inclusion.

Section 12 of the ICA Reads;

> *"a decision of the CDR Empowered Group relating to prima facie feasibility and/or final approval of a Restructuring Scheme shall be taken by a Super-Majority Vote at a duly convened meeting, after giving reasonable notice, to the Lenders and to the Eligible Borrower".*

Where a foreign lender becomes party to the ICA as per section 9 above and signs the ICA for particular companies debt restructuring, the question that arises is, whether such lender will be included in the super majority vote? To answer that question it is important to understand the definitions of Super majority Vote and Lender.

Section 1 (z) of the ICA Defines, "Super-Majority Vote" as;

> *"Votes cast in favour of a proposal by not less than sixty percent (60%) of number of Lenders and holding not less than seventy-five percent (75%) of the aggregate Principal Outstanding Financial Assistance".*

Section 1 (q) Defines Lender as;

> *"The Participating Financial Institutions and/ or Banks, which have granted Financial Assistance to such Eligible Borrower and a party to this Agreement".*

Once a foreign lender signs the ICA as per section 9 above, it falls within the definition of Lender as a 'party to the agreement'. A lender shall vote in the super majority vote as per the definition of Super Majority Vote above. Hence, the foreign Lender gets voice in the decision making process and is counted towards calculating the 60% and 75% thresholds.

The CDR system favours the Indian banks. While foreign lenders do get the right to vote in the super majority vote once they sign the ICA, What tilts the mechanism in favour of Indian banks is that it is the existing group of participating financial institutions and banks who get to choose on a case by case basis if they want to include a new lender to the CDR mechanism.

It could be debated that the existing members may not be keen to allow a foreign lender with an exposure that could account for more than 25% of the voting in the Super Majority Vote. For this reason foreign lenders who have minor exposure to a company prefers to deal with the company independently rather than becoming part of the CDR mechanism as signing the ICA would bind them to the final approved package.

Hypothetical

Assume that a company has the following structure of debt on its books;

(a) Domestic bank lending- 45%

(b) External commercial borrowing- 38%

(c) FCCBs (Foreign currency convertible bonds) – 17%

In a CDR mechanism for such company there is an omnipresent spectre of favour towards domestic banks as they may choose not to include the lenders falling under category (b) and (c) in the CDR mechanism. Once the final restructuring package is formulated it will most likely have an effect on lenders falling under category (b) and (c) as well. For example where as per the terms of the package the company decides to sell some of its assets on which the foreign lenders had a charge. CDR Empowered Group has quasi judicial powers and its decision and approved package are final. The only recourse left to the foreign lenders is to petition the court for winding up of the company and not give a no objection certificate which is usually required from the Lenders for sale of an asset by the company.

Other Aspects

Category 1 and 2: One of the main features of restructuring under the CDR system is the provision of two categories of debt restructuring. Accounts which are classified as 'standard' and 'sub-standard' in the books of the creditors are restructured under the first category (category 1). Accounts which are classified as 'doubtful' in the books of the creditors are restructured under the second category (category 2).

To understand this classification it is important to understand how accounts are classified as standard and sub-standard.

Firstly, a Non-Performing Asset is a loan or an advance where:

- Interest and/or instalment of principal remain overdue for a period of more than 90 days in respect of a Term Loan
- The account remains 'Out of order'@ for a period of more than 90 days, in respect of an Overdraft/ Cash Credit (OD/CC)
- The bill remains overdue for a period of more than 90 days in the case of bills purchased and discounted
- Any amount to be received remains overdue for a period of more than 90 days in respect of other accounts.

Secondly, Non Performing Assets are classified as Sub-standard, Doubtful and Loss Assets.

- Standard asset (or loan) is a loan which is less risky.
- Sub-standard asset is one which has remained a Non Performing Asset for a period less than or equal to 12 months. In this case, the current net worth of the borrower or guarantor or the current market value of the security charged is not enough to ensure recovery of the dues to the banks in full. In other words, such assets have well defined credit weakness with a distinct possibility that the banks will suffer some loss.
- Doubtful asset is one which has remained in the sub standard category for a period of 12 months. These have all the characteristics of a sub standard asset and additionally the weakness is so defined that it makes collection in full highly questionable or improbable.

What's the Difference between Category 1 and Category 2?

Under category 2 it is not binding on the creditors to provide additional financing worked out under the CDR package, so what happens is that the existing loans are restructured and it is on the promoter to firm up additional financing. All other features under category 1 and category 2 such as standstill, asset classification etc are the same.

Stand still clause- One of the most important elements of the DCA is the stand still clause whereby both parties commit themselves not to take recourse to any other legal action during the standstill period, which is the period of 90 or 180 days as the case may be. This helps the system work well and undertake the necessary debt restructuring exercise without any outside intervention, judicial or otherwise.

Additional financing and Exit Option- Additional finance as per the terms of the final CDR package is to be provided by all creditors of a standard or sub-standard account irrespective of whether they are working capital or term creditors on a pro rata basis. In case for any internal reason, any creditor who is outside the minimum 75% and 60% Super Majority Vote threshold does not wish to commit additional financing, that creditor will have an exit option. However, such creditor has to either, (a) arrange for its share of additional finance to be provided by a new or existing creditor, or (b) agree to the deferment of first year's interest due to it after the CDR package becomes effective. The first year's deferred interest without compounding is payable along with the last installment of the principal due to the creditor.

Conversion option- The CDR Empowered Group while deciding the restructuring package should also decide regarding the issue of convertibility (into equity) option as part of the restructuring exercise whereby the banks and financial institutions shall have a right to convert a portion of the restructured amount into equity investment.

Meaning of Corporate Restructuring

The term corporate restructuring is a wide and varied term. It has no legal definition as the term has not been defined in any legal legislation. Hence, neither it has clear and precise meaning nor can it be defined with precision.

Etymologically the term" Restructuring" means 'giving new structure or rebuild or rearrange'. In this perspective, 'Corporate Restructuring' is defined as a process of rearranging the organisational or business structure of the company for increased efficiency and profitable growth.

Simply stated, Corporate Restructuring is a comprehensive process by which a company can consolidate or rearrange its organisational set up or business operations and strengthen its position so as to achieve its short-term or /and long term objectives and establish itself as a synergetic , dynamic , continuing as well as successful independent corporate entity in the competitive environment.

In the words of hon'ble Justice D.Y. Chandrachud "Corporate Restructuring" is the means that can be employed to meet challenges which confronts businesses. To conclude, it is a process undertaken by a business / corporate/ any other such entity whether proprietorship or partnership for the purpose of bringing about changes for better and to make the business competitive.

Need and Scope of Corporate Restructuring

Today, corporate restructuring has become common to the corporate sector in order to grow and survive in the present ongoing corporate environment for increased efficiency and profitable growth. It is mainly concerned with reorganising or restructuring or rearranging the organisational or business activities of the company as a whole in the form of Merger, Amalgamation or Takeover or Joint Venture etc, so as to achieve certain predetermined objectives at corporate level.

Some of Such Corporate Objectives are as Follows:-

Orderly Redirection of the Firms Activities: Deploying the firm's surplus funds from one business to another for profitable growth.

Exploiting the inter dependence among the present and perspective business within corporate Portfolio.

Risk Reduction and Development of Core Competencies

Therefore, when the corporate enterprises consider the scheme of restructuring their business activities they have to take a wholesome view of the business activities so as to introduce a scheme of restructuring at all level in a phase manner. It also aims at improving the competitive position of an individual business, maximizing its contribution to the corporate level objectives and exploiting the strategic assets accumulated by a business to enhance the competitive advantage. Thus, restructuring would help bringing an edge over competitors.

Needs of Corporate Restructuring

The various needs of undertaking the scheme of corporate restructuring in this modern competitive business / corporate world are discussed briefly as follows:-

a. To focus on core strengths, operational synergy , and efficient allocation of managerial capabilities and infrastructure
b. Consolidation and economies of scale by expansion and diversion to exploit the extended domestic and international markets
c. Revival and rehabilitation of sick unit by adjusting the losses of such sick units with profits of healthy company
d. Acquiring the constant supply of raw materials and access to scientific research and technological development
e. Capital restructuring by appropriate mix up of loans and equity capital to reduce cost of servicing and to increase return on capital employed
f. Improve the corporate performances to bring it at par with competitors.

Corporate Restructuring Law and Legal Definition

The process of corporate restructuring involves evaluating the business/turnaround strategy, providing valuation analysis of the business, its components and assets and assessing the financial alternatives available for consideration. Some of the tasks involved may include, among others:

1. Stabilizing operations and financial crisis
2. Analyzing operational economics and cash flow dynamics
3. Restructuring financial obligations to match cash flow potential
4. Redesigning business models to be more competitive, including the rationalization of SKUs, channels of distribution and management layers

5. Evaluation of management
6. Turnaround plan development and implementation
7. Financial restructuring
8. Management of relations with debtholder/investors
9. Analysis of financial alternatives
10. Development & management of wind-down and liquidation strategies
11. Cash flow forecasting and management
12. Viability analysis
13. Operational analysis and forecasting
14. Refinancing and recapitalization
15. Evaluation of systems and controls
16. Bankruptcy consulting

Corporations Corporate Restructuring Law & Legal Definition

Corporate restructuring can be defined as the act or process by which the organisation and existing interests of a corporation is changed. Reorganisation usually occurs as a result of financial difficulties under the existing corporate structure, operation, or management, and often as an alternative to dissolution. It may consist of changes within an existing corporation, such as recapitalization; it may involve transactions with another existing corporation, such as a transfer of stock or assets in exchange for voting stock; or it may involve the formation of a new corporation to take over the business of the old one.

Corporate reorganisations may be either judicial or nonjudicial. Judicial reorganisation can be voluntary or involuntary. Judicial reorganisations may be carried out through receivership, judicial sale, and other equitable procedures, but most judicial reorganisations are carried out under the "reorganisation" provisions of Chapter 11 of the Bankruptcy Code A nonjudicial reorganisation is one conducted by agreement between the interested parties.

Corporate reorganisations may qualify for partial or complete tax-free treatment where they satisfy special requirements of the Internal Revenue Code.

The Activities or Changes Which are not Termed

'Corporate Restructuring'

(a) Initial creation of a company: Here, an instructor should explain the concept and distinguish between

- a limited company
- a proprietary concern and a company
- a partnership firm and company
- a private company and a public company

Its various examples are:

1. Incorporation of a limited company
2. Conversion of a proprietary concern into a company
3. Conversion of a partnership firm into a company
4. Conversion of a private company into a public company

(b) Change in the internal command structure or hierarchy: The command structure of an organisation or its hierarchy simply means the reporting relationships among the employees, managers, top management and their various functions.

- Functional organisation
- Divisional organisation
- Matrix organisation

With businesses having become more complex along with the acceptance of newer concepts of organisation building such as tutorship, mentorship, etc., the hierarchies have stopped strictly falling into one of the three types mentioned above.

Any migration of an organisation from functional to divisional or to matrix type or to any new or hybrid type or vice-versa would not be a case of 'corporate restructuring'.

(c) Change in the business process: Re-engineering is the fundamental rethinking and redesign of business processes to achieve dramatic improvement in critical, contemporary measures of performance such as, cost, quality, service and speed.

Thus, It refers to the radical redesigning of business processes and not to the ownership and control or to the capital structure of the organisation.

(d) Downsizing: It is another form of organisational change in which the business organisation substantially cuts down on its manpower, recurring cost and/or capital expenditure, either as an objective itself or as a result of re-engineering.

(e) Other Activities: Since there is no standard definition of corporate restructuring, activities such as outsourcing, enterprise resource planning, total quality management, licensing, etc., have not been termed as corporate restructuring activities.

Main Forms of Corporate Restructuring

Major Forms of Corporate Restructuring:

- Merger
- Consolidation
- Acquisition
- Divestiture
- Demerger (spin-off/split-up/split-off)
- Carve-Out
- Joint Venture
- Reduction of Capital
- Buy-back of Securities
- Delisting of Securities/Company

Corporate Financial Restructuring

Corporate restructuring entails any fundamental change in a company's business or financial structure, designed to increase the company's value to shareholders or creditor. Corporate restructuring is often divided into two parts: financial restructuring and operational restructuring. Financial restructuring relates to improvements in the capital structure of the firm. An example of financial restructuring would be to add debt to lower the corporation's overall cost of capital. For otherwise viable firms under stress it may mean debt rescheduling or equity-for-debt swaps based on the strength of the firm. If the firm is in bankruptcy, this financial restructuring is laid out in the plan of reorganisation. The second meaning, operational restructuring, is the process of increasing the economic viability of the underlying business model. Examples include mergers, the sale of divisions or abandonment of product lines, or cost-cutting measures such as closing down unprofitable facilities. In most turnarounds and bankruptcy situations, both financial and operational restructuring must occur simultaneously to save the business.

Corporate financial restructuring involves restructuring the assets and liabilities of corporations, including their debt-to-equity structures, in line with their cash-flow needs to promote efficiency, support growth, and maximize the value to shareholders, creditors and other stakeholders. These objectives make it sound like restructuring is done pro-actively, that it is initiated by management or the board of directors. While that is sometimes the case — examples include share buybacks and leveraged recapitalizations — more often the existing structure remains in place until a crisis emerges. Then the motives are defencive — as in defences against a hostile takeover — or distress-induced, where creditors threaten to enforce their rights.

Financial restructuring may mean refinancing at every level of capital structure, including:

- Securing asset-based loans (accounts receivable, inventory, and equipment)
- Securing mezzanine and subordinated debt financing
- Securing institutional private placements of equity
- Achieving strategic partnering
- Identifying potential merger candidates

Just because a company needs restructuring — financial or operational — does not mean it will undertake the necessary reforms. Management and controlling shareholders may prevail for an extended period, during which time minority shareholders and/or creditors suffer an erosion of value.

A number of East Asian corporations, saddled with debt, nearly collapsed during the financial crisis of 1997. Many have managed to avoid both repayment and restructuring, however, and remain overly indebted and invested in unprofitable businesses.

Corporate Restructuring in India

In earlier years, India was a highly regulated economy. To set-up an industry various licenses and registration under various enactments were required. The scope and mode of corporate restructuring was, therefore, very limited due to restrictive government policies and rigid regulatory framework.

Consequent upon the raid of DCM Limited and Escorts Limited launched by Swaraj Paul, the role of the financial institutions became quite important. In fact, Swaraj Paul's bids were a forerunner and constituted a 'watershed' in the corporate history of India. The Swaraj Paul episode also gave rise to a whole new trend. Financially strong entrepreneurs made their presence felt as industrialists – Ram Prasad Goenka, M.R.Chabria, Sudarshan Birla, Srichand Hinduja, Vijay Mallya and Dhirubhai Ambani and were instrumental in corporate restructuring.

The real opening up of the economy started with the Industrial Policy, 1991 whereby 'continuity with change' was emphasized and main thrust was on relaxations in industrial licensing, foreign investments, and transfer of foreign technology etc. For instance, amendments were made in MRTP Act, within all restrictive sections discouraging growth of industrial sector. With the economic liberalization, globalization and opening up of economies, the Indian corporate sector started restructuring to meet the opportunities and challenged of competition.

Today, a restructuring wave is sweeping the corporate sector over the world, taking within its fold both big and small entities, comprising old economy businesses conglomerates and new economy companies and even the infrastructure and service sector. Mergers, amalgamations, acquisitions, consolidation and takeovers have become an integral part of new economic paradigm. Conglomerates are being formed to combine businesses and where synergies are not achieved, Demergers have become the order of the day. With the increasing competition and the economy, heading towards globalization, the corporate restructuring activities are expected to occur at a much larger scale than at any time in the past, and are stated to pay a major role in achieving the competitive edge for India in international market place.

The process of restructuring through mergers and amalgamations has been a regular feature in the developed and free economy nations like Japan, USA and European countries with special reference to UK where hundreds of mergers take place every year. The mergers and takeovers of multinational corporate houses across the borders has become a normal phenomenon.

The unleashing of Indian economy has opened up lucrative and dependable opportunities to business community as a whole. The absence of strict regulations about the size and volume of business encouraged the enterprises to opt for mergers and amalgamations so as to produce on a massive scale, reduce costs of production, make prices internationally competitive etc. Today Indian economy is passing through recession. In such a situation, corporates which are capable of restructuring can contribute towards economic revival and growth. Despite the sluggish economic scenario in India, merger and amalgamation deals have been on the increase. The obvious reason is – as the size of the market shrinks, it becomes extremely difficult for all the companies to survive, unless they cut costs and maintain prices. In such a situation, merger eliminates duplication of administrative and marketing expenses. The other important reason is that it prevents price war in a shrinking market. Companies, by merging, reduce the number of competitors and increase their market share.

Corporate Restructuring is One of the Means that can be Employed to Meet the Challenges which Confront Business

The sweeping wave of economic reforms and liberalization, has transformed the business scenario all over the world. The most significant development has been the integration of national economies with 'Market-oriented Globalized Economy'. The multilateral trade agenda and the World Trade Organisation (WTO) have been facilitating easy and free flow of technology, capital and expertise across the globe.

Globalization gives the consumer many choices – technologies are changing, established brands are being challenged by value – for money products, the movement of goods across countries is on the rise and entry barriers are being reduced. As markets consolidate into fewer and larger entities, economies become more concentrated. In this international scenario, there is a heavy accent on the quality, range, cost and reliability of product and services. Companies all over the world have been reshaping and repositioning themselves to meet the challenges and seize the opportunities thrown open by globalization. The management strategy in turbulent times is to focus on core competencies – selling loss making companies and acquiring those, which can contribute to profit and growth of the group. The underlying objective is to achieve and sustain superior performance. In fact, most companies in the world are merging to achieve an economic size as a means of survival and growth in the competitive economy. There has been a substantial increase in quantum of funds flowing across nations in search of restructuring and takeover candidates.

Corporate restructuring involves restructuring the assets and liabilities of corporations, including their debt-to-equity structures, in line with their cash flow needs in order to,

- Promote efficiency,
- Restore growth,
- And minimize the cost to tax payers.

Corporate governance refers to the framework of rules and regulations that enable the stakeholders to exercise appropriate oversight of a company to maximize its value and to obtain a return on their holdings.

Fundamental cultural and institutional changes are required if a new corporate governance structure is to be established with arm's-length, transparent relations between corporations, government, and banks. Changing corporate governance, however, is a long-term process Global enterprises may be motivated to reorganise their worldwide tax and legal structure for a variety of reasons. For example,

- To fully realise the value anticipated from a strategic merger or acquisition, a global enterprise must quickly reorganise and integrate its combined business operations from a tax and legal perspective.
- On the other hand, a fully integrated global enterprise may be forced to quickly realign its worldwide structure in order to effect a strategic spin-off or disposition of business operations that the management no longer deems desirable or essential.
- Finally, a global enterprise may wish to reorganise its worldwide structure to accommodate a down-sizing or transformation of its existing business operations or simply to generate tax and legal efficiencies that will contribute to its overall earnings per share.

Whatever the objective, to be truly successful, a global reorganisation must be structured in a manner that not only,

- Optimizes the ultimate tax position of the enterprise,
- But also addresses a multitude of legal issues that arise as a result of the restructuring.

Restructuring Techniques

Corporate restructuring can take several forms,

- Mergers and acquisitions
- Portfolio restructurings
- Financial restructurings.

Restructuring may also be classified into following forms,

- Financial restructuring
- Technological restructuring
- Organisational restructuring

The most commonly applied tools of corporate restructuring are

- Amalgamation
- Joint venture
- Merger
- Divestment

- Demerger
- Strategic alliance
- Slump sale
- Franchises
- Acquisition

Corporate Failures

"God, but its hard making predictions!........ Especially about the future" – Alphonse Allais.

The under mentioned causes result is increased number of corporate failures.

Business Failure and Reorganisation

Business failure occurs due to different reasons. While few firms fail within first year or two of life, few others grow, mature and fail much later. The failure can occur in a number of ways and also from different reasons. Business failure can be considered from,

- Economic and,
- Financial view point.

Why Business Firms Fail

Let's see different reasons same makes failure to corporate:

- An imbalance of skills within the top echelon.
- A chief executive who dominates a firms operations without regard for the inputs of peers
- An inactive board of directors. The board of Directors lack of interest in the financial position of the company may lead to insolvency.
- A deficient finance function within the firm's management.
- The absence of responsibility for the chief executive officer.

Apart from the above mistakes the firm usually is vulnerable to several mistakes,

- Management may be negligent in developing effective accounting system
- The company may be unresponsive to change
- Management may be inclined to undertake an investment project that is disproportionately large relative to firm size. If the project fails the probability of insolvency is greatly increased.

- Finally the management may rely heavily on debt financing that even a minor problem can place the firm in a dangerous position.

Symptoms of Bankruptcy or Failure: Having understood the causes for a firm's sickness, the next important question is – is it possible to with reasonable accuracy predict a firm's failure using some modelling technique.

Research shows that as a company enters the final stage prior to failure – a pattern may develop in terms of – changing financial ratios which prove to be useful indicators of an impending disaster.

Altman has developed a statistical model and found the statistical ratios best predicting bankruptcy. Based upon Altman's sample of bankrupt firms the study yielded an equation that used five ratios to predict bankruptcy.

Accordingly,

Bankruptcy score = 1.2X 1+ 1.4X2 + 3.3X3 + 0.6X4 + 0.999X5

Where,

X1 = Networking Capital / Total assets

X2 = Retained earnings / Total assets

X3 = Earnings before interest and taxes / total assets

X4 = Total market value of stock / book value of total debt

X5 = Sales / total assets

The Analysis:- The Z-score was developed from an analysis of 33 – Bankrupt manufacturing companies with average assets of $6.4 million, and, as controls, another 33 companies with assets between $1 million and $25 million.

Atman's Z-score calculates 5 ratios,

1 return on total assets

2 sales to total assets

3 working capital to total assets

4 retained earnings to total assets

These ratios are then multiplied by a predetermined weight fact or and the results are added together. The final number–the Z-score–yields a number between -4 and +8.

The research showed that Financially-sound companies show Z-scores above 2.99, while those scoring below 1.81 are in fiscal danger, maybe even heading toward bankruptcy. Scores that fall between these ends indicate potential trouble.

In Altman's initial study of 33 bankrupt companies, Z-scores for 95 % of these companies pointed to trouble or imminent bankruptcy.

Although the numbers that go into calculating the Z-score (and a company's financial soundness) are sometimes influenced by external factors, it provides a good quick analysis of where the company under study stands compared to the competition, and provides a good tool for analyzing the ups and downs of the company's financial stability over time.

The Altman Z-Score Analysis – 5 Ratios :

RATIO	***FORMULA***	***WEIGHT FACTOR***	***WEIGHTED RATIO***
Return on Total Assets			
Earnings Before Interest and Taxes ———— ———— – Total Assets	x. 3.3	-4 to +8.0	
Sales to Total Assets			
Net Sales ——— ———— ——— Total Assets	x 0.999	-4 to +8.0	
Equity to Debt			
Market Value of Equity ———— ———— —— Total Liabilities	x 0.6	-4 to +8.0	
Working Capital to Total Assets			
Working Capital ———— ———— Total Assets	x 1.2	-4 to +8.0	
Retained Earnings to Total Assets			
Retained Earnings ——— ———— ——— Total Assets	x1.4	-4 to +8.0	

The Physiology of Business Failure

In an economic sense business failure is associated with success in business relates to firms that earn adequate return on their investment. Similarly business failure is associated with forms that cannot earn adequate returns on their investments.

What is important is whether a business failure is permanent or temporary. In fact the appropriate course of action depends on whether the business failure is permanent or temporary. Thus if the failure is temporary the firm may have to be liquidated and if the failure is permanent the firm may have to take steps to the speed the company's return to business.

Types of Business Failure:-

- *Insolvency:* A firm may fail if its returns are negative or even low. A firm that consistently reports losses at operational level would experience decline in market share and eventual closure.
- *Technical insolvency:* A firm is said to be facing technical insolvency when it is unable to pay its liabilities as they become due. Thus when a firm faces technical insolvency its assets are still greater than the liabilities but the firm is confronted with liquidity crisis.
- *Bankruptcy:* When a firm has technical insolvency some of its assets could be converted to cash to escape complete failure. If this is not done at right time, the firm may have to face a more serious type of failure – Bankruptcy. It occurs when firm's assets are less than the liabilities. A bankrupt firm has a negative shareholder's equity. Although bankruptcy is a more obvious form of business failure courts treat technical insolvency and bankruptcy in the same way.

The challenge:-When a firm faces severe problems, either the problems must be resolved or the firm must be liquidated. At such point an important question has to be answered – "is the firm worth more dead or alive".

The decision to continue operating has to be based upon – The feasibility and fairness of reorganising the firms as opposed to the benefits of liquidating the business.

When technical insolvency occurs management must either modify the operating financial conditions or terminate the firm's life

If a decision is made to alter the company in the hopes of revitalizing its operations,

- Either voluntary agreements with the investors, or
- A formal court arranged reorganisation must be used.

If on the other hand the difficulties are believed to be insurmountable, then liquidation will take place either by assignments of assets to an independent party for liquidation or by formal bankruptcy proceedings.

Voluntary Remedies to Insolvency

Once a firm begins to encounter these difficulties the firm's owners and management have to consider the alternatives available to failing business. Such a firm has two remedies,

- Attempt to resolve its difficulties with its creditors on voluntary or informal process.
- Petition the courts for assistance and formally declare bankruptcy.

The company creditors also may petition to courts and get the company involuntarily declared bankrupt.

To Reorganise or Liquidate

Regardless of whether a business chooses informal or formal methods to deal with its difficulties eventually the decision has to be made whether to reorganise or liquidate the business. Before this decision can be made both the business liquidation value and its going concern value has to determine.

Liquidation value: equals the proceeds that would be received from the sale of the business less its liabilities.

Going concern value: equals the capitalized value of the company's operating earnings less its liabilities.

Normally, If the going-concern value exceeds the liquidation value the company needs to be reorganised otherwise it should be liquidated.

However in practice the determination of the going concern and liquidation values is not easy due to following reasons,

- Uncertainty as to estimating the price the company's assets will bring at auction.
- The company's future operating earnings
- Appropriate discount rate at which to capitalize the earning may be difficult to determine.
- Management understandably is not in a position to be completely –objective, about the above values.

Informal Alternatives for Failing Business

Regardless of exact reasons why a business begins to experience difficulties Regardless of the exact reasons why a business begins to experience difficulties the result is often same – Cash flow problems

Frequently,

- The first step taken by troubled company involves stretching its payable. In some occasions this can keep the company busy for several weeks of needed time before creditors take action. If the difficulties are more than just minor and temporary the company may turn to its bankers with request for additional working capital loans.
- Another possible action is the company bankers and creditors take up to restructure the company's debt.

Restructuring of debt by bankers can be quite complex. However debt restructuring basically involves either

- Extension,
- Composition, or
- A combination of both above.
- *In Extension:–* The failing company tries to reach an agreement with its creditors that will permit it to lengthen the time for meeting its obligations.
- *In composition:–* The firm's creditors accept some percentage amount lees than their original claim and the company is permitted to discharge its debt obligations by paying less than the full amounts and are protected from any further actions on part of creditors while it attempts to work out a plan of re-organisation.

What to do with the Failing Firm

Another important aspect of the bankruptcy procedures involves what to do with the failing firm. Just as in case of informal alternatives a decision has to be made about whether a firm's value as a going concern is greater than its liquidation value. Generally if this is so a suitable plan of reorganisation can be formulated and the firm is reorganised otherwise it is liquidated.

Reorganisation

If a voluntary remedy such as an extension or composition is not workable a company can declare or be forced by its creditors into bankruptcy.

As a part of this process a firm is either reorganised or dissolved. Reorganisation is similar to an extension or composition, the objective being to revitalize the firm by changing its capital structure – like,

- Reduction of fixed charges by substituting equity and limited income securities in place of fixed income securities, etc.

Corporate restructuring can occur in myriad ways. Mergers, takeovers, divestitures, spin-offs, and so on referred to collectively as corporate restructuring have become a major force in the financial and economic environment all over the world.

Dynamics of Restructuring

In an incisive study on corporate restructuring covering a number of companies over an extended period of time Gordon Donalson examined the dynamics of corporate restructuring.

He tried to look at issues like why corporate restructuring occurs periodically, what conditions or circumstances induce corporate restructuring and how should corporate governance be reformed to make it more responsive to the needs of restructuring. The key insights of this study are as below,

- Even though the environmental change which warrants corporate restructuring is a gradual process, corporate restructuring is often an episodic and convulsive exercise. Why? Typically an organisation can tolerate only one vision of future, articulated by its chief executive and it takes time to communicate that vision and mobilize collective commitment. Once the strategy and structure that reflect that vision are in place, they acquire a life of their own. A constituency develops with a vested interest in that strategy and structure which resists change unless it becomes inescapable.
- Hence Gordon Donalson says "hence resistance to change often preserves the status quo well beyond its period of relevance so that when change comes the pent up forces like an earthquake capture in one violent moment a decade of gradual change.
- The conditions or circumstances which seem to enhance the probability of voluntary corporate restructuring but not necessarily guarantee same are,
- persuasive evidence that the strategy and structure in place have substantially eroded the benefits accruing to one or more principal corporate constituencies

- a shift in the balance of power in favour of the disadvantaged constituency
- availability of options to improve performance
- Presence of leadership which is capable of and willing to act.
- Corporate restructuring occurs periodically due to an on going tension between the organisational need for stability and continuity on one hand and economic compulsion to adapt to changes on the other. As Gordon Donald son says, " the 'wrongs' that develop during one period of stable strategy and structure are never permanently rightened because each new restructuring becomes the platform on which the next era of stability and continuity is constructed.

Organisational Restructuring Exercise

Many firms have begun organisational exercises for restructuring in recent years to cope with heightened competition. The common elements in most organisational restructuring and performance enhancement programmes are described below,

- *Regrouping of business:* firms are regrouping the existing businesses into a few compact strategic business units which are often referred to as profit centres. For example L&T has been advised by Mckinsey Consultants to regroup its twelve businesses into five compact divisions.
- *Decentralization:* to promote a quicker organisational response to dynamic environmental developments, companies are resorting to decentralization, de-layering, and delegation aimed at empowering people down the line. For example, Hindustan lever Ltd., has embarked on an initiative to reduce.

Portfolio Restructurings

Mergers, asset purchases, and takeovers lead to expansion in some way or the other. They are based on the principle of synergy which says 2 +2=5 !

Portfolio restructuring, on the other hand, involves some kind of contraction through a Divestiture or a De-merger is based on the principle of "synergy" which says 5 -3 = 3!

Corporate Strategy

Towards reorganising themselves companies need to develop a strategy.

The conditions companies must satisfy if they are to conserve their essential characteristics over time may be summed up as –

- Consistency between their strategy, and
- The characteristics of the external environment in which they operate.

Owing to technological change and evolution as well as owing to heightened competitive pressures following,

- Market globalization and,
- Deregulation,

Companies increasingly have to cope with altered conditions of competition. In response they are forced to change their strategic framework.

Companies also need to change the way they compete and also the basic assumptions underlying the planning criteria that they adopt for their more general strategic design/architecture and those that govern the ways in which they interact with the external environment.

These Changes have a Bearing on,

- The companies ability to control environment variables
- The degree of company dependence on the external environment
- The very nature of the variability to be controlled.

Uncertainty has become the central element of competitiveness and business environment. In a world defined by turbulence surprise and a lack of continuity predictions are increasingly erroneous and therefore dangerous. This turbulence is being caused by,

- Acceleration of technological process
- The globalization of competition
- The restructuring of capitalism on a global scale.
- The slowing down of growth in some key sectors
- The political changes
- The high growth rates of Asian countries
- The large imbalance in global economy.

In a world, where prediction is becoming less reliable, decision-making and management models are perennially evolving, successful companies are organising to become progressively "ready for anything".

They are equipping themselves to be able to seize unexpected opportunities and retreat rapidly from bad risks. This evolution is centred on,

- Improvement of strategic analysis and thinking in terms of scenarios
- The anticipated development of additional capabilities in key resources
- Increased speed of action and reaction through efficient process of learning and change.

Conclusion

Organisations are restructuring themselves to meet changing environment. For three decades after world war two most economies around the world witnessed historically unparalleled progress. However after the early 1970s growth in most of industrialized economies began to slow down, affecting much of the developing world particularly adversely during the 1980's and 1990's. There were a variety of causes of this change in the trajectory of growth some of a macro economic nature and others rooted in the structure of corporate organisation and in inter-firm linkages.

The response to these pressures has been a significant change in macroeconomic policies amongst countries. Throughout the world there has been a surge toward deregulation and a feeling of barriers to the global flow of many resources. For some countries this has resulted in significant enhancement to economic growth but for others globalization has done little to enhance living standards and security. Thus the gains from globalization is not automatic they depend on response of producers to the changing competitive environment.

One critical area of change is to be found in organisation of production. To cope with new competitive pressures firms have to deliver not just low-priced goods and services but also products of greater quality and diversity. This requires in the first instance that they reorient their internal organisation, changing production layout, introducing new methods of quality assurance and instituting processes to ensure continuous improvement.

Different Modes of Corporate Restructuring

The 1980's bore witness to a decade of aggressive mergers, acquisitions and takeovers. The mergers and acquisitions scenario is hotting up in India. According to PricewaterhouseCoopers, the value of M&A deals announced in the first six months of 2005 was $6.9 billion, compared to $2.9 billion in the first half of 2004, and more than the $5.2 billion in the whole of 2004. The corporate are being concerned at cocktail parties by people who are eager to explain their system for making creamy profits by investing in common stock. Fortunately, these bores go into temporary hibernation whenever the market goes down.

There are a number of factors depicting the significance of this study. All innovations and inventions in terms of corporate and principles happen abroad, and then are being carried to Indian environment. Corporate restructuring, out of all emerging concepts of findings ways to serve shareholders better, has been a very successful concept abroad and its been followed all the more in high context cultures like India. The rapidity with corporate finance due to external factors like increased price volatility, a general globalisation of the markets, tax asymmetric, development in technology, regulatory change, liberalisation, increased competition and reduction in information and transaction costs and also intrafirm factors like liquidity needs of business, capital costs and growth perspective have lead to practice of corporate restructuring as a strategic move to maximise the shareholder's value.

The "Corporate restructuring" is an umbrella term that includes mergers and consolidations, divestitures and liquidations and various types of battles for corporate control. The essence of corporate restructuring lies in achieving the long run goal of wealth maximisation. This study is an attempt to highlight the impact of corporate restructuring on the shareholders value in the Indian context. Thus, it helps us to know, if restructuring generates value gains for shareholders (both those who own the firm before the restructuring and those who own the firm after the restructuring), how these value gains have be created and achieved or failed.

Further, it will also focus on issues involving ownership and controls. This leads logically to the subject of leveraged buyouts. It was during 1980s that many of the new tools which made leveraged buyouts possible, including high yield or junk bonds, found favour.

Last year, M&A activities were largely restricted to IT and telecom sectors. They have now spread across the economy. As Businessworld recently reported, this is the fourth wave of corporate deal-making in India.

The first happened in the 1980s, led by corporate raiders such as Swaraj Paul, Manu Chhabria and R P Goenka, in the very early days of reforms. In view of the license raj prevailing then, buying a company was one of the best ways to generate growth, for ambitious corporates.

In the early 1990s, in the liberalised economy, Indian business houses began to feel the heat of competition. Conglomerates that had lost focus were forced to sell non-core businesses that could not withstand competitive pressures. The Tatas, for instance, sold TOMCO to Hindustan Lever. Corporate restructuring, largely drove this second wave of M&As.

The third wave started about five years ago, driven by consolidation in key sectors like cement and telecommunications. Companies like Bharti Tele-Ventures and Hutch bought smaller competitors to establish a national presence.

What makes the most recent wave of M&As different from the three previous ones is the involvement of global players. Foreign private equity is coming into Indian companies, like Newbridge's recent investment in Shriram Holdings.

Multinational corporations are also entering India. Swiss cement major Holcim's investment in ACC and Oracle's purchase of a 41 per cent stake in i-flex solutions (for $593 million) are good examples.

Meanwhile, Indian companies, sensing attractive opportunities outside the country are also venturing abroad. Tata Steel has bought Singapore-based NatSteel for $486 million. Videocon has bought the colour picture tubes business of Thomson for $290 million.

Such global forays have become a possibility because foreign exchange is no longer a scarce commodity. They have also become a necessity because in globalising industries, only players with global scale and reach can survive.

At the same time, the difficulties involved in making M&As click must not be underestimated. A paradigm shift is likely in the coming years. Friendly deals could give way to aggressive ones. In future, we may see hostile bids and leveraged buyouts. Most M&As so far have been cash deals. With the Sensex crossing 9000, stock deals may become more common. As the appetite for deal making increases, the valuation is also bound to go up. In short, exciting times are ahead.

The term corporate restructuring encompasses three distinct, but related, groups of activities; expansions – including mergers and consolidations, tender offers, joint ventures, and acquisitions; contraction – including sell offs, spin offs, equity carve outs, abandonment of assets, and liquidation; and ownership and control – including the market for corporate control, stock repurchases program, exchange offers and going private (whether by leveraged buyout or other means). Mergers and acquisitions (M&A) and corporate restructuring are a big part of the corporate finance world. One plus one makes three: this equation is the special alchemy of a merger or an acquisition. The key principle behind buying a company is to create shareholder value over and above that of the sum of the two companies. Two companies together are more valuable than two separate companies - at least, that's the reasoning behind M&A.

This rationale is particularly alluring to companies when times are tough. Strong companies will act to buy other companies to create a more competitive, cost-efficient company. The companies will come together hoping to gain a greater market share or to achieve greater efficiency. Because of these potential benefits, target companies will often agree to be purchased when they know they cannot survive alone.

We will briefly look at each of the three major categories of restructuring in the section which follow as:

Expansions

Expansions include mergers, consolidations, acquisitions and various other activities which result in an enlargement of a firm or its scope of operations. There is a lot of ambiguity in the usage of the terms associated with corporate expansions.

A Merger involves a combination of two firms such that only one firm survives. Mergers tend top occur when one firm is significantly larger than the other and the survivor is usually the larger of the two. A Merger can take the form of :

- Horizontal merger involves two firms in similar businesses. The combination of two oil companies or two solid waste disposal companies, for example would represent horizontal mergers.
- Vertical mergers involves two firms involve in different stages of production of the same end product or related end product.
- Conglomerate mergers involves two firms in unrelated business activities.

A consolidations involves the creation of an altogether new firm owning the assets of both of the first two firms and neither of the first two survive. This form of combination is most common when the two firms are of approximately equal size.

The joint ventures, in which two separate firms pool some of their resources, is another such form that does not ordinarily lead to the dissolution of either firm. Such ventures typically involve only a small portion of the cooperating firms overall businesses and usually have limited lives.

The term acquisitions is another ambiguous term. At the most general, it means an attempts by one firm, called the acquiring firm to gain a majority interest in another firm called the target firm. The effort to gain control may be a prelude to a subsequent merger to establish a parent subsidiary relationship, to break up the target firm and dispose of its assets or to take the target firm private by a small group of investors.

There are a number of strategies that can be employed in corporate aquisitions like friendly takeovers, hostile takeovers etc. The specialist have engineered a number of strategies which often have bizarre nicknames such as shark repellents and poison pills terms which accurately convey the genuine hostility involved.

In the same vain, the acquiring firm itself is often described as a raider. One such strategy is to emply a target block repurchase with an accompanying stanstill agreement. This combination sometimes describes as greenmail.

Contractions

Contraction, as the term implies, results in a maller firm rather than a larger one. If we ignore the abandonment of assets, occasionally a logical course of action, corporate contraction occurs as the result of disposition of assets. The disposition of assets, sometimes called sell-offs, can take either of three board form:

- Spin-offs
- Divestitures
- Carve outs.

Spin-offs and carve outs create new legal entities while divestitres do not.

Ownership and Control

The third mahor area encompassed by the term corporate restructuring is that of ownership and control. It has been wrested from the current board, the new management will often embark on a full or partial liquidating strategy involving the sale of assets. The leveraged buyout preserves the integrity of the firm as legal entity but consolidates ownership in the hands of a small groups. In the 1980s, many large publicly traded firms went private and employs a similar strategy called a leveraged buyout or LBO.

Whether a purchase is considered a merger or an acquisition really depends on whether the purchase is friendly or hostile and how it is announced. In other words, the real difference lies in how the purchase is communicated to and received by the target company's board of directors, employees and shareholders.

Synergy

Synergy is the magic force that allows for enhanced cost efficiencies of the new business. Synergy takes the form of revenue enhancement and cost savings. By merging, the companies hope to benefit from the following:

Staff reductions - As every employee knows, mergers tend to mean job losses. Consider all the money saved from reducing the number of staff members from accounting, marketing and other departments. Job cuts will also include the former CEO, who typically leaves with a compensation package.

Economies of Scale - Yes, size matters. Whether it's purchasing stationery or a new corporate IT system, a bigger company placing the orders can save more on costs. Mergers also translate into improved purchasing power to buy equipment or office supplies - when placing larger orders, companies have a greater ability to negotiate prices with their suppliers.

Acquiring New Technology - To stay competitive, companies need to stay on top of technological developments and their business applications. By buying a smaller company with unique technologies, a large company can maintain or develop a competitive edge.

Improved market reach and industry visibility - Companies buy companies to reach new markets and grow revenues and earnings. A merge may expand two companies' marketing and distribution, giving them new sales opportunities. A merger can also improve a company's standing in the investment community: bigger firms often have an easier time raising capital than smaller ones.

That said, achieving synergy is easier said than done - it is not automatically realised once two companies merge. Sure, there ought to be economies of scale when two businesses are combined, but sometimes a merger does just the opposite.

Mergers and Acquisitions : Valuation Matters

Investors in a company that is aiming to take over another one must determine whether the purchase will be beneficial to them. In order to do so, they must ask themselves how much the company being acquired is really worth.

Naturally, both sides of an M&A deal will have different ideas about the worth of a target company: its seller will tend to value the company at as high of a price as possible, while the buyer will try to get the lowest price that he can.

There are, however, many legitimate ways to value companies. The most common method is to look at comparable companies in an industry, but deal makers employ a variety of other methods and tools when assessing a target company . Here are just a few of them:

Comparative Ratios - The following are two examples of the many comparative metrics on which acquiring companies may base their offers:

Price-Earnings Ratio (P/E Ratio) - With the use of this ratio, an acquiring company makes an offer that is a multiple of the earnings of the target company. Looking at the P/E for all the stocks within the same industry group will give the acquiring company good guidance for what the target's P/E multiple should be.

Enterprise-Value-to-Sales Ratio (EV/Sales) - With this ratio, the acquiring company makes an offer as a multiple of the revenues, again, while being aware of the price-to-sales ratio of other companies in the industry.

Replacement Cost - In a few cases, acquisitions are based on the cost of replacing the target company. For simplicity's sake, suppose the value of a company is simply the sum of all its equipment and staffing costs. The acquiring company can literally order the target to sell at that price, or it will create a competitor for the same cost. Naturally, it takes a long time to assemble good management, acquire property and get the right equipment.

This method of establishing a price certainly wouldn't make much sense in a service industry where the key assets - people and ideas - are hard to value and develop.

Discounted Cash Flow (DCF) - A key valuation tool in M&A, discounted cash flow analysis determines a company's current value according to its estimated future cash flows. Forecasted free cash flows (operating profit + depreciation + amortization of goodwill – capital expenditures – cash taxes - change in working capital) are discounted to a present value using the company's weighted average costs of capital (WACC). Admittedly, DCF is tricky to get right, but few tools can rival this valuation method.

Mergers and Acquisitions : Break Ups

As mergers capture the imagination of many investors and companies, the idea of getting smaller might seem counterintuitive. But corporate break-ups, or de-mergers, can be very attractive options for companies and their shareholders.

Advantages

The rationale behind a spinoff, tracking stock or carve-out is that "the parts are greater than the whole." These corporate restructuring techniques, which involve the separation of a business unit or subsidiary from the parent, can help a company raise additional equity funds. A break-up can also boost a company's valuation by providing powerful incentives to the people who work in the separating unit, and help the parent's management to focus on core operations. Most importantly, shareholders get better information about the business unit because it issues separate financial statements. This is particularly useful when a company's traditional line of business differs from the separated business unit. With separate financial disclosure, investors are better equipped to gauge the value of the parent corporation. The parent company might attract more investors and, ultimately, more capital. Also, separating a subsidiary from its parent can reduce internal competition for corporate funds. For investors, that's great news: it curbs the kind of negative internal wrangling that can compromise the unity and productivity of a company. For employees of the new separate entity, there is a publicly traded stock to motivate and reward them. Stock options in the parent often provide little incentive to subsidiary managers, especially because their efforts are buried in the firm's overall performance.

Disadvantages

That said, de-merged firms are likely to be substantially smaller than their parents, possibly making it harder to tap credit markets and costlier finance that may be affordable only for larger companies. And the smaller size of the firm may mean it has less representation on major indexes, making it more difficult to attract interest from institutional investors. Meanwhile, there are the extra costs that the parts of the business face if separated. When a firm divides itself into smaller units, it may be losing the synergy that it had as a larger entity. For instance, the division of expenses such as marketing, administration and research and development (R&D) into different business units may cause redundant costs without increasing overall revenues.

Restructuring Methods

There are several restructuring methods: doing an outright sell-off, doing an equity carve-out, spinning off a unit to existing shareholders or issuing tracking stock. Each has advantages and disadvantages for companies and investors. All of these deals are quite complex.

Sell-Offs

A sell-off, also known as a divestiture, is the outright sale of a company subsidiary. Normally, sell-offs are done because the subsidiary doesn't fit into the parent company's core strategy. The market may be undervaluing the combined businesses due to a lack of synergy between the parent and subsidiary. As a result, management and the board decide that the subsidiary is better off under different ownership.

Besides getting rid of an unwanted subsidiary, sell-offs also raise cash, which can be used to pay off debt. In the late 1980s and early 1990s, corporate raiders would use debt to finance acquisitions. Then, after making a purchase they would sell-off its subsidiaries to raise cash to service the debt. The raiders' method certainly makes sense if the sum of the parts is greater than the whole. When it isn't, deals are unsuccessful.

Equity Carve-outs

More and more companies are using equity carve-outs to boost shareholder value. A parent firm makes a subsidiary public through an initial public offering (IPO) of shares, amounting to a partial sell-off. A new publicly-listed company is created, but the parent keeps a controlling stake in the newly traded subsidiary.

A carve-out is a strategic avenue a parent firm may take when one of its subsidiaries is growing faster and carrying higher valuations than other businesses owned by the parent. A carve-out generates cash because shares in the subsidiary are sold to the public, but the issue also unlocks the value of the subsidiary unit and enhances the parent's shareholder value.

The new legal entity of a carve-out has a separate board, but in most carve-outs, the parent retains some control. In these cases, some portion of the parent firm's board of directors may be shared. Since the parent has a controlling stake, meaning both firms have common shareholders, the connection between the two will likely be strong.

That said, sometimes companies carve-out a subsidiary not because it's doing well, but because it is a burden. Such an intention won't lead to a successful result, especially if a carved-out subsidiary is too loaded with debt, or had trouble even when it was a part of the parent and is lacking an established track record for growing revenues and profits.

Carve-outs can also create unexpected friction between the parent and subsidiary. Problems can arise as managers of the carved-out company must be accountable to their public shareholders as well as the owners of the parent company. This can create divided loyalties.

Spinoffs

A spinoff occurs when a subsidiary becomes an independent entity. The parent firm distributes shares of the subsidiary to its shareholders through a stock dividend. Since this transaction is a dividend distribution, no cash is generated. Thus, spinoffs are unlikely to be used when a firm needs to finance growth or deals. Like the carve-out, the subsidiary becomes a separate legal entity with a distinct management and board.

Like carve-outs, spinoffs are usually about separating a healthy operation. In most cases, spinoffs unlock hidden shareholder value. For the parent company, it sharpens management focus. For the spinoff company, management doesn't have to compete for the parent's attention and capital. Once they are set free, managers can explore new opportunities.

Investors, however, should beware of throw away subsidiaries the parent created to separate legal liability or to off-load debt. Once spinoff shares are issued to parent company shareholders, some shareholders may be tempted to quickly dump these shares on the market, depressing the share valuation.

Tracking Stock

A tracking stock is a special type of stock issued by a publicly held company to track the value of one segment of that company. The stock allows the different segments of the company to be valued differently by investors. Let's say a slow-growth company trading at a low price-earnings ratio (P/E ratio) happens to have a fast growing business unit. The company might issue a tracking stock so the market can value the new business separately from the old one and at a significantly higher P/E rating.

Why would a firm issue a tracking stock rather than spinning-off or carving-out its fast growth business for shareholders? The company retains control over the subsidiary; the two businesses can continue to enjoy synergies and share marketing, administrative support functions, a headquarters and so on. Finally, and most importantly, if the tracking stock climbs in value, the parent company can use the tracking stock it owns to make acquisitions.

Still, shareholders need to remember that tracking stocks are class B , meaning they don't grant shareholders the same voting rights as those of the main stock. Each share of tracking stock may have only a half or a quarter of a vote. In rare cases, holders of tracking stock have no vote at all.

Review of Existing Literature

Review of existing literature has a great relevance in the research of any project as it acts as a backbone for new studies. Review of existing literature includes the history of the study, previous studies that had already being done on the subject. It lets the researcher explore on all these dimensions which have remain untouched in previous studies on the said topic. Therefore, it provides a necessary base and acts as a broader frame work and guideline to give researcher a clear cut focus for the fresh attempt.

Here are some of the views and studies by some of the researchers about the impact of corporate restructuring on shareholders value:

Guru of Corporate Restructuring: Bruce Wasserstein

In the mid-1980s, there was an avalanche of takeovers of underperforming companies, the targets of institutions and arbitrageurs who suspected that, with the help of plentiful leverage, they could increase corporate values by 'mobilizing assets'. Often that term meant disposal of non-performing assets.

In his 1998 book Big Deal, Wasserstein surveys 'the battle for control of America's leading corporations'. He describes five waves of mergers beginning in the mid-1800s: the first involved the building of the railroad empires; the second, in the 1920s, saw merger mania fuelled by a frothy stock market and rapid industrial growth; the third happened in 1960s featured the rise of the conglomerate; the fourth occurred with the hostile takeovers of the 1980s, driven by names such as Icahn, Boesky and Milken; and finally, a fifth wave happening today. Wasserstein attributes the explosion of M&A activity at the turn of the century to the need for companies to reposition themselves in today's ever changing competitive environment.

Porter (1987) attempted to study this relationship in a slightly different way. He took rate of divestment of new acquisitions by companies within a few years as an indicator of success or failure. He found that about 75 percent of all unrelated acquisition in the sample was divested after few years and 60 percent of acquisitions in entirely new industry.

In 1992, Aggarwal, Jaffe and Mandelkar studied post merger performance of the companies with a different perspective. They adjusted data for size effect and beta weighted market return and found that shareholders of the acquiring firms experienced a wealth loss of about 10% over the period of five years following the merger completion.

A study done by J. Fred Weston and Samual C. Weaver shows that around 50% mergers are successful in terms of creation of values for shareholders.

Anslinger and Copeland (1996) studied returns to shareholders in unrelated acquisition covering the 1985 to 1995 and they found that in two third cases companies were failed to earn their cost of acquisition.

Robert W. Holthausen "The Nomura Securities Company Professor, Professor of Accounting and Finance and Management": Various studies have shown that mergers have failure rates of more than 50 percent. One recent study found that 83 percent of all mergers fail to create value and half actually destroy value. This is an abysmal record. What is particularly amazing is that in polling the boards of the companies involved in those same mergers, over 80% of the board members thought their acquisitions had created value.

Corporate India - Still counting costs of restructuring : S. Vaidya Nathan : Not one company has restructured itself in a way that could rekindle investor interest and improve valuations substantively.

Wockhardt has come the closest : Restructuring, painful and protracted: Numerous companies — big and small — have traversed the restructuring route and shown some improvement in stock prices. But this aspect is only from the point of view of shareholders who had entered the stocks at lows, post-1996. No domestic company pursuing restructuring has shown conclusive and sustainable improvement in valuation in the long-term interest of the shareholders. As far as companies with a presence in a range of businesses go, though most have shed a few businesses, they still retain the profile of unfocussed business entities with limited competitive edge. And they are still in the process of restructuring despite having had a few rounds of mergers, de-mergers, asset sell-offs, one-time special dividend payments, stock buybacks and capital reduction.

Prashant Kale of University of Michigan, and Harbir Singh of Wharton, a study on M&As between 1992 and 2002, concluded that in the initial years of economic liberalisation, Indian companies failed to create sufficient value from acquisitions, as compared to MNCs. However, with the passage of time, Indian companies have begun developing the necessary capabilities to create more value from deals. But returns on acquisitions fell after 1998.

Stressing on the importance on changes required in the restructuring environment in the country, Ashwani Puri, Head, Corporate Finance and Recovery Services-PricewaterhouseCoopers

India said, "Business Restructuring in India has been slow and expensive. Lack of conducive regulatory environment, a complex tax framework, court processes and an endless list of compliance issues impede the process and impair efficient and effective realignment of resources through restructuring.

Evidences and several studies suggests that "Intense competition, rapid technological change, major corporate accounting scandals, and rising stock market volatility have increased the burden on managers to deliver superior performance and value for their shareholders. In the modern "winner takes all" economy, companies that fail to meet this challenge will face the certain loss of their independence, if not extinction. Corporate restructuring has enabled thousands of organisations around the world to respond more quickly and effectively to new opportunities and unexpected pressures, there by reestablishing their competitive advantage".

Takeover Tactics

Corporate Takeover Defence: A Shareholder's Perspective

Much has been written, often in dramatic and ominous language, about hostile takeovers and the various steps companies take to prevent them. While most articles and books view such events from the perspective of investment bankers and corporate officers, little has been written about the impact of hostile takeovers on shareholders of target companies. Yet these shareholders can experience significant financial consequences when the target company's board activates a defence or signals its intention to do so by adding defencive strategies to the corporate charter after the news of an impending takeover breaks.

To assess the ramifications of a takeover, shareholders need to identify and understand the various defencive strategies companies employ to avoid one. These shark repellent tactics, named for the well-known circling predator, can be both effective in repelling a takeover and detrimental to shareholder value. This article will discuss the effects of some typical shark-repellent and poison pill strategies.

Shareholders Rights Plan

The most common form of takeover defence is the shareholders' rights plans, which activates at the moment a potential acquirer announces its intentions. Under such plans, shareholders can purchase additional company stock at an attractively discounted price, making it far more difficult for the corporate raider to take control.

But today, more than ever, there are steep consequences to the poison pill reaction. While it can indeed complicate matters for the acquirer, it is often enacted to protect the interests of the elite upper echelon of corporate executives, rather than the company or its investors. It can also discourage the average, well-intentioned investor and drag down share prices. This destructive scenario played out the day after Yahoo! (Nasdaq:YHOO) announced it had added a poison pill clause to the company charter in 2000 and its shares plummeted 94%, from a high of $118.75 to $6.78.

While the poison pill defence may help ward off unwanted suitors, it also makes it more difficult for shareholders to profit from the announcement of a takeover. Rights issued to existing shareholders can effectively thwart a takeover by diluting the acquirer's ownership percentage, making a takeover more expensive and preventing or delaying control of the board and the company. But shareholders are often punished when their stock drops after a company adds a poison pill clause to its charter and they are unable to reap profits from a successful takeover.

Voting Rights Plans

Targeted companies may also implement a voting-rights plan, which separates certain shareholders from their full voting powers at a predetermined point. For instance, shareholders who already own 20% of a company may lose their ability to vote on such issues as the acceptance or rejection of a takeover bid.

The presence of corporate predators may also trigger super-majority voting, which requires that a full 80% of shareholders approve a merger, rather than a simple 51% majority. This requirement can make it difficult - if not impossible - for a raider to gain control of a company. It is very difficult for management to convince shareholders that voter-rights clauses benefit them, and the addition of such clauses to the corporate charter is often followed by a drop in stock price.

Staggered Board of Directors

Clauses involving shareholders are not the only escape routes available to targeted companies. A staggered board of directors (B of D), in which groups of directors are elected at different times for multiyear terms, can challenge the prospective raider. The raider now has to win multiple proxy fights over time and deal with successive shareholder meetings in order to successfully take over the company. It's important to note, however, that such a plan holds no direct shareholder benefit.

Greenmail

A company may also pursue the greenmail option by buying back its recently acquired stock from the putative raider at a higher price in order to avoid a takeover. This technique was popular during one of the final mergers and acquisitions trends in the 1980s, and it typically comes with the requirement that the raider not pursue another takeover attempt. Because the shares must be purchased at a premium over the takeover price, this "payout" strategy is a prime example of how shareholders can lose out even while avoiding a hostile takeover. The practice was effectively curtailed in the U.S. by an amendment to the U.S. Internal Revenue Code, which applied a punishing 50% tax on greenmail profits.

White Knight

If a determined hostile bidder thwarts all defences, a possible solution is a white knight, a strategic partner that merges with the target company to add value and increase market capitalization. Such a merger can not only deter the raider, but can also benefit shareholders in the short term, if the terms are favourable, as well as in the long term if the merger is a good strategic fit. A good example of this is the acquisition of Bear Stearns by white knight JPMorgan Chase (NYSE:JPM) in 2008. At the time of the acquisition, Bear Stearns' market cap had declined by 92% on concerns of its vulnerability to the global credit crisis at that time, making it extremely vulnerable to hostile takeover and even insolvency. Although a white knight defence is generally considered beneficial to shareholders, this is not always the case when the merger price is low or when the synergies and efficiencies of the combined entities do not materialize.

Increasing Debt

Increasing debt as a defencive strategy has been deployed in the past. By increasing debt significantly, companies hope to deter raiders concerned about repayment after the acquisition. However, adding a large debt obligation to a company's balance sheet can significantly erode stock prices.

Making an Acquisition

Perhaps a better strategy for target shareholders is for the company to make an acquisition, preferably through stock swaps or a combination of stock and debt. This has the effect of diluting the raider's ownership percentage and makes the takeover significantly more expensive. Although stock prices may drop upon the target's acquisition of the third party, shareholders can benefit in the longer term from operational efficiencies and increased revenues. When InBev made an unsolicited bid for Anheuser-Busch (NYSE:BUD) in 2008, the latter company immediately sought to purchase outright both Grupo Modelo of Mexico and Crown International of India in an attempt to make the acquisition too costly for its suitor.

Acquiring the Acquirer

Ironically, a takeover defence that has been successful in the past, albeit rarely, is to turn the tables on the acquirer and mount a bid to take over the raider. This requires resources and shareholder support, and it removes the possibility of activating the other defencive strategies. This strategy, called the Pac-Man defence, after Bendix Corporation's attempted to acquire Martin Marietta in 1982, very rarely benefits the shareholders. Martin Marietta defended itself by purchasing Bendix stock and sought a white knight in Allied Corporation.

Triggered Option Vesting

A triggered stock option vesting strategy for large stakeholders in a company can be used as a defence, but it rarely benefits anyone involved because it often results in massive talent migration. Generally, the share price drops when the clause is added to the charter as executives sell off the stock and leave the company.

Takeover

In business, a takeover is the purchase of one company (the *target*) by another (the *acquirer*, or *bidder*). In UK, the term refers to the acquisition of a public company whose shares are listed on a stock exchange, in contrast to the acquisition of a private company.

Friendly Takeovers

A "friendly takeover" is an acquisition which is approved by the management. Before a bidder makes an offer for another company, it usually first informs the company's board of directors. In an ideal world, if the board feels that accepting the offer serves the shareholders better than rejecting it, it recommends the offer be accepted by the sharcholders.

In a private company, because the shareholders and the board are usually the same people or closely connected with one another, private acquisitions are usually friendly. If the shareholders agree to sell the company, then the board is usually of the same mind or sufficiently under the orders of the equity shareholders to cooperate with the bidder.

This point is not relevant to the UK concept of takeovers, which always involve the acquisition of a public company.

Hostile Takeovers

A "hostile takeover" allows a bidder to take over a target company whose management is unwilling to agree to a merger or takeover. A takeover is considered "hostile" if the target company's board rejects the offer, but the bidder continues to pursue it, or the bidder makes the offer directly after having announced its firm intention to make an offer. Development of the hostile tender is attributed to Louis Wolfson.

A hostile takeover can be conducted in several ways. A tender offer can be made where the acquiring company makes a public offer at a fixed price above the current market price. Tender offers in the United States are regulated by the Williams Act. An acquiring company can also engage in a proxy fight, whereby it tries to persuade enough shareholders, usually a simple majority, to replace the management with a new one which will approve the takeover. Another method involves quietly purchasing enough stock on the open market, known as a "creeping tender offer", to affect a change in management. In all of these ways, management resists the acquisition, but it is carried out anyway.

The main consequence of a bid being considered hostile is practical rather than legal. If the board of the target cooperates, the bidder can conduct extensive due diligence into the affairs of the target company, providing the bidder with a comprehensive analysis of the target company's finances. In contrast, a hostile bidder will only have more limited, publicly available information about the target company available, rendering the bidder vulnerable to hidden risks regarding the target company's finances. An additional problem is that takeovers often require loans provided by banks in order to service the offer, but banks are often less willing to back a hostile bidder because of the relative lack of target information which is available to them.

A well known example of an extremely hostile takeover was Oracle's hostile bid to acquire PeopleSoft.

Reverse Takeovers

A "reverse takeover" is a type of takeover where a private company acquires a public company. This is usually done at the instigation of the larger, private company, the purpose being for the private company to effectively float itself while avoiding some of the expense and time involved in a conventional IPO. However, in the UK under AIM rules, a reverse take-over is an acquisition or acquisitions in a twelve-month period which for an AIM company would:

- exceed 100% in any of the class tests; or
- result in a fundamental change in its business, board or voting control; or
- in the case of an investing company, depart substantially from the investing strategy stated in its admission document or, where no admission document was produced on admission, depart substantially from the investing strategy stated in its pre-admission announcement or, depart substantially from the investing strategy.

An individual or organisation, sometimes known as corporate raider, can purchase a large fraction of the company's stock and, in doing so, get enough votes to replace the board of directors and the CEO. With a new agreeable management team, the stock is a much more attractive investment, which would likely result in a price rise and a profit for the corporate raider and the other shareholders.

Backflip Takeovers

A "backflip takeover" is any sort of takeover in which the acquiring company turns itself into a subsidiary of the purchased company. This type of takeover can occur when a larger but less well-known company purchases a struggling company with a very well-known brand. Example include:

- The Texas Air Corporation takeover of Continental Airlines but taking the Continental name as it was better known.
- The SBC takeover of the ailing AT&T and subsequent rename to AT&T.
- NationsBank's takeover of the Bank of America, but adopting Bank of America's name.

Financing a Takeover

Funding

Often a company acquiring another pays a specified amount for it. This money can be raised in a number of ways. Although the company may have sufficient funds available in its account, remitting payment entirely from the acquiring company's cash on hand is unusual. More often, it will be borrowed from a bank, or raised by an issue of bonds. Acquisitions financed through debt are known as leveraged buyouts, and the debt will often be moved down onto the balance sheet of the acquired company. The acquired company then has to pay back the debt. This is a technique often used by private equity companies. The debt ratio of financing can go as high as 80% in some cases. In such a case, the acquiring company would only need to raise 20% of the purchase price.

Loan Note Alternatives

Cash offers for public companies often include a "loan note alternative" that allows shareholders to take a part or all of their consideration in loan notes rather than cash. This is done primarily to make the offer more attractive in terms of taxation. A conversion of shares into cash is counted as a disposal that triggers a payment of capital gains tax, whereas if the shares are converted into other securities, such as loan notes, the tax is rolled over.

All Share Deals

A takeover, particularly a reverse takeover, may be financed by an all share deal. The bidder does not pay money, but instead issues new shares in itself to the shareholders of the company being acquired. In a reverse takeover the shareholders of the company being acquired end up with a majority of the shares in, and so control of, the company making the bid. The company has managerial rights.

Mechanics

In the United Kingdom

Takeovers in the UK (meaning acquisitions of public companies only) are governed by the City Code on Takeovers and Mergers, also known as the 'City Code' or 'Takeover Code'. The rules for a takeover can be found in what is primarily known as 'The Blue Book'. The Code used to be a non-statutory set of rules that was controlled by city institutions on a theoretically voluntary basis. However, as a breach of the Code brought such reputational damage and the possibility of exclusion from city services run by those institutions, it was regarded as binding. In 2006, the Code was put onto a statutory footing as part of the UK's compliance with the European Takeover Directive (2004/25/EC).

The Code requires that all shareholders in a company should be treated equally. It regulates when and what information companies must and cannot release publicly in relation to the bid, sets timetables for certain aspects of the bid, and sets minimum bid levels following a previous purchase of shares.

In particular:

- a shareholder must make an offer when its shareholding, including that of parties acting in concert (a "concert party"), reaches 30% of the target;
- information relating to the bid must not be released except by announcements regulated by the Code;
- the bidder must make an announcement if rumour or speculation have affected a company's share price;
- the level of the offer must not be less than any price paid by the bidder in the three months before the announcement of a firm intention to make an offer;
- if shares are bought during the offer period at a price higher than the offer price, the offer must be increased to that price;

The Rules Governing the Substantial Acquisition of Shares, which used to accompany the Code and which regulated the announcement of certain levels of shareholdings, have now been abolished, though similar provisions still exist in the Companies Act 1985.

Strategies

There are a variety of reasons why an acquiring company may wish to purchase another company. Some takeovers are *opportunistic* - the target company may simply be very reasonably priced for one reason or another and the acquiring company may decide that in the long run, it will end up making money by purchasing the target company. The large holding company Berkshire Hathaway has profited well over time by purchasing many companies opportunistically in this manner.

Other takeovers are *strategic* in that they are thought to have secondary effects beyond the simple effect of the profitability of the target company being added to the acquiring company's profitability. For example, an acquiring company may decide to purchase a company that is profitable and has good distribution capabilities in new areas which the acquiring company can use for its own products as well. A target company might be attractive because it allows the acquiring company to enter a new market without having to take on the risk, time and expense of starting a new division. An acquiring company could decide to take over a competitor not only because the competitor is profitable, but in order to eliminate competition in its field and make it easier, in the long term, to raise prices. Also a takeover could fulfill the belief that the combined company can be more profitable than the two companies would be separately due to a reduction of redundant functions.

Agency Problems

Takeovers may also benefit from principal–agent problems associated with top executive compensation. For example, it is fairly easy for a top executive to reduce the price of his/her company's stock – due to information asymmetry. The executive can accelerate accounting of expected expenses, delay accounting of expected revenue, engage in off-balance-sheet transactions to make the company's profitability appear temporarily poorer, or simply promote and report severely conservative (e.g. pessimistic) estimates of future earnings. Such seemingly adverse earnings news will be likely to (at least temporarily) reduce share price. (This is again due to information asymmetries since it is more common for top executives to do everything they can to window dress their company's earnings forecasts). There are typically very few legal risks to being 'too conservative' in one's accounting and earnings estimates.

A reduced share price makes a company an easier takeover target. When the company gets bought out (or taken private) – at a dramatically lower price – the takeover artist gains a windfall from the former top executive's actions to surreptitiously reduce share price. This can represent tens of billions of dollars (questionably) transferred from previous shareholders to the takeover artist. The former top executive is then rewarded with a golden handshake for presiding over the fire sale that can sometimes be in the hundreds of millions of dollars for one or two years of work. (This is nevertheless an excellent bargain for the takeover artist, who will tend to benefit from developing a reputation of being very generous to parting top executives). This is just one example of some of the principal–agent / perverse incentive issues involved with takeovers.

Similar issues occur when a publicly held asset or non-profit organisation undergoes privatization. Top executives often reap tremendous monetary benefits when a government owned or non-profit entity is sold to private hands. Just as in the example above, they can facilitate this process by making the entity appear to be in financial crisis. This perception can reduce the sale price (to the profit of the purchaser) and make non-profits and governments more likely to sell. It can also contribute to a public perception that private entities are more efficiently run, reinforcing the political will to sell off public assets.

Pros and Cons of Takeover

While pros and cons of a takeover differ from case to case, there are a few reoccurring ones worth mentioning.

Pros

1. Increase in sales/revenues (e.g. Procter & Gamble takeover of Gillette)
2. Venture into new businesses and markets
3. Profitability of target company
4. Increase market share
5. Decreased competition (from the perspective of the acquiring company)
6. Reduction of overcapacity in the industry
7. Enlarge brand portfolio (e.g. L'Oréal's takeover of Body Shop)
8. Increase in economies of scale
9. Increased efficiency as a result of corporate synergies/ redundancies (jobs with overlapping responsibilities can be eliminated, decreasing operating costs)
10. Expand Strategic Distribution Network

Cons

1. Goodwill, often paid in excess for the acquisition
2. Culture clashes within the two companies causes employees to be less-efficient or despondent
3. Reduced competition and choice for consumers in oligopoly markets. (Bad for consumers, although this is good for the companies involved in the takeover)
4. Likelihood of job cuts
5. Cultural integration/conflict with new management
6. Hidden liabilities of target entity
7. The monetary cost to the company
8. Lack of motivation for employees in the company being bought.

Takeovers also tend to substitute debt for equity. In a sense, any government tax policy of allowing for deduction of interest expenses but not of dividends, has essentially provided a substantial subsidy to takeovers. It can punish more-conservative or prudent management that do not allow their companies to leverage themselves into a high-risk position.

High leverage will lead to high profits if circumstances go well, but can lead to catastrophic failure if circumstances do not go favourably. This can create substantial negative externalities for governments, employees, suppliers and other stakeholders.

Occurrence

Corporate takeovers occur frequently in the United States, Canada, United Kingdom, France and Spain. They happen only occasionally in Italy because larger shareholders (typically controlling families) often have special board voting privileges designed to keep them in control. They do not happen often in Germany because of the dual board structure, nor in Japan because companies have interlocking sets of ownerships known as keiretsu, nor in the People's Republic of China because the state majority-owns most publicly listed companies.

Mergers and Acquisitions: Understanding Takeovers

Terms like "dawn raid", "poison pill", and "shark repellent" might seem like they belong in James Bond movies, but there's nothing fictional about them - they are part of the world of mergers and acquisitions (M&A). Owning stock in a company means you are part owner, and as we see more and more sector-wide consolidation, mergers and acquisitions are the resultant proceedings. So it is important to know what these terms mean for your holdings.

Mergers, acquisitions and takeovers have been a part of the business world for centuries. In today's dynamic economic environment, companies are often faced with decisions concerning these actions - after all, the job of management is to maximize shareholder value. Through mergers and acquisitions, a company can (at least in theory) develop a competitive advantage and ultimately increase shareholder value.

There are several ways that two or more companies can combine their efforts. They can partner on a project, mutually agree to join forces and merge, or one company can outright acquire another company, taking over all its operations, including its holdings and debt, and sometimes replacing management with their own representatives. It's this last case of dramatic unfriendly takeovers that is the source of much of M&A's colourful vocabulary.

Hostile Takeover

This is an unfriendly takeover attempt by a company or raider that is strongly resisted by the management and the board of directors of the target firm. These types of takeovers are usually bad news, affecting employee morale at the targeted firm, which can quickly turn to animosity against the acquiring firm. Grumblings like, "Did you hear they are axing a few dozen people in our finance department..." can be heard by the water cooler. While there are examples of hostile takeovers working, they are generally tougher to pull off than a friendly merger.

Dawn Raid

This is a corporate action more common in the United Kingdom; however it has also occurred in the Unites States. During a dawn raid, a firm or investor aims to buy a substantial holding in the takeover-target company's equity by instructing brokers to buy the shares as soon as the stock markets open. By getting the brokers to conduct the buying of shares in the target company (the "victim"), the acquirer (the "predator") masks its identity and thus its intent.

The acquirer then builds up a substantial stake in its target at the current stock market price. Because this is done early in the morning, the target firm usually doesn't get informed about the purchases until it is too late, and the acquirer now has controlling interest. In the U.K., there are now restrictions on this practice.

Saturday Night Special

A Saturday night special is a sudden attempt by one company to take over another by making a public tender offer. The name comes from the fact that these maneuvers used to be done over the weekends. This too has been restricted by the Williams Act in the U.S., whereby acquisitions of 5% or more of equity must be disclosed to the Securities Exchange Commission.

Takeovers are announced practically everyday, but announcing them doesn't necessarily mean everything will go ahead as planned. In many cases the target company does not want to be taken over. What does this mean for investors? Everything! There are many strategies that management can use during M&A activity, and almost all of these strategies are aimed at affecting the value of the target's stock in some way. Let's take a look at some more popular ways that companies can protect themselves from a predator. These are all types of what is referred to as "shark repellent".

Golden Parachute

A golden parachute measure discourages an unwanted takeover by offering lucrative benefits to the current top executives, who may lose their job if their company is taken over by another firm. Benefits written into the executives' contracts include items such as stock options, bonuses, liberal severance pay and so on. Golden parachutes can be worth millions of dollars and can cost the acquiring firm a lot of money and therefore act as a strong deterrent to proceeding with their takeover bid.

Greenmail

A spin-off of the term “blackmail”, greenmail occurs when a large block of stock is held by an unfriendly company or raider, who then forces the target company to repurchase the stock at a substantial premium to destroy any takeover attempt. This is also known as a “bon voyage bonus” or a “goodbye kiss”.

Macaroni Defence

This is a tactic by which the target company issues a large number of bonds that come with the guarantee that they will be redeemed at a higher price if the company is taken over. Why is it called macaroni defence? Because if a company is in danger, the redemption price of the bonds expands, kind of like macaroni in a pot! This is a highly useful tactic, but the target company must be careful it doesn’t issue so much debt that it cannot make the interest payments.

Takeover-target companies can also use leveraged recapitalization to make themselves less attractive to the bidding firm.

People Pill

Here, management threatens that in the event of a takeover, the management team will resign at the same time en masse. This is especially useful if they are a good management team; losing them could seriously harm the company and make the bidder think twice. On the other hand, hostile takeovers often result in the management being fired anyway, so the effectiveness of a people pilldefence really depends on the situation.

Poison Pill

With this strategy, the target company aims at making its own stock less attractive to the acquirer. There are two types of poison pills. The ‘flip-in’ poison pill allows existing shareholders (except the bidding company) to buy more shares at a discount.

This type of poison pill is usually written into the company’s shareholder-rights plan. The goal of the flip-in poison pill is to dilute the shares held by the bidder and make the takeover bid more difficult and expensive.

The ‘flip-over’ poison pill allows stockholders to buy the acquirer’s shares at a discounted price in the event of a merger. If investors fail to take part in the poison pill by purchasing stock at the discounted price, the outstanding shares will not be diluted enough to ward off a takeover.

An extreme version of the poison pill is the "suicide pill" whereby the takeover-target company may take action that may lead to its ultimate destruction.

Sandbag

With the sandbag tactic the target company stalls with the hope that another, more favourable company (like "a white knight") will make a takeover attempt. If management sandbags too long, however, they may be getting distracted from their responsibilities of running the company.

White Knight

A white knight is a company (the "good guy") that gallops in to make a friendly takeover offer to a target company that is facing a hostile takeover from another party (a "black knight"). The white knight offers the target firm a way out with a friendly takeover.

Conclusion

The next time you read a news release that says that your company is using a poison pill to ward off a takeover attempt, you'll now know what it means. More importantly, you'll know that you have the opportunity to purchase more shares at a cheap price. M&A has an entire vocabulary of its own, expressed through some of the rather creative strategies employed in the process, such as the ones we've touched on above. Hopefully by reading this article you are at least a bit wiser in the wacky world of M&A terminology. By understanding what is happening to your holdings during a takeover or attempted takeover, you may one day even save money.

Get Out of Debt – Start Making Money

Want to get out of debt, get a mortgage and save for retirement?

Corporate Take-over and Defencive Tactics

Corporate take-overs are currently riding a wave of unprecedented popularity. In 1995 both the frequency and the value of the recorded take-overs in Canada and the United States far surpassed those of any other era in history. The *motivations* underlying these consolidations are assorted, ranging from the potential revenue stability of diversification, to the cost-savings of economies of scale, to the ego-oriented desires of business leaders to own an empire. Likewise, the *consequences* of take-overs are numerous and distinct, varying according to the make-up of the particular corporations, the skills of the players involved, and the ambitions underlying the transaction.

Nevertheless, notwithstanding the peculiarities which serve to highlight the contrasts between corporate reorganisations, all take-over scenarios possess at least one fundamental similarity: the potential to inflict change on the personalities involved in the deal.

Every take-over situation is characterized by the presence of a variety of interested parties, or stakeholders, whose interests may be fundamentally affected (beneficially or detrimentally) by a merger. These stakeholders include the target corporation (the offeree), the buying corporation (the offeror), employees, and an offeree's management and shareholders. In an effort to help safeguard the rights and interests of such stakeholders, the federal government of Canada responded by installing take-over laws and regulations within the Canada Business Corporations Act.

A second response to the take-over phenomenon, in this case originating from the corporations targeted for take-over, was a plethora of defencive tactics - such as poison pills, golden parachutes, and white knights - which could be used by an offeree's management to thwart its acquisition by an offeror. Such defences, however, present the danger that an offeree's directors may exercise them for purely self-motivated reasons. In an effort to prevent such an abuse of power, and to protect the rights and interests of shareholders of offerees, the Canadian courts proceeded to strike down defencive strategies which were inconsistent with the fiduciary duties owed by directors to their shareholders under the CBCA.

Thus, the intent of this paper is two-fold. First of all, to review the objectives behind the CBCA's take-over provisions, to analyze the degree to which the objectives have so far been satisfied, and to propose regulatory changes which would allow the CBCA to better protect and balance the rights and interests of the stakeholders in take-overs. Second, to review the most common take-over defences, to analyze the fiduciary duties of directors of Canadian corporations during a take-over attempt, and to propose methods of achieving a fairer, more effective means in Canada of controlling such defences.

The paper is divided into five sections, as follows: Part I contains an introduction; Part II provides background information on take-overs, including an analysis of how various stakeholders are affected by consolidatory transactions; Part III addresses the numerous issues related to the regulation of take-overs by the CBCA; Part IV is devoted to the topics of defencive tactics and fiduciary duties; and Part V provides a conclusion to the paper.

Definition of Take-overs (v. Mergers)

The term *take-over* is broadly defined in Canada by both corporate and securities law. Generally, it is considered to be an offer to all or most shareholders to purchase shares of a target (offeree) corporation, where the offeror, if successful, will obtain enough shares to control the target corporation. For the purposes of this paper, a take-over will have the meaning specified in Section 194 of the CBCA:

> *an offer, other than an exempt offer, made by an offeror to shareholders at approximately the same time to acquire shares that, if combined with shares already beneficially owned or controlled, directly or indirectly, by the offeror or an affiliate or associate of the offeror on the date of the take-over bid, would exceed ten per cent of any class of issued shares of an offeree corporation and includes every offer, other than an exempt offer, by an issuer to repurchase its own shares.*

The Ontario Securities Act provides a similar definition, the most notable exception being that the OSA doesn't deem a take-over to have occurred until a 20 percent share of ownership is exceeded.

While the focus of this paper is take-overs, it is important to note the distinction that exists between take-overs and other forms of corporate reorganisations such as mergers and acquisitions. For example, although the term *merger* doesn't have a legal meaning in Canadian corporate law, it is generally employed to refer to "any transaction whereby one corporation acquires control of another, whether by take-over bid, amalgamation or arrangement." Thus, a take-over is just one form of the various types of mergers.

Categories of Takeovers

Take-overs can generally be grouped into one of three major categories: horizontal, vertical and conglomerate take-overs. A horizontal take-over occurs when the offeror and the offeree corporations are both engaged in the same broad sector of industry or commerce, and are actual or potential market competitors of each other.

In a vertical take-over the offeror and the offeree are actual potential suppliers or customers, such as when a motor manufacturer purchases a producer of electrical components. A conglomerate or diversifying take-over is the catch-all category, taking place where the offeror and the offeree belong to different sectors of business, and stand in neither a competitive nor a buyer-seller relationship to one another.

Motivating Factors behind Take-overs

It would be imprudent to conduct an analysis of corporate take-overs and their regulation without first being aware of the motivating factors underlying take-overs. A review of the pertinent scholarly research reveals at least seven major theories of takeover motives: synergy, diversification, economics, tax, the improved management hypothesis, the undervaluation theory, and the hubris hypothesis.

Synergy

Synergy is the most cited motive for takeovers. Its basic assumption is that the value of the combination of the offeror and the offeree is greater than the sum of the individual values of the two corporations. The source of such gains in a take-over is the potential cost-savings realised from the integration of the production and investment infrastructure of the offeror and the offeree, especially economies of scale, enhanced organisational efficiencies and increased market power.

Diversification

Take-overs are frequently inspired by the offeror's desire to avoid "putting all its eggs in one basket." Instead, a corporation may wish to "hedge its bets." The coinsurance theory suggests that by acquiring another corporation having imperfectly correlated earnings (irrespective of whether the offeree is inside or outside of the offeror's industry); such an offeror corporation will be able to derive a combined earnings stream that is less volatile than either of the individual companies' earnings stream.

Economics

In addition to the synergy benefit of economies of scale, two other economic motives that stimulate take-overs are horizontal and vertical integration. In theory, horizontal integration, or the acquisition of competitors, provides the offeror corporation with an increase in market share and market power, and in turn, allows the corporation to set and maintain prices above previously competitive levels. Furthermore, vertical integration, or the acquisition of potential buyer or seller firms, offers a variety of possible benefits to the offeror corporation, including a more dependable source of supplies, and lower inventory costs.

Tax

A variety of tax savings may result from a take-over. To illustrate, the offeror obtains a valuable savings if the offeree possesses transferable tax losses that the offeror is able to offset against its own income. Another potential tax benefit arises where the market value of the offeree's depreciable assets is greater than their book value.

Inefficient Management Hypothesis

The inefficient management hypothesis suggests that where a corporation has inefficient management, there exists an incentive for an offeror company to acquire it and install new leaders who are better able to harness the full potential of the offeree's assets. If more effective and efficient management of the offeree's assets is ultimately achieved, then the resulting gains accrue directly to the offeror.

Undervaluation Theory

The undervaluation theory is based on the assumption that the offeree firm is undervalued by the market, and that the offeror is in possession of such special or inside information which will not become available to the market generally, until after the take-over. Thus, the offeror is motivated to acquire the offeree with the expectation of reaping the gain that will result once the market valuation adjusts upward.

Hubris Hypothesis

The hubris hypothesis of take-overs, proposed by Richard Roll, implies that managers of an offeror corporation may pay a premium to acquire an offeree that the market has already correctly valued for their own personal motives rather than for pure economic gains. Roll suggests that the pride of the offeror's managers may cause them to place greater significance on their own valuation of the offeree than on that of the market's valuation.

History of Take-overs

The history of take-overs in the United States and Canada has been characterized by four cycles or waves - periods of high levels of take-overs followed by periods of relatively low activity. The four waves occurred between 1897 and 1904; 1916 and 1929; 1965 and 1969; and 1984 and 1989. The first wave, beginning after the Depression of 1883, was stimulated in the United States and Canada by the development of large national markets and the expanding overseas markets for manufactured products. Firms wanting to grow as quickly as possible during these opportunistic times bought other corporations in the same industry in order to acquire their additional manufacturing capacity. Lax federal anti-trust laws and the relaxing of corporate laws made it easier for corporations to finance their take-overs, thus further strengthening this period of horizontal integration.

The second wave of take-overs, commencing in 1916, was founded on a desire to reduce operating costs and maintain profit margins through the economies of scale offered by vertical integration. As a result, offeror corporations acquired both supplier and buyer firms in their attempts to internalize previously external risks. Contrasting the first and second waves, George Stigler, the economics Nobel Laureate, described the former as a "merging for monopoly" and the latter as a "merging for oligopoly." This period of consolidation came to an abrupt halt in 1929 with the crash of the stock market that had been partially fuelling it.

The third take-over wave led to the rise of corporate conglomeration in Canada and the United States. While the previous waves had been directed at the integration of firms within one's own industry, 80% of the mergers that took place throughout this period were conglomerate-oriented and involved the take-over by offerors of offerees from different industries. This cycle was driven by a variety of different corporate motivations, including a desire to circumvent tough anti-trust laws which had made it very difficult to pursue either horizontal or vertical integration strategies of expansion, and an attempt to achieve greater financial stability through diversification of products and industries.

The fourth wave of take-overs that swept through Canada and the United States in the 1980s was characterized by the mega size and prominence of the offerees, and by the more hostile, aggressive tactics of the offerors. As well, this period witnessed a transformation in industries, spurred on both by the deregulation of industries such as airlines and banks, and by the arrival of primarily speculative investors who rapidly purchased and resold corporations purely for profit.

Although it has yet to be labelled as such, the period between 1992 and the present has seen the rise of a fifth wave of take-overs and mergers in Canada and the United States. Following the recovery of the United States economy from the 1990-91 recession, as corporations once again began to seek to expand, take-overs were viewed as a quick and efficient manner in which to do exactly that. This "fifth wave" of consolidation has thus far largely avoided the super-leveraged, debt-financed transactions of the 1980s, observing instead take-overs financed primarily through the increased use of equity instruments.

The quantity and economic value of the mergers and acquisitions that have occurred in North America since 1990 have steadily increased, with there being no hint of the trend slowing down in either Canada or the United States. This continued and substantial growth in corporate take-overs signifies the importance of ensuring that the take-over regulatory regime be as efficient, effective and fair as possible.

Stakeholders in Take-overs

As observed in the Introduction to this paper, take-overs have the potential to fundamentally affect a number of stakeholders, the most notable of which are the offeror and offeree corporations, the employees of both firms, and the management and shareholders of the offeree. While it is understood that the fallout from take-overs will vary according to the facts of a particular case, studies have revealed certain patterns or trends in how each group is affected.

Offeror and Offeree Corporations

Involvement in a take-over scenario is *prima facie* a risky venture for both the offeror and the offeree. Although the extensive varieties and complexities of the take-overs that have occurred in Canada and the United States have served as a barrier to an all-encompassing, and generally applicable research project on the consequences of take-overs on the companies involved, a number of more limited studies have been conducted. Many of these have revealed ambivalent conclusions. For example, research conducted by Tarasofsky and Corvari, building upon earlier work of Jog and Riding, held that, in the context of Canadian take-overs, the number of acquired firms that report an increase in their profits 3-5 years after the take-over is virtually equivalent to the number that report a decrease. As well, a study of take-overs based on firm-specific accounting data in the United States carried out by Ravenscraft and Scherer revealed that the profitability of acquired assets in their sample deteriorated significantly after being acquired.

In addition to the effects on profitability, take-overs can also cause more fundamental changes in the merging firms, such as divestitures of portions of the offeror or offeree (or both), dramatic shifts in corporate culture, and in certain cases, the collapse of one or both of the merged corporations.

Employees

The employees of the offeror and offeree are probably the most vulnerable stakeholders throughout a take-over. Economists have recognised that take-overs threaten the two most important pillars of an employee's career: job security and job satisfaction. First of all, consolidations are frequently accompanied by a loss of jobs. An increase in economies of scale may result in the closure of certain sections of the merged companies, and in turn, corresponding layoffs. As well, studies indicate that take-overs are often accompanied by the divestiture of divisions or departments of the acquired company for a quick profit, again resulting in considerable loss of jobs.

With respect to job satisfaction, take-overs may result in a deterioration of employee morale due to problems such as uncertainty of job description, shifts in corporate culture or separation anxiety. Astrachan, in his book *Mergers, Acquisitions and Employee Anxiety*, observed that job separation anxiety, or the fear by employees that relationships will be severed as a result of dismissals, transfers, or restructuring, skyrockets during a take-over. Furthermore, on the basis of a study of 150 large mergers and acquisitions in the United States, Harlow Unger reported in 1986 that the turnover of senior executives of acquired companies is almost 50% within the first year after the merger, and nearly 75% by the end of three years. Similarly, John Humpal has presented data, again restricted to samples in the United States, which demonstrate that the likelihood to quit was three times higher among acquired employees than parent employees.

Management and Shareholders of Offeree

An offeree's management and shareholders are the two most integral groups in the determination of whether a take-over is successful. The offeree's directors may, or may not, choose to recommend to the shareholders to accept the offeror's bid. As well, corporate management may choose to deploy a strategic defencive tactic to fend off the predator company. The shareholders, on the other hand, as owners, must make the ultimate decision as to whether to acquiesce to or to fight the offeror. Thus, the participation of and the interaction between these two stakeholders during a take-over is essential to the ultimate result.

However, the balance within this relationship is constantly threatened by the reality that an offeree's management and shareholders fundamentally possess conflicting objectives. For example, studies indicate that there is a high managerial turnover following take-overs, thus making management naturally adverse to successful changes in ownership. As well, corporate managers typically possess keen competitive and possessive instincts which propel directors to fight for their companies' independence and survival.

In contrast, the motivations of the shareholders of an offeree are generally based on share wealth maximization. The key consideration in deciding whether to accept or reject a take-over bid is the share price being offered. A study of the take-overs of ten Canadian firms by Patry and Poitevin revealed that the target's shareholders tend to do very well, averaging a gain of 35.6% over their estimated market value. As well, a study by Professor Espin Eckbo of the 1,930 mergers and take-overs of Canadian public companies between 1964 and 1983 found that the offerees' shares averaged an 11.87 percent increase in share value over the twelve months preceding and four months following the first public announcement of a possible pending reconsolidation. Thus, an offeree's shareholders generally benefit from a take-over.

While it would be misleading to suggest that all directors and shareholders of target companies behave in the stereotyped manner suggested above, on a theoretical plane these two stakeholders do have fundamentally adverse ambitions which create the potential for serious problems such as conflicts of interest and breaches of fiduciary duties.

Having identified the groups whose rights and interests are affected by take-overs, the next step is to determine the role which the CBCA should play in providing regulatory protection to these stakeholders. Should the federal law attempt to safeguard all stakeholders equally? To what extent should federal legislation interfere with the operation of the commercial markets?

The Regulation of Takeovers and Proposed Amendments

Origins of Take-over Legislation

Take-over legislation in Canada has its roots in the 1965 report of the Attorney General's Committee on Securities Legislation in Ontario (the "Kimber Report"). Responding to concerns about how an increasing number of take-overs would affect offeree shareholders, the Kimber Report established the following rationale for all subsequent Canadian take-over laws:

> *...the primary objective of any recommendations for legislation with respect to the take-over bid transaction should be the protection of the bona fide interests of the shareholders of the offeree company. Shareholders should have made available to them, as a matter of law, sufficient up-to-date relevant information to permit them to come to a reasoned decision as to the desirability of accepting a bid for their shares. In arriving at its conclusions, however, the Committee attempted to ensure that its recommendations would not unduly impede*

potential bidders or put them in a commercially disadvantageous position vis a vis...[a] board of directors of an offeree company.

In 1966 the OSA adopted the recommendations of the Kimber Report, and implemented rules for take-over bids, including disclosure and timing requirements, rights of withdrawal of tender by offeree shareholders, and rules requiring the equal treatment of offeree shareholders. The first take-over provisions of the CBCA were enacted shortly thereafter, in 1970, as amendments to the Canada Corporations Act, and were later largely transferred to the CBCA in 1975. These original federal take-over provisions were virtually identical to those of the OSA and have remained unchanged to this day.

An Introduction to the CBCA Take-over Provisions

The CBCA's take-over regulatory regime generally applies to all CBCA corporations whose shares are publicly-traded or which have 15 or more shareholders. Pursuant to the Kimber Report, these provisions hinge upon the identification of a take-over bid - an offer to shareholders to purchase shares of a corporation, that, if combined with shares already beneficially owned or controlled, directly or indirectly, by the offeror would exceed ten percent of any class of issued shares of an offeree corporation. Once such an offer to purchase shares is deemed to be a take-over bid, then the offeror is required to extend the offer to all the shareholders of that class of shares. The CBCA rules then specify procedures and time periods for disclosure, solicitation and take-up of shares tendered pursuant to the offer.

The fundamental objective of the CBCA provisions is to protect the rights and interests of the four main parties involved in a take-over bid: the offeror, the offeree, and the shareholders and directors of the offeree. While much of the legislation is pointed at safeguarding the *bona fide* interests of the shareholders of the offeree corporation, there is a concerted effort made by the legislators to balance this protection with a desire not to unduly impede potential bidders.

For example, the rules are structured so as to counterbalance the offeror's informational and time advantage by requiring it to disclose to both the shareholders and directors of the offeree all the information which it possesses which is relevant to the decision to accept or reject the bid. As well, the legislation attempts to ensure that both the offeree's shareholders and directors have sufficient time to digest the information, seek advice and make a reasoned decision. The rules also require that a bid be made to all shareholders of the shares sought, and that all shareholders be treated equally with respect to the taking up of their shares in an oversubscribed partial bid. Yet, at no place in the statute, does the CBCA attempt to arbitrarily prohibit any bid by an offeror. The result is a body of provisions which strives to produce a regime of fair and orderly take-over bids by means of a legal system which specifies the rights and obligations of each of the parties involved.

While four of the five main categories of stakeholders are given some degree of protection by the CBCA's take-over laws, no comparable relief is designated to help preserve the rights and interests of the employees of the offeror and offeree corporations. As discussed earlier in this paper, employees represent one of the groups that is generally most negatively affected by a take-over transaction. Nevertheless, the absence of employee-related take-over legislation in the CBCA is likely justifiable on the basis that employment issues in Canada are already regulated by labour and contract laws. Thus, if the CBCA attempted to regulate the corporate-employee relationship, it would be overstepping its legislative bounds and improperly, if not, illegally, intervening.

Having concluded a brief sketch of the policy objectives and legislative approach of the CBCA take-over provisions, a detailed examination of specific sections of the rules will now be undertaken with a dual purpose in mind: 1) to identify the protection offered to stakeholders by existing provisions; and 2) to determine ways in which the existing provisions may be amended so as to achieve a more efficient and effective system of regulatory protection.

Proposed Amendments of the CBCA's Take-over Provisions

It is recognised that the present CBCA take-over rules have been instrumental in creating a regulatory system in Canada which is characterized by order, stability and stakeholder protection. However, there are several opportunities by which this legislation may be improved so as to make it more efficient and effective for the key parties to take-overs.

Take-over Bid Threshold: Section 194

At present the CBCA's take-over provisions are triggered if an offeror, after making a bid for shares of an offeree, would control or own 10 percent or more of any class of the shares of the offeree. This threshold ensures that the offeror becomes subject to the take-over regulatory scheme of the CBCA before being able to secretly accumulate *de facto* or effective control of an offeree, thus providing protection to the offeree's directors and shareholders. However, the CBCA's 10 percent threshold deviates from the 20 percent level used by all provincial securities acts. Given that most take-over bids are captured by one of the provincial statutes, parties who make offers to CBCA corporations are therefore usually forced to endure the burdensome compliance costs of satisfying two different but overlapping sets of regulations. The result is an unnecessary cost expenditure by the offeror and a reduction in the overall efficiency of the regulatory process.

While a possible solution to this problem would be to increase the CBCA's threshold to 20 percent, that approach has been criticized on the basis that it could delay the availability of key ownership information to shareholders of the offeree, and thus potentially injure their position by allowing predators to acquire significant shares without anyone's knowledge. The significance of these fears, however, is diminished by the fact that there are a very limited number of widely-held corporations in Canada, leading one to the conclusion that in most situations, a potential offeror would have to acquire at least 20 percent of a publicly-traded corporation's class of shares in order to achieve *de facto* control. As well, the 1983 Report of the Securities Industry Committee on Take-over Bids concluded that the 20% mark should be adopted by the CBCA as "there [was] no evidence that the benefits of a lower threshold outweigh the costs that flow from the lack of uniformity in take-over bid rules."

It would appear, therefore, that an increase in the threshold would have only minor negative effects on the management and shareholders of offerees, and that these would be more than offset by the gains that would accrue to offerors by removing the inconvenience and unnecessary administrative costs associated with meeting the requirements of two different legislative systems.

Early Warning Disclosure

In order to compensate for the limited loss of shareholder and director protection that could result from an increase in the CBCA take-over threshold, it has been suggested that the CBCA adopt an "early warning disclosure" regime. Based on existing provisions of the OSA, the new CBCA provision could require any offeror that acquires 10 percent or more of a class of shares of a CBCA corporation to file a report disclosing information concerning the purchase. Subsequently, such an offeror could be obligated to file similar reports for any additional acquisition of that class of shares constituting 2 percent or more of the total class. The implementation of such a provision was strongly recommended by the 1983 Securities Industry Committee on Take-over Bids which recognised that a holding of 10 percent or more of a class of shares was "a significant development in the marketplace - it may be a signal of a potential acquisition of control - and should be disclosed."

The integration of this early warning system into the CBCA take-over rules would allow an offeree's shareholders and directors as much advanced notice of a potential power struggle as they currently enjoy under the 10 percent threshold. Unfortunately, the proposed provision would virtually duplicate existing provincial securities legislation on the subject, while at the same time, encompassing very few additional share acquisitions that would not have already been captured by the provincial statutes. As a consequence, any potential savings to offerors generated from the harmonization of the take-over thresholds of the CBCA and provincial securities law would be counteracted by the additional expense of satisfying the nearly identical early warning requirements of two separate regulatory regimes.

Perhaps the best solution to this situation would be for the Director (as appointed under section 260) to take advantage of new section 258.2 of the CBCA which would allow him/her to issue blanket exemption orders in cases where similar or overlapping information is required to be filed under other legislation. Applying this power to early warning reports in particular, only those acquisitions not currently captured by early warning provisions in provincial securities laws could be made subject to a CBCA early warning regime. The result would be a significantly improved set of take-over rules which would efficiently and fairly balance the offeree's desire for early disclosure with the offeror's need to reduce duplicative compliance costs.

Private Agreement Exemption

One definition of an *exempt offer* according to the CBCA's take-over provisions is "an offer to fewer than fifteen shareholders to purchase shares by way of separate agreements." Otherwise known as a *private agreement exemption*, the purpose of such an exemption is to permit holders of large blocks of shares, including controlling shareholders, to sell their shares without committing the buyers to making a formal take-over bid to all the owners of that class of shares. The underlying philosophy of the private agreement exemption, as originally voiced by the Kimber Report, is that "questions of fairness between shareholders [are] a matter for company law and the courts." The 1983 Securities Industry Committee on Take-over Bids reluctantly accepted this philosophy, holding that the elimination of private agreement exemptions could be deemed to constitute an undue "limiting [of] the freedom of parties to contract privately, [especially] where such a restriction was unnecessary to achieve the legislative objectives."

However, while this exemption protects the rights of offerors and significant shareholders to freely contract in private, it fundamentally violates a general principle of take-over regulations that "all shareholders of the same class of an offeree shall be treated similarly by an offeror." Private agreement exemptions discriminate between significant and minor shareholders, allowing a relatively small number of owners to sell their shares and, in turn, a controlling interest in the offeree, to an offeror in exchange for a premium price. The remainder of the shareholders, who have not negotiated private agreements with the offeror, are given no opportunity to sell their shares or to share in the premium being offered.

In an attempt to balance the conflicting rights and interests of these stakeholders, it is proposed that two amendments of the exemption be pursued. First of all, it is suggested that the maximum number of shareholders under the private agreement exemption be reduced to five. This would harmonize the CBCA rules with those of the provincial securities statutes, and as such, provide more clarity and uniformity to the law. Furthermore, the 1983 Securities Industry Committee on Take-over Bids concluded that it is very rare for more than five shareholders to be legitimate members of a controlling block, and that the extension of the number beyond five would only serve to "detract from the organised markets and invite privileged participation by shareholders who merely have an association with the offeror or a major selling shareholder." Thus, a limit of five shareholders would help protect the interests of the minority shareholders where the offeree is fairly widely-held.

Secondly, it is recommended that the CBCA take-over rules adopt a maximum premium of 15 percent over market price that can be paid for securities purchased under the exemption. One benefit that would be derived from such a ceiling would be the further harmonization of the CBCA with provincial securities statutes. As well, even though opponents of the amendment protest that it lacks a "rational, theoretical or evidentiary basis" for requiring that the premium be shared with minority shareholders, it ultimately represents the best balance between the views of those advocating the principle of equal treatment of shareholders in the context of take-over bids, and those favouring the private property perspective that major shareholders should be allowed to sell their shares at a premium, irrespective of whether or not a similar is made to the other shareholders.

Integration Periods

The primary purpose of integration periods is to ensure equal treatment for all the shareholders of an offeree corporation. The CBCA currently attempts to accomplish this objective by preventing holders of significant blocks of targeted shares (subject to certain exemptions such as the private agreement exemption) from selling them at a premium to an offeror during the take-over bid deposit period. As outlined in sections 197(d) and 197(f) of the CBCA, all shares acquired by an offeror pursuant to a take-over bid must be purchased for the same price. Thus, if the terms of a take-over bid are amended by increasing the price offered for the shares, the offeror is then obligated to pay this increased consideration to each offeree whose shares are taken up pursuant to the take-over bid.

However, the potential still exists for shareholders to secure advantages over one another by obtaining large premiums in private purchases which occur either shortly before or after the official take-over bid period. To prevent transactions which violate the underlying spirit of the CBCA take-over regime, it is recommended that both a pre-bid and a post-bid integration period be introduced.

Modelling it after similar provisions contained in provincial securities statutes, it is suggested that the CBCA's pre-bid integration period begin 90 days immediately preceding a take-over bid. An offeror would be required to pay the same or higher price for shares purchased during the take-over period as was paid for the same class of shares during the pre-bid interval. It is further proposed that a post-bid integration period be established prohibiting, for twenty days following the expiry of the bid, the purchase of the same class of shares for a price that is not generally available to all shareholders.

Expanding Minimum Period and Other Time Period Related Issues

At the heart of the CBCA's take-over rules are provisions specifying certain minimum and maximum periods which regulate the deposit and purchase of shares pursuant to a take-over bid. For example, an offeree's directors currently have 10 days from the date of a bid to make recommendations to their shareholders in the form of the director's circular. As well, shareholders of the offeree have a maximum of 35 days from the date of a partial bid to deposit their shares for sale. There is no such limit with respect to a bid for all the shares of a class. Furthermore, the CBCA provides that a minimum of 10 days for a full bid, and 21 days for a partial bid, must expire from the date of the respective take-over offer before the offeror can actually purchase the shares.

These minimum and maximum period provisions are aimed at allowing an offeree's directors to adequately analyze an offer, make recommendations to shareholders, and to seek or consider competing bids. Likewise, they are intended to ensure that an offeree's shareholders have sufficient time to consider an initial and all subsequent take-over offers. Thus, they attempt to achieve one of the underlying goals of take-over bid regulation, namely the protection of the rights and interests of shareholders. However, they may still be too short to allow an offeree to acquire, assess, and output properly all of the overwhelming amount of information that accompanies any take-over attempt.

In 1990 the Canadian Securities Administrators proposed a number of changes to the provincial securities statutes, in particular that the minimum period for depositing shares pursuant to a take-over bid be increased from 21 to 35 days [in the case of the CBCA, it is currently 35 days for a partial bid and 21 days for a full bid], that the period for withdrawing securities deposited pursuant to an offer be raised from 21 days to 35 days [in the case of the CBCA, it is currently only 10 days for full bids, and 21 days for partial bids], and that directors of the offeree corporation be given 21 instead of 10 days to respond to the take-over bid in the directors' circular. Both of these modifications would result in greater protection of the rights and interests of the offeree by providing it more time in order to make the crucial determination of whether to accept or reject a take-over offer. As well, an extension of the take-over bid period would likely increase the possibility of other firms expressing interest in the offeree, and in turn, raise the probability of the offered share price being forced upwards as a result of competitive bids. While such a scenario would worsen the position of initial offerors and possibly serve as a deterrent to take-over activity in general, it would also lead to greater premiums for an offeree's shareholders.

Finally, the view that offeree's shareholders and directors consider the existing time provisions to be inadequate is supported by the increasing use of shareholder rights/poison pills plans in Canada. While these defencive instruments have been criticized as being mere instruments by which management may entrench itself, their officially stated purpose is to extend the period in which shareholders may consider a take-over bid. Thus, an amendment which extended the CBCA's take-over bid period would, on one hand, provide greater protection to offerees, and on the other, serve to weaken the foundation on which the use of the controversial defence tactics is based.

Having seen the variety of benefits that would flow to an offeree's shareholders by an extension of the time periods specified in the CBCA's take-over provisions, one must conclude that such extensions should be implemented in the legislation. While the Industry Canada Discussion Paper on Take-overs advocates a number of specific, and seemingly arbitrary changes, I would recommend more generally that an offeree's shareholders be granted an increased period in which to deposit their shares, that shares deposited pursuant to the bid not be taken up by the offeror until the expiration of the take-over period, and that directors be given additional time in which to respond to a take-over bid in the director's circular.

In summary, the preceding examination of key sections of the CBCA's take-over provisions revealed numerous examples of the extensive protection which the legislation affords to take-over stakeholders. However, it also exposed a variety of areas - threshold level, early warning signals, private agreement exemptions, integration periods and minimum time periods - where the rules could be improved to make them more sensitive to the safeguarding of the interests of the vulnerable parties to a take-over, especially the shareholders. An issue which impacts strongly upon this relationship between stakeholders and the CBCA's take-over rules is the use of defencive tactics by the management of offeree corporations. A number of questions must be answered. What objectives underlie their employment, whose interests do they protect and what role should the CBCA play in administrating their use?

Anti-takeover Defences and Fiduciary Duties

Anti-takeover defencive tactics represent one of the most contentious areas of corporation law. From their crude beginnings as novel agents of corporate preservation in the midst of the wave of hostile take-overs of the 1980s, they have evolved into an elaborate and sophisticated corporate armoury. Approximately 85% of large U.S. corporations now have in place some form of anti-takeover defence , and despite being relatively rare in Canada, their presence on the Canadian landscape is increasing rapidly.

The circle of controversy that has engulfed these defence measures stems from the theory that the interests of an offeree's directors and shareholders during a take-over are polar. While the survival of an offeree's management group is generally contingent upon the successful activation of a defence tactic to defeat a potential offeror, an offeree's shareholders are generally better off by selling their shares to the highest bidder at a large premium.

Therefore, the employment of an anti-takeover strategy by an offeree's directors begs the question: in fighting the take-over, were the directors acting honestly and in good faith with a view to the best interests of the corporation [and thus satisfying their fiduciary duties], or were they acting out of their personal self-interest [and thus in breach of their fiduciary duties]? A detailed analysis of this question requires a brief outline of the various categories of anti-takeover measures, a discussion of the motivations underlying these measures, an examination of the fiduciary duties of directors in a take-over situation and a review of the role that courts and legislators have thus far played in attempting to clarify this matter.

Categories and Motivations of Anti-takeover Defences

The corporate armoury of anti-takeover defencive tactics is well stocked. Falling into two major categories - preventative and active - there is an overwhelming variety of defences now available to corporations. Whereas preventative measures are intended to decrease the likelihood of a financially successful take-over and thus deter potential bidders, active defences are instigated after a bid has been made.

Preventative Anti-takeover Defences

Patrick Gaughan describes the installation in a corporation of preventative defences as "an exercise in wall building." The goal of preventative defences is to alter some, if not all, of the value-enhancing characteristics of a target firm - i.e. healthy cash flows, low debt levels, and low share price-to-assets ratio - either in advance of, or upon completion of, a take-over bid. While they don't guarantee that a company will be able to avoid a take-over fight, these defences do tend to make a take-over far more difficult and costly to the offeror, the hope being that bidders will decide to bypass such a well-defended target in favour of a more vulnerable company. These preventative measures include poison pills, corporate charter amendments and golden parachutes.

Poison pills vary from company to company but generally retain certain common characteristics. As one of the most popular and common of all anti-takeover defences, they will be described in relative detail in this paper. Poison pills are essentially shareholders' rights plans developed by a corporation's directors under which typically one right is distributed per common share. The rights do not detach and are not exercisable until some triggering event occurs. This event is usually defined in one of two ways: either 1) a potential offeror has acquired a certain percentage of common shares of a class, or 2) a specified number of days has passed since an offeror has launched a take-over bid that is intended to make that offeror the effective owner of the offeree.

The integral feature of most poison pills is a flip-in provision that generally stipulates that once the triggering event has occurred then all the holders of the rights, excluding the offeror, may exchange them for common shares at half their normal price. The offeror's rights are nullified upon the crossing of the triggering threshold. The result of the flip-in is, therefore, that the offeror's holdings become considerably diluted and the cost of acquiring effective ownership becomes prohibitively expensive. The flip-in provision combined with the fact that an offeree's board of directors usually retain the power to redeem the rights at a minimal price up until the triggering event takes place, forces potential offerors to negotiate with the offeree's board of directors in order reach some kind of deal.

Another more recent feature of poison pills is the "permitted bid" clause which allows a potential offeror who has satisfied certain conditions to by-pass the offeree's board of directors and to negotiate directly with the offeree's shareholders without creating a flip-in event. Whatever the exact structure of the instrument, all poison pills either deter a potential offeror from continuing with its bid, or else forces the offeror to work with the offeree directly. In the end, poison pills delay the take-over process, which, in turn, provides the offeree with valuable additional time to consider a take-over bid, negotiate a higher price from the offeror, or to find a competitive bidder to drive share price offers higher.

Corporate charter amendments are defencive tactics intended to make it difficult for a potential offeror to initiate changes in the managerial control of an offeree. Some examples include staggered boards of directors, dual capitalizations, and supermajority clauses.

Golden parachutes are special compensation packages that a company provides to its upper management, and although not usually primarily aimed at deterring take-overs, they may have some anti-takeover effects. A typical golden parachute agreement provides a lump-sum payment to an executive upon the occurrence of a specific change in the control or ownership of the company, or upon his/her voluntary or involuntary departure from the company after such a change in control. Thus, an offeror upon obtaining control of a company having these compensation devices is forced to pay a large sum of money in order to replace existing managers with the offeror's desired people. Since the cost of paying off the golden parachute packages is usually only a small percentage of the take-over purchase price, their anti-takeover effects are relatively small.

Active Anti-takeover Defences

Anti-takeover defencive defences are only applicable after an offeree has received an unwanted bid. Some examples of these tactics include greenmail, white knights, and the pacman defence. Greenmail involves the payment by an offeree of a substantial premium for a significant shareholder's stock in return for the shareholder's promise not to initiate a bid for control of the company. The white knight defencive strategy involves seeking out a friendly bidder, or white knight, as an alternative buyer to the hostile one. Finally, the pacman defence is an extreme strategy involving a take-over attempt by the offeree on the offeror.

Hypotheses of the Motivations of Anti-takeover Defences

The nature and extent of the potential conflict of interests between an offeree's shareholders and directors must be considered in light of the motivations which induce directors to make use of anti-takeover defences. There are two competing accounts of the function and purpose of these defences: the *shareholder interest hypothesis* (SIH) and the *management entrenchment hypothesis* (MEH). According to the SIH, management employs anti-takeover tactics for the ultimate benefit of the shareholders. The use of defencive strategies such as poison pills to make an acquisition prohibitively expensive without the cooperation of the board of directors allows corporate management to compel the potential offeror to negotiate with them.

In the effective capacity as bargaining agents for the shareholders, the SIH suggests that the objective of management is to obtain for the shareholders the "full and fair value" of their shares. This may be accomplished by either rejecting a bid that is too low, forcing the offeror to introduce a more generous bid, or by soliciting competing bids to drive up the share premium offer. At the other end of the spectrum, the MEH holds that since a successful take-over often results in the dismissal of an offeree's existing directors, the offeree's incumbent management group may be more motivated to save their jobs than act in the best interests of its shareholders.

Thus, according to the MEH the power from a defence such as a poison pill may be used by management to reject take-over bids that threaten its survival. The result is a loss to the shareholders of large take-over premiums that would otherwise have been paid by the thwarted offeror.

If one accepts the management entrenchment hypothesis as correct, then the answer to the question underlying this part of the paper would be immediately discernible: an offeree's corporate managers' use of defencive strategies *does* result in a breach of their fiduciary duties since they *prima facie* place their own self-interests ahead of those of the corporation or shareholders.

Likewise, if the SIH represents the operating motive then again the central issue is immediately resolved: the offeree's corporate managers' use of defencive strategies *does not* result in a breach of their fiduciary duties since they *prima facie* place the interests of the shareholders ahead of their own self-interests. The better answer is that the two hypotheses operate and interact simultaneously such that the aversion of management to take-over bids is balanced by management's objective to maximize shareholders' wealth.

The result then becomes realistic: the implementation of defence instruments such as poison pills has "the effect of increasing premiums in successful take-overs, while also reducing the probability of a successful take-over." This hybrid view of the management objectives underlying the use of defence tactics, or the *dual purpose hypothesis*, (DPH) suggests that both conflicting purposes are constantly at play within the collective mind of management. The determination of which, if either, of these motivations was dominant is fundamental to concluding whether or not an offeree's directors breached their fiduciary duties in their exercise of a take-over defence.

The Fiduciary Duty Analysis

In examining the fiduciary duties of an offeree's directors in the context of a take-over bid, one must first consider the source of the directors' duties. Subsection 122(1) of the CBCA requires that a director, in discharging his/her duties, "act honestly and in good faith with a view to the best interests of the corporation" and "exercise the care, diligence and skill that a reasonably prudent person would exercise in comparable circumstances." Thus, the question is whether or not the actions of the directors of a target corporation in using an anti-takeover instrument satisfied these legislative requirements.

Notwithstanding the CBCA's specific formulation of the components of a director's duties, the courts in Canada have struggled to determine how these duties may be discharged by a director defending a corporation from a take-over bid. This judicial setback may be linked to the limited number of Canadian cases that have dealt with the issue, and to the fact that those which do exist often contradict one another. To facilitate a comprehensive and linear review of the approaches taken by the courts in Canada, it is recommended that the law be surveyed in three major stages: the state of the law preceding the leading Canadian case on this issue, Teck. Corp. v. Millar, the law as set out in the Teck decision itself, and the state of the law since Teck.

Law Before Teck

The law before Teck followed the *proper purpose doctrine,* an approach laid out in the leading case of Hogg v. Cramphorn Ltd. Based on the premise that directors' powers were conferred upon them for a particular purpose or purposes, this doctrine holds that the exercise of a power for a purpose other than the specific one for which it was conferred to be invalid. The proper purpose test consists of two parts. First of all, the proper purpose for which the power was conferred to the directors must be determined.

Second, it must be ascertained whether the power was exercised for that proper purpose. Since the proper purpose analysis is applied only to the primary purpose of the directors in exercising their power, so long as the directors' primary purpose is a proper one, then a secondary purpose will not invalidate the action. The burden of proof is on the plaintiff to establish that the directors' primary motive was an improper purpose. Turning to Cramphorn, the directors of the company established a trust for the benefit for the company's employees, under which shares were issued to the directors as trustees for the employees. However, the court found that the directors' primary purpose in setting up the fund and issuing shares was to prevent a certain individual seeking control of the company from acquiring a majority of the shares. Finding that the primary purpose of the directors' power to issue shares was to raise capital when required, and that the power had actually been exercised for the primary purpose of retaining control, the court invalidated the action.

Teck

The most significant Canadian case in the past sixty years on the subject of directors' fiduciary duties in resisting a take-over bid, Teck proposed a more lenient version of the proper purpose test.

The facts are briefly as follows. The plaintiff Teck, a major mining company, desired to join with a junior mine, Afton Mines, in a venture to develop a promising deposit already owned by Afton. Afton's directors, however, led by Millar, chose instead to negotiate a deal with Teck's rival, Canex. In the face of Afton's continued rejection of Teck's offers, even though they were better than the terms offered by Canex, Teck decided to obtain control of Afton through share purchases. To stave off Teck's hostile bid, Afton accordingly accelerated its negotiations with Canex and ultimately reached a deal which entailed the issuance of sufficient shares to deny Teck control, one day after Teck had accumulated a fifty percent ownership in Afton. Teck subsequently brought a derivative action as a shareholder of Afton against its directors, alleging that the agreement with Canex was void because it was made for an improper purpose.

Concluding that it was not "sound to limit the directors' exercise of their powers to the extent required by Cramphorn," Berger J. for the British Columbia Supreme Court held that directors are entitled to resist a take-over bid if they meet a two-part test:

(1) they must act in good faith in resisting the bid; and

(2) they must believe, on reasonable grounds, that the take-over will cause substantial damage to the their company's interests.

In this particular case he found that the directors of Afton had satisfied their fiduciary obligations. Berger J. placed the burden of proof on the plaintiff to show either that the directors' purpose in rejecting a bid was not in the best interests of the company, or that the directors did not have reasonable grounds for believing that the take-over would have caused the company substantial damage.

Furthermore, in assessing the *best interests* of the corporation, Teck provided that the directors may consider a variety of differing interests:

1) who is seeking control and why (assess the reputation of the offeror, previous experiences with the offeror, policies of the offeror, etc.);

2) the interests of employees and consequences to the community in general; and

3) the impact on the corporation and shareholders.

Thus, Teck represented a clear departure from the strict proper purpose test of Cramphorn, with Berger J. concluding that the courts should only find a directors' exercise of power to be improper if their purpose was not to serve the best interests of the corporation.

Law After Teck

One of the difficulties in determining the judicial effects of the Teck decision is the fact that it has been thoughtfully applied in only two subsequent Canadian cases: Re Olympia & York Enterprises and Hiram Walker Resources Ltd and Exco Corp. v. Nova Scotia Savings & Loan Co. Prior to those two cases, however, it had been considered by the Judicial Committee of the Privy Council in Howard Smith Ltd. v. Ampol Petroleum Ltd.

First of all, Howard Smith's analysis of Teck created uncertainty as to Teck's appropriate interpretation and application. By recognising that there was no set purpose for the power of directors to issue shares, the Privy Council in Howard Smith appeared likely to follow Teck's lead and adopt a more moderate proper purpose test. However, the Privy Council observed that Teck was consistent with the traditional view of defencive measures, and then proceeded to apply the strict proper purpose test of Cramphorn to its own facts.

Re Olympia & York reinforces the test outlined by Berger J. in Teck. The facts of Re Olympia & York may be summarized as follows. The hostile bidder, Olympia & York, tried to block financing extended by the board of the target, Hiram Walker, to Fingas, a corporation jointly owned by Hiram Walker and Allied Lyons, a white knight purchaser of a portion of Hiram Walker's business. This financing allowed Fingas to make a higher bid for Hiram Walker's shares than Olympia and York's initial offer. As a result, Olympia and York sought injunctions, arguing that the action of the Hiram Walker directors was for the purpose of entrenching themselves in the management of the corporation, and as such, a breach of their fiduciary duties.

Applying the Teck formulation, Montgomery J. held that the directors of Hiram Walker had acted in the best interests of the corporation and in good faith and, that as a consequence, it was irrelevant that they had also benefitted from their actions [by becoming more entrenched in the company]. While reinforcing the existing rules of the Teck test for directors' use of anti-takeover defences, Re Olympia & York also supplements it with the following additional principles :

1) it is the duty of directors in a take-over contest to maximize the value to all shareholders;
2) directors are entitled to rely on professional advice as to the adequacy of a bid, and such reliance will constitute evidence of acting in good faith and upon reasonable grounds; and

3) self-entrenchment will not necessarily be inferred where retaining control is secondary to the primary purpose of acting in the best interests of the corporation and in good faith.

While Teck and Re Olympia & York helped to build a modern, consistent framework in which to analyze the duties of directors in defending take-overs, the decision of the court in Exco served to dismantle it. The case involved an allegation that a series of share issues by the offeree, Nova Scotia Savings and Loan (NSSL), were improperly made to facilitate the accumulation of control by a corporation "not unfriendly" to NSSL's management and to defeat a hostile bid made by Exco. Richard J., in finding there had been an abuse of directors' powers, articulated a new restricted proper purpose doctrine. This new rule provides that in order for directors to discharge their fiduciary duties, they must demonstrate that their actions were motivated by "considerations consistent only with the best interests of the company and inconsistent with any other interests."

Exco's considerably more narrow approach alters the Teck and Re Olympia & York framework in three major ways. First of all, it limits the considerations directors may undertake. While under Teck directors could consider a number of parties' interests, including the reputation of the offeror, the community, the employees and of the corporation, Exco requires directors to consider only the best interests of the corporation. As well, Exco prohibits directors from receiving any secondary benefit from their actions. Thus although both Teck and Re Olympia & York held that if the primary purpose was proper, then any secondary benefit to the directors would not invalidate the actions, Exco would conclude there to be a breach of duty if directors' actions were even secondarily consistent with self-interest. Finally, Exco places the burden of proof on the target directors.

In the aftermath of Exco, legal analysts agree that the law in Canada is unsettled. There is an ongoing struggle between Exco's restricted proper purpose test and Teck's moderate proper purpose test which will probably continue until a string of cases are consistently decided on the basis of one of the approaches. It is a struggle which should be won by the supporters of Teck. While Teckprovides an analytical framework in which the decision of directors to defeat a take-over may be viewed with respect to its effect on a wide variety of groups - including the corporation, shareholders, employees and the community, Exco views the decision solely within the context of the best interests of the corporation. Thus, the Teck rule strives to consider and, in turn, possibly protect, the rights and interests of a much larger number of stakeholders to a take-over, which is more consistent with the policy rationale underlying the CBCA's take-over rules. A second major flaw in the Exco rule is the requirement that target directors demonstrate that the considerations upon which their decision was based are consistent only with the best interests of the corporation and inconsistent with any other interests. This problem with this element is that in many cases the proper exercise of directors' duties will be in the best interests of both the corporation and shareholders. For example, by rejecting a bid which doesn't appear beneficial for the shareholders and company as a whole, the directors would be simultaneously benefitting themselves. The consequence of Exco, therefore, is that target directors will rarely, if ever, be capable of discharging their fiduciary duties.

A third weakness of Exco is the assumption that all directorial powers are conferred with a particular, restricted purpose in mind. To determine the purpose of such powers one must look to the statutory grant by which they are given. However, the statutory language inevitably tends to be very broad with little indication of the specific reason for which the power has been provided. This assumption also dictates that the courts must be able to ascertain the exact primary purpose behind the directors' use of a defence strategy, as opposed to any secondary purposes. Since it is generally impossible for courts to read the minds of directors, this requirement is impossible to achieve in real terms. In contrast, Teck offers a more objective test, requiring only that directors decide, on reasonable grounds, that a take-over will cause substantial damage to the company's interests before exercising a defencive strategy.

American Jurisprudence

Any analysis of the fiduciary test for corporate directors in defeating take-overs should include an examination of American jurisprudence. While Canada is limited to very few cases on the issue, the American experience is rich with related cases. The most common approach in the United States is known as the *Business Judgment Rule*. The business judgment rule provides that a court should evaluate a decision by directors to employ an anti-takeover defence in the same way as they would evaluate any other business judgment. Flowing from this rule are several conditions that directors must meet in order to demonstrate that they fulfilled their fiduciary duty in good faith. For example, a director must show that he/she is not interested in the subject of the business judgment. As well, he/she must be informed with respect to the subject of the business judgment to the extent that he/she reasonably believes to be appropriate under the circumstances. A director must rationally believe that his/her business judgment is in the best interests of the corporation. A final requirement is that there be a valid, legitimate business purpose underlying the director's actions. However, due to the possibility that the interests of directors may conflict with those of the corporation, American jurisprudence has held that before one may conduct the business judgment analysis, the defendant directors must first discharge an initial burden of proof. As introduced by the decision in Cheff v. Mathes and later modified by the courts in Unocal Corp. v. Mesa Petroleum Co, the test for discharging this initial burden of proof requires the defendant director to show two things: 1) that they had reasonable grounds for believing that a danger to corporate policy and effectiveness existed by the presence of the potential offeror; and 2) that the defencive measure was reasonable in relation to the threat posed.

It is evident from the preceding description of the American approach on this issue that it is remarkably similar to that of the British Columbia Supreme Court in Teck. For example, the American courts have adopted the central requirement of Teck, that being that the decisions by directors to employ anti-takeover defences must be made in good faith and on reasonable grounds. As well, both Teck and the business judgment rule allow directors to base their decisions on a number of considerations, including the best interests of both the corporation and the employees, and the identity of the offeror.

The Role of the CBCA

A final point that should be considered is whether or not the CBCA should expand its role in the regulation of the fiduciary duties of directors in the context of a take-over bid by introducing a detailed code of conduct for directors. This question is examined thoroughly in Industry Canada's 1996 discussion paper on take-overs in which it is recommended that provisions be added to the CBCA requiring directors to obtain shareholder approval of all anticipatory defencive measures. Yet, such a legislative response appears to constitute an excessive and unnecessary intervention in the affairs of a corporation. The potential abuse of an anti-takeover instrument by an offeree's directors is already controlled by subsection 122(1) of the CBCA which requires that directors not act contrary to their fiduciary duties. If anything, a CBCA code of conduct would be best used to outline to directors certain prerequisites that they must satisfy in order to discharge their duties in the context of a take-over bid. It could, in the process, help to crystallize the Canadian position on the fiduciary duty test. The

Canadian Securities Administrators have already made some progress in this area, issuing National Policy 38 which, among other things, recognises the potential conflict between the interests of shareholders and management in a take-over situation, emphasizes that the primary objective of take-over legislation is to protect shareholders, and provides that ultimately the shareholders have the right to make the take-over decision. In fact, the courts have already begun to turn to National Policy 38 as an interpretative guide for their examination of anti-takeover defencive measures.

In summary, anti-takeover defencive strategies continue to present directors with the potential to misuse their powers at the expense of shareholders. However, the Canadian courts have successfully responded by invalidating any exercise of defencive measures which constitutes a breach of directors' fiduciary duties. In order to continue to discourage directors from abusing these defence instruments, and to foster a more balanced, trusting relationship between shareholders and directors, we should aspire to two goals. First, the Teck fiduciary test must be adopted as the only true test for directors' take-over fiduciary duties. Second, the CBCA should draft a guideline outlining the keys to avoiding a breach of duty during a take-over.

Chapter 3

Monte Carlo Method

In its pure mathematical form, the Monte Carlo method consists of finding the definite integral of a function by choosing a large number of independent-variable samples at random from within an interval or region, averaging the resulting dependent-variable values, and then dividing by the span of the interval or the size of the region over which the random samples were chosen. This differs from the classical method of approximating a definite integral, in which independent-variable samples are selected at equally-spaced points within an interval or region.

The Monte Carlo method is most famous for its use during the Second World War in the design of the atomic bomb. It has also been used in diverse applications, such as the analysis of traffic flow on superhighways, the development of models for the evolution of stars, and attempts to predict fluctuations in the stock market. The scheme also finds applications in integrated circuit (IC) design, quantum mechanics , and communications engineering.

Definition of 'Monte Carlo Simulation'

A problem solving technique used to approximate the probability of certain outcomes by running multiple trial runs, called simulations, using random variables.

Monte Carlo Simulation

"It's mandated [at Suncor] to do Monte Carlo simulation on all major projects' capital cost estimates."

Risk analysis is part of every decision we make. We are constantly faced with uncertainty, ambiguity, and variability. And even though we have unprecedented access to information, we can't accurately predict the future. Monte Carlo simulation (also known as the Monte Carlo Method) lets you see all the possible outcomes of your decisions and assess the impact of risk, allowing for better decision making under uncertainty.

What is Monte Carlo Simulation?

Monte Carlo simulation is a computerized mathematical technique that allows people to account for risk in quantitative analysis and decision making. The technique is used by professionals in such widely disparate fields as finance, project management, energy, manufacturing, engineering, research and development, insurance, oil & gas, transportation, and the environment.

Monte Carlo simulation furnishes the decision-maker with a range of possible outcomes and the probabilities they will occur for any choice of action.. It shows the extreme possibilities—the outcomes of going for broke and for the most conservative decision—along with all possible consequences for middle-of-the-road decisions.

The technique was first used by scientists working on the atom bomb; it was named for Monte Carlo, the Monaco resort town renowned for its casinos. Since its introduction in World War II, Monte Carlo simulation has been used to model a variety of physical and conceptual systems.

How Monte Carlo Simulation Works

Monte Carlo simulation performs risk analysis by building models of possible results by substituting a range of values—a*probability distribution*—for any factor that has inherent uncertainty. It then calculates results over and over, each time using a different set of random values from the probability functions. Depending upon the number of uncertainties and the ranges specified for them, a Monte Carlo simulation could involve thousands or tens of thousands of recalculations before it is complete. Monte Carlo simulation produces distributions of possible outcome values.

By using probability distributions, variables can have different probabilities of different outcomes occurring. Probability distributions are a much more realistic way of describing uncertainty in variables of a risk analysis. Common probability distributions include:

Normal – Or "bell curve." The user simply defines the mean or expected value and a standard deviation to describe the variation about the mean. Values in the middle near the mean are most likely to occur.

It is symmetric and describes many natural phenomena such as people's heights. Examples of variables described by normal distributions include inflation rates and energy prices.

Lognormal – Values are positively skewed, not symmetric like a normal distribution. It is used to represent values that don't go below zero but have unlimited positive potential. Examples of variables described by lognormal distributions include real estate property values, stock prices, and oil reserves.

Uniform – All values have an equal chance of occurring, and the user simply defines the minimum and maximum. Examples of variables that could be uniformly distributed include manufacturing costs or future sales revenues for a new product.

Triangular – The user defines the minimum, most likely, and maximum values. Values around the most likely are more likely to occur. Variables that could be described by a triangular distribution include past sales history per unit of time and inventory levels.

PERT- The user defines the minimum, most likely, and maximum values, just like the triangular distribution. Values around the most likely are more likely to occur. However values between the most likely and extremes are more likely to occur than the triangular; that is, the extremes are not as emphasized. An example of the use of a PERT distribution is to describe the duration of a task in a project management model.

Discrete – The user defines specific values that may occur and the likelihood of each. An example might be the results of a lawsuit: 20% chance of positive verdict, 30% change of negative verdict, 40% chance of settlement, and 10% chance of mistrial.

During a Monte Carlo simulation, values are sampled at random from the input probability distributions. Each set of samples is called an *iteration,* and the resulting outcome from that sample is recorded. Monte Carlo simulation does this hundreds or thousands of times, and the result is a probability distribution of possible outcomes. In this way, Monte Carlo simulation provides a much more comprehensive view of what may happen. It tells you not only what could happen, but how likely it is to happen.

Monte Carlo simulation provides a number of advantages over *deterministic,* or "single-point estimate" analysis:

- *Probabilistic Results.* Results show not only what could happen, but how likely each outcome is.

- *Graphical Results.* Because of the data a Monte Carlo simulation generates, it's easy to create graphs of different outcomes and their chances of occurrence. This is important for communicating findings to other stakeholders.
- *Sensitivity Analysis.* With just a few cases, deterministic analysis makes it difficult to see which variables impact the outcome the most. In Monte Carlo simulation, it's easy to see which inputs had the biggest effect on bottom-line results.
- *Scenario Analysis:* In deterministic models, it's very difficult to model different combinations of values for different inputs to see the effects of truly different scenarios. Using Monte Carlo simulation, analysts can see exactly which inputs had which values together when certain outcomes occurred. This is invaluable for pursuing further analysis.
- *Correlation of Inputs.* In Monte Carlo simulation, it's possible to model interdependent relationships between input variables. It's important for accuracy to represent how, in reality, when some factors goes up, others go up or down accordingly.

An enhancement to Monte Carlo simulation is the use of Latin Hypercube sampling, which samples more accurately from the entire range of distribution functions.

What is the Monte Carlo Method?

Any method which solves a problem by generating suitable random numbers and observing that fraction of the numbers obeying some property or properties.

The method is useful for obtaining numerical solutions to problems which are too complicated to solve analytically. It was named by S. Ulam, who in 1946 became the first mathematician to dignify this approach with a name, in honour of a relative having a propensity to gamble. Nicolas Metropolis also made important contributions to the development of such methods.

In general terms, the Monte Carlo method (or Monte Carlo simulation) can be used to describe any technique that approximates solutions to quantitative problems through statistical sampling. As used here, 'Monte Carlo simulation' is more specifically used to describe a method for propagating (translating) uncertainties in model inputs into uncertainties in model outputs (results).

Hence, it is a type of simulation that explicitly and quantitatively represents uncertainties. Monte Carlo simulation relies on the process of explicitly representing uncertainties by specifying inputs as probability distributions.

If the inputs describing a system are uncertain, the prediction of future performance is necessarily uncertain. That is, the result of any analysis based on inputs represented by probability distributions is itself a probability distribution.

Whereas the result of a single simulation of an uncertain system is a *qualified statement* ("if we build the dam, the salmon population could go extinct"), the result of a probabilistic (Monte Carlo) simulation is a *quantified probability* ("if we build the dam, there is a 20% chance that the salmon population will go extinct").

Such a result (in this case, quantifying the risk of extinction) is typically much more useful to decision-makers who utilise the simulation results.

In order to compute the probability distribution of predicted performance, it is necessary to *propagate* (translate) the input uncertainties into uncertainties in the results. A variety of methods exist for propagating uncertainty. Monte Carlo simulation is perhaps the most common technique for propagating the uncertainty in the various aspects of a system to the predicted performance.

In Monte Carlo simulation, the entire system is simulated a large number (e.g., 1000) of times. Each simulation is equally likely, referred to as a realisation of the system.

For each realisation, all of the uncertain parameters are sampled (i.e., a single random value is selected from the specified distribution describing each parameter). The system is then simulated through time (given the particular set of input parameters) such that the performance of the system can be computed.

This results is a large number of separate and independent results, each representing a possible "future" for the system (i.e., one possible path the system may follow through time). The results of the independent system realisations are assembled into probability distributions of possible outcomes. As a result, the outputs are not single values, but probability distributions.

A Simple Example: Rolling Dice

As a simple example of a Monte Carlo simulation, consider calculating the probability of a particular sum of the throw of two dice (with each die having values one through six). In this particular case, there are 36 combinations of dice rolls:

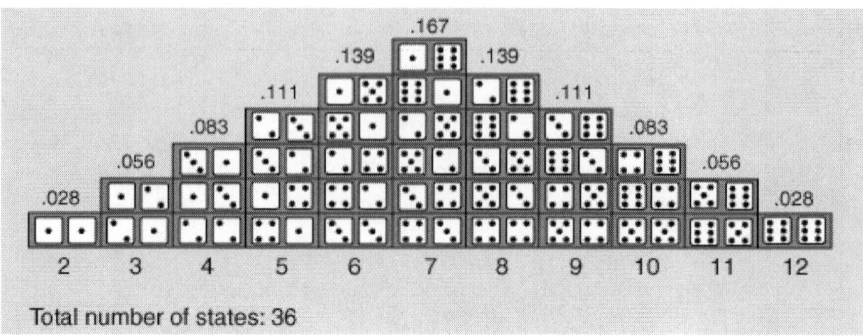

Figure: *Based on this, you can manually compute the probability of a particular outcome. For example, there are six different ways that the dice could sum to seven. Hence, the probability of rolling seven is equal to **6** divided by **36** = **0.167**.*

Instead of computing the probability in this way, however, we could instead throw the dice a hundred times and record how many times each outcome occurs. If the dice totaled seven 18 times (out of 100 rolls), we would conclude that the probability of rolling seven is approximately 0.18 (18%). Obviously, the more times we rolled the dice, the less approximate our result would be. Better than rolling dice a hundred times, we can easily use a computer to simulate rolling the dice 10,000 times (or more).

Because we know the probability of a particular outcome for one die (1 in 6 for all six numbers), this is simple. The output of 10,000 realisations (using GoldSim software):

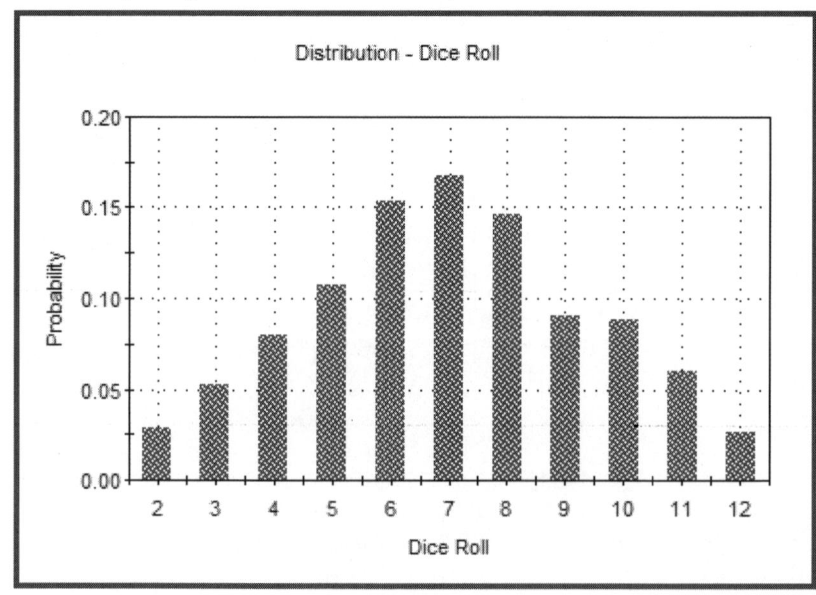

How Accurate are the Results?

The accuracy of a Monte Carlo simulation is a function of the number of realisations. That is, the confidence bounds on the results can be readily computed based on the number of realisations. The two examples below show the 5% and 95% confidence bounds on the value for each outcome (i.e., there is a 90% chance the true value lies between the bounds):

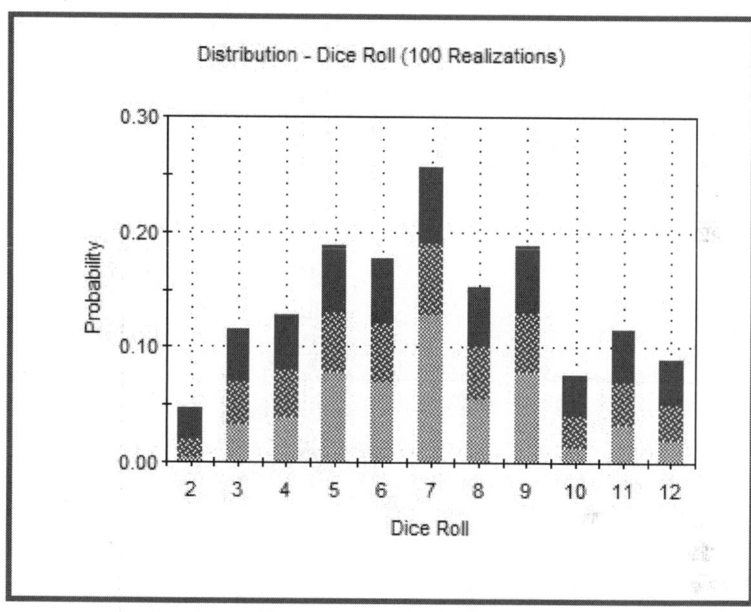

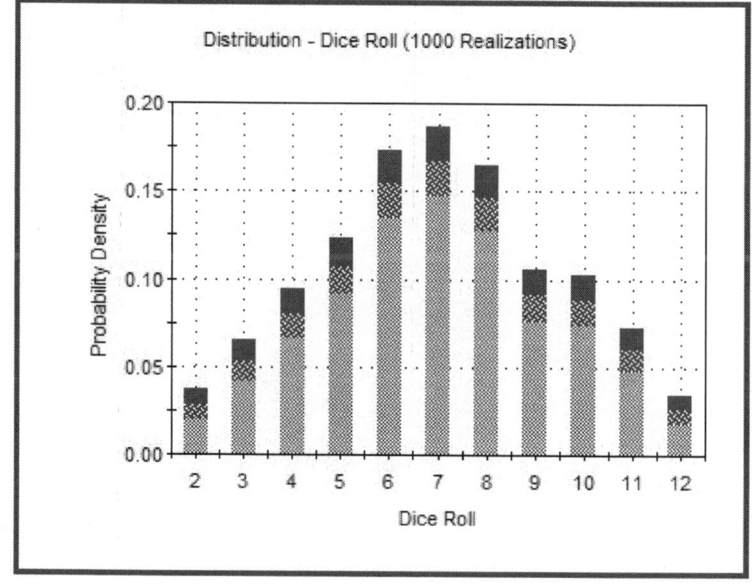

History of the Monte Carlo Method

Monte Carlo simulation was named after the city in Monaco (famous for its casino) where games of chance (e.g., roulette) involve repetitive events with known probabilities. Although there were a number of isolated and undeveloped applications of Monte Carlo simulation principles at earlier dates, modern application of Monte Carlo methods date from the 1940s during work on the atomic bomb. Mathematician Stanislaw Ulam is credited with recognising how computers could make Monte Carlo simulation of complex systems feasible:

> *The first thoughts and attempts I made to practice [the Monte Carlo Method] were suggested by a question which occurred to me in 1946 as I was convalescing from an illness and playing solitaires. The question was what are the chances that a Canfield solitaire laid out with 52 cards will come out successfully? After spending a lot of time trying to estimate them by pure combinatorial calculations, I wondered whether a more practical method than "abstract thinking" might not be to lay it out say one hundred times and simply observe and count the number of successful plays. This was already possible to envisage with the beginning of the new era of fast computers, and I immediately thought of problems of neutron diffusion and other questions of mathematical physics, and more generally how to change processes described by certain differential equations into an equivalent form interpretable as a succession of random operations. Later ... [in 1946, I] described the idea to John von Neumann, and we began to plan actual calculations.*

Monte Carlo and Random Numbers

Monte Carlo simulation methods do not always require truly random numbers to be useful — while for some applications, such as primality testing, unpredictability is vital. Many of the most useful techniques use deterministic, pseudorandom sequences, making it easy to test and re-run simulations. The only quality usually necessary to make good simulations is for the pseudo-random sequence to appear "random enough" in a certain sense.

What this means depends on the application, but typically they should pass a series of statistical tests. Testing that the numbers are uniformly distributed or follow another desired distribution when a large enough number of elements of the sequence are considered is one of the simplest, and most common ones. Weak correlations between successive samples is also often desirable/necessary.

Sawilowsky lists the characteristics of a high quality Monte Carlo simulation:

- the (pseudo-random) number generator has certain characteristics (*e.g.*, a long "period" before the sequence repeats)
- the (pseudo-random) number generator produces values that pass tests for randomness
- there are enough samples to ensure accurate results
- the proper sampling technique is used
- the algorithm used is valid for what is being modelled
- it simulates the phenomenon in question.

Pseudo-random number sampling algorithms are used to transform uniformly distributed pseudo-random numbers into numbers that are distributed according to a given probability distribution.

Low-discrepancy sequences are often used instead of random sampling from a space as they ensure even coverage and normally have a faster order of convergence than Monte Carlo simulations using random or pseudorandom sequences. Methods based on their use are called quasi-Monte Carlo methods.

Monte Carlo Simulation versus "What If" Scenarios

There are ways of using probabilities that are definitely not Monte Carlo simulations — for example, deterministic modelling using single-point estimates. Each uncertain variable within a model is assigned a "best guess" estimate. Scenarios (such as best, worst, or most likely case) for each input variable are chosen and the results recorded.

By contrast, Monte Carlo simulations sample probability distribution for each variable to produce hundreds or thousands of possible outcomes. The results are analyzed to get probabilities of different outcomes occurring. For example, a comparison of a spreadsheet cost construction model run using traditional "what if" scenarios, and then run again with Monte Carlo simulation and Triangular probability distributions shows that the Monte Carlo analysis has a narrower range than the "what if" analysis. This is because the "what if" analysis gives equal weight to all scenarios, while Monte Carlo method hardly samples in the very low probability regions. The samples in such regions are called "rare events".

Applications

Monte Carlo methods are especially useful for simulating phenomena with significant uncertainty in inputs and systems with a large number of coupled degrees of freedom. Areas of application include:

Physical Sciences

Monte Carlo methods are very important in computational physics, physical chemistry, and related applied fields, and have diverse applications from complicated quantum chromodynamics calculations to designing heat shields and aerodynamic forms. In statistical physics Monte Carlo molecular modelling is an alternative to computational molecular dynamics, and Monte Carlo methods are used to compute statistical field theories of simple particle and polymer systems. Quantum Monte Carlo methods solve the many-body problem for quantum systems. In experimental particle physics, Monte Carlo methods are used for designing detectors, understanding their behaviour and comparing experimental data to theory. In astrophysics, they are used in such diverse manners as to model both the evolution of galaxies and the transmission of microwave radiation through a rough planetary surface. Monte Carlo methods are also used in the ensemble models that form the basis of modern weather forecasting.

Engineering

Monte Carlo methods are widely used in engineering for sensitivity analysis and quantitative probabilistic analysis in process design. The need arises from the interactive, co-linear and non-linear behaviour of typical process simulations. For example,

- In microelectronics engineering, Monte Carlo methods are applied to analyze correlated and uncorrelated variations in analog and digital integrated circuits.
- In geostatistics and geometallurgy, Monte Carlo methods underpin the design of mineral processing flowsheets and contribute to quantitative risk analysis.
- In wind energy yield analysis, the predicted energy output of a wind farm during its lifetime is calculated giving different levels of uncertainty
- impacts of pollution are simulated and diesel compared with petrol.
- In Fluid Dynamics, in particular Rarefied Gas Dynamics, where the Boltzmann equation is solved for finite Knudsen number

fluid flows using the Direct Simulation Monte Carlo method in combination with highly efficient computational algorithms.

- In autonomous robotics, Monte Carlo localization can determine the position of a robot. It is often applied to stochastic filters such as the Kalman filter or Particle filter that forms the heart of the SLAM (Simultaneous Localization and Mapping) algorithm.
- In telecommunications, when planning a wireless network, design must be proved to work for a wide variety of scenarios that depend mainly on the number of users, their locations and the services they want to use. Monte Carlo methods are typically used to generate these users and their states. The network performance is then evaluated and, if results are not satisfactory, the network design goes through an optimization process.
- In reliability engineering, one can use Monte Carlo simulation to generate mean time between failures and mean time to repair for components.

Computational Biology

Monte Carlo methods are used in various fields of computational biology, for example for Bayesian inference in phylogeny, or for studying biological systems such as genomes, proteins, or membranes. The systems can be studied in the coarse-grained or *ab initio* frameworks depending on the desired accuracy. Computer simulations allow us to monitor the local environment of a particular molecule to see if some chemical reaction is happening for instance. We can also conduct thought experiments when the physical experiments are not feasible, for instance breaking bonds, introducing impurities at specific sites, changing the local/global structure, or introducing external fields.

Computer Graphics

Path Tracing, occasionally referred to as Monte Carlo Ray Tracing, renders a 3D scene by randomly tracing samples of possible light paths. Repeated sampling of any given pixel will eventually cause the average of the samples to converge on the correct solution of the rendering equation, making it one of the most physically accurate 3D graphics rendering methods in existence.

Applied Statistics

In applied statistics, Monte Carlo methods are generally used for two purposes:

1. To compare competing statistics for small samples under realistic data conditions. Although Type I error and power properties of statistics can be calculated for data drawn from classical theoretical distributions (*e.g.*, normal curve, Cauchy distribution) for asymptotic conditions (*i. e*, infinite sample size and infinitesimally small treatment effect), real data often do not have such distributions.
2. To provide implementations of hypothesis tests that are more efficient than exact tests such as permutation tests (which are often impossible to compute) while being more accurate than critical values for asymptotic distributions.

Monte Carlo methods are also a compromise between approximate randomization and permutation tests. An approximate randomization test is based on a specified subset of all permutations (which entails potentially enormous housekeeping of which permutations have been considered). The Monte Carlo approach is based on a specified number of randomly drawn permutations (exchanging a minor loss in precision if a permutation is drawn twice – or more frequently—for the efficiency of not having to track which permutations have already been selected).

Artificial Intelligence for Games

Monte Carlo methods have been developed into a technique called Monte-Carlo tree search that is useful for searching for the best move in a game. Possible moves are organised in a search tree and a large number of random simulations are used to estimate the long-term potential of each move. A black box simulator represents the opponent's moves.

The Monte Carlo Tree Search (MCTS) method has four steps:

1. Starting at root node of the tree, select optimal child nodes until a leaf node is reached.
2. Expand the leaf node and choose one of its children.
3. Play a simulated game starting with that node.
4. Use the results of that simulated game to update the node and its ancestors.

The net effect, over the course of many simulated games, is that the value of a node representing a move will go up or down, hopefully corresponding to whether or not that node represents a good move.

Monte Carlo Tree Search has been used successfully to play games such as Go, Tantrix, Battleship, Havannah, and Arimaa.

Design and Visuals

Monte Carlo methods are also efficient in solving coupled integral differential equations of radiation fields and energy transport, and thus these methods have been used in global illumination computations that produce photo-realistic images of virtual 3D models, with applications in video games, architecture, design, computer generated films, and cinematic special effects.

Finance and Business

Monte Carlo methods in finance are often used to evaluate investments in projects at a business unit or corporate level, or to evaluate financial derivatives. They can be used to model project schedules, where simulations aggregate estimates for worst-case, best-case, and most likely durations for each task to determine outcomes for the overall project.

Use in Mathematics

In general, Monte Carlo methods are used in mathematics to solve various problems by generating suitable random numbers and observing that fraction of the numbers that obeys some property or properties. The method is useful for obtaining numerical solutions to problems too complicated to solve analytically. The most common application of the Monte Carlo method is Monte Carlo integration.

Integration

Deterministic numerical integration algorithms work well in a small number of dimensions, but encounter two problems when the functions have many variables. First, the number of function evaluations needed increases rapidly with the number of dimensions. For example, if 10 evaluations provide adequate accuracy in one dimension, then 10^{100} points are needed for 100 dimensions—far too many to be computed. This is called the curse of dimensionality. Second, the boundary of a multidimensional region may be very complicated, so it may not be feasible to reduce the problem to a series of nested one-dimensional integrals. 100 dimensions is by no means unusual, since in many physical problems, a "dimension" is equivalent to a degree of freedom.

Monte Carlo methods provide a way out of this exponential increase in computation time. As long as the function in question is reasonably well-behaved, it can be estimated by randomly selecting points in 100-dimensional space, and taking some kind of average of the function values at these points. By the central limit theorem, this method displays $1/\sqrt{N}$ convergence—i.e., quadrupling the number of sampled points halves the error, regardless of the number of dimensions.

A refinement of this method, known as importance sampling in statistics, involves sampling the points randomly, but more frequently where the integrand is large. To do this precisely one would have to already know the integral, but one can approximate the integral by an integral of a similar function or use adaptive routines such as stratified sampling, recursive stratified sampling, adaptive umbrella sampling or the VEGAS algorithm.

A similar approach, the quasi-Monte Carlo method, uses low-discrepancy sequences. These sequences "fill" the area better and sample the most important points more frequently, so quasi-Monte Carlo methods can often converge on the integral more quickly.

Another class of methods for sampling points in a volume is to simulate random walks over it (Markov chain Monte Carlo). Such methods include the Metropolis-Hastings algorithm, Gibbs sampling and the Wang and Landau algorithm.

Simulation and Optimization

Another powerful and very popular application for random numbers in numerical simulation is in numerical optimization. The problem is to minimize (or maximize) functions of some vector that often has a large number of dimensions. Many problems can be phrased in this way: for example, a computer chess program could be seen as trying to find the set of, say, 10 moves that produces the best evaluation function at the end. In the travelling salesman problem the goal is to minimize distance travelled. There are also applications to engineering design, such as multidisciplinary design optimization.

The travelling salesman problem is what is called a conventional optimization problem. That is, all the facts (distances between each destination point) needed to determine the optimal path to follow are known with certainty and the goal is to run through the possible travel choices to come up with the one with the lowest total distance. However, let's assume that instead of wanting to minimize the total distance travelled to visit each desired destination, we wanted to minimize the total time needed to reach each destination. This goes beyond conventional optimization since travel time is inherently uncertain (traffic jams, time of day, etc.). As a result, to determine our optimal path we would want to use simulation - optimization to first understand the range of potential times it could take to go from one point to another (represented by a probability distribution in this case rather than a specific distance) and then optimize our travel decisions to identify the best path to follow taking that uncertainty into account.

Simulating industry problems using spreadsheet software is a powerful application of Monte Carlo simulation. With a basic spreadsheet tool and some formulas built into the sheet, industry can often attain good solutions without having to procure expensive simulation software.

Inverse Problems

Probabilistic formulation of inverse problems leads to the definition of a probability distribution in the model space. This probability distribution combines prior information with new information obtained by measuring some observable parameters (data). As, in the general case, the theory linking data with model parameters is nonlinear, the posterior probability in the model space may not be easy to describe (it may be multimodal, some moments may not be defined, etc.).

When analyzing an inverse problem, obtaining a maximum likelihood model is usually not sufficient, as we normally also wish to have information on the resolution power of the data. In the general case we may have a large number of model parameters, and an inspection of the marginal probability densities of interest may be impractical, or even useless. But it is possible to pseudorandomly generate a large collection of models according to the posterior probability distribution and to analyze and display the models in such a way that information on the relative likelihoods of model properties is conveyed to the spectator. This can be accomplished by means of an efficient Monte Carlo method, even in cases where no explicit formula for the *a priori* distribution is available.

The best-known importance sampling method, the Metropolis algorithm, can be generalized, and this gives a method that allows analysis of (possibly highly nonlinear) inverse problems with complex *a priori* information and data with an arbitrary noise distribution.

Monte Carlo Algorithm

In computing, a Monte Carlo algorithm is a randomized algorithm whose running time is deterministic, but whose output may be incorrect with a certain (typically small) probability.

The related class of Las Vegas algorithms are also randomized, but in a different way: they take an amount of time that varies randomly, but always produce the correct answer. A Monte Carlo algorithm can be converted into a Las Vegas algorithm whenever there exists a procedure to verify that the output produced by the algorithm is indeed correct. If so, then the resulting Las Vegas algorithm is merely to repeatedly run the Monte Carlo algorithm until one of the runs produces an output that can be verified to be correct.

The name refers to the grand casino in the Principality of Monaco at Monte Carlo, which is well-known around the world as an icon of gambling.

One-Sided vs Two-Sided Error

Whereas the answer returned by a deterministic algorithm is always expected to be correct, this is not the case for Monte Carlo algorithms. For decision problems, these algorithms are generally classified as either false-biased or true-biased. A false-biased Monte Carlo algorithm is always correct when it returns false; a true-biased algorithm is always correct when it returns true. While this describes algorithms with *one-sided errors*, others might have no bias; these are said to have *two-sided errors.* The answer they provide (either true or false) will be incorrect, or correct, with some bounded probability.

For instance, the Solovay–Strassen primality test is used to determine whether a given number is a prime number. It always answers true for prime number inputs; for composite inputs, it answers false with probability at least ½ and true with probability at most ½. Thus, false answers from the algorithm are certain to be correct, whereas the true answers remain uncertain; this is said to be a *½-correct false-biased algorithm.*

Amplification

For a Monte Carlo algorithm with one-sided errors, the failure probability can be reduced (and the success probability amplified) by running the algorithm k times. Consider again the Solovay–Strassen algorithm which is *½-correct false-biased.* One may run this algorithm multiple times returning a false answer if it reaches a false response within k iterations, and otherwise returning true. Thus, if the number is prime then the answer is always correct, and if the number is composite then the answer is correct with probability at least 1"(1"½)^k = 1"2^{-k}.

For Monte Carlo decision algorithms with two-sided error, the failure probability may again be reduced by running the algorithm k times and returning the majority function of the answers.

Complexity Classes

The complexity class BPP describes decision problems that can be solved by polynomial-time Monte Carlo algorithms with a bounded probability of two-sided errors, and the complexity class RP describes problems that can be solved by a Monte Carlo algorithm with a bounded probability of one-sided error: if the correct answer is no, the algorithm always says so, but it may answer no incorrectly for some instances where the correct answer is yes.

In contrast, the complexity class ZPP describes problems solvable by polynomial expected time Las Vegas algorithms. ZPP †" RP †" BPP, but it is not known whether any of these complexity classes is distinct from each other; that is, Monte Carlo algorithms may have more computational power than Las Vegas algorithms, but this has not been proven. Another complexity class, PP, describes decision problems with a polynomial-time Monte Carlo algorithm that is more accurate than flipping a coin but where the error probability cannot be bounded away from ½.

Topics in Going Private Transactions

Litigation: Lessons Learned from the Dell Saga in Going-private Transactions

The Special Committee Meets Several Requirements Imposed on Corporate Boards by Corporate Law: Michael Dell recently succeeded in taking Dell Inc., the computer company he founded in 1984, private in a $25 billion dollar buyout. The transaction was consummated following months of drama involving Dell himself, veteran investor Carl Icahn (who tried to derail the deal) and a number of other institutional shareholders.

But a starring role in the drama was played by the special committee of Dell's board of directors, formed to evaluate Dell's initial offer and all subsequent offers. The committee was critical to Dell's defeat of Icahn's legal challenge to the buyout. The role of that special committee, and the ways in which the committee was effective in protecting the transaction from legal attack, are worth further consideration.

The special committee has become a standard feature of going-private transactions because it meets several requirements imposed on corporate boards by corporate law, particularly as interpreted by the influential Delaware courts. Dell Inc., like many large corporations, is incorporated in Delaware, and the struggle to control the company was fought in part in Delaware courthouses. A fundamental principle of Delaware corporate law is that corporate directors owe fiduciary duties to their corporation, including the duties of care and loyalty. They discharge those duties by remaining informed about the corporation and its affairs and acting in a way that they in good faith believe to be in the corporation's best interest. Provided that they fulfill their fiduciary duties, directors are protected by the business judgment rule. The business judgment rule shields them from liability for their decisions, even if those decisions turn out to be wrong, and further provides that courts will not second-guess those decisions.

The analytical framework shifts, however, in the context of a going private transaction led by a dominant, related party shareholder (such as Michael Dell in the Dell, Inc. transaction). Michael Dell and his investors, led by private equity firm Silver Lake, proposed to acquire 75 percent of the company. Dell owned 16 percent at the outset and sat on the board of directors.

In a going-private transaction led by a controlling shareholder, presumptions of the business judgment rule will frequently not apply to protect against a shareholder challenge, shifting the burden to the directors to show that the proposed transaction is "entirely fair" to the corporation and its shareholders. The entire fairness standard, as enunciated by the Delaware courts, is sufficiently demanding to be characterized as outcome-determinative by many observers. That is, if the burden shifts to the directors to show the entire fairness of the going-private transaction, they may abandon the transaction altogether.

Enter the special committee. If a court finds that a properly constituted special committee, supported by adequate resources, sufficiently investigated the merits of the going private transaction, canvassed for alternatives, and engaged in vigorous arms-length negotiations with the shareholder seeking to take the corporation private, the court will likely conclude that the demanding standard of entire fairness is satisfied.

Furthermore, if the special committee conditions approval of the transaction on a vote of the majority of the remaining disinterested shareholders, the committee can shift the burden back to the challenging shareholder to demonstrate a lack of entire fairness. To ensure that the special committee will have the desired legal effect, the committee should be composed entirely of disinterested and independent directors who are authorized to evaluate and negotiate the going-private transaction on behalf of the minority shareholders.

The special committee should retain independent financial and legal advisors to assist in evaluating the proposal and negotiating with the controlling shareholder.

In the Dell, Inc. transaction, the special committee acted with vigor, contacting 67 potential bidders during a 45-day "go shop" period following Dell's announcement of his offer in February 2013. Icahn informed the board in March that he had acquired a substantial block of shares and would fight the transaction. Blackstone made a competing bid for the company. And several other large shareholders, including Southeastern Asset Management, Harris Associates, and Yacktman Asset Management, also expressed opposition to the going-private transaction.

During the course of the special committee's evaluation of the transaction, Michael Dell's group benefited from continuing weakness in Dell, Inc.'s PC business, which discouraged competing offers. Blackstone abandoned its bid in April, citing a 14 percent drop in PC volume. Moreover, the special committee was able to determine that Michael Dell's was the only credible offer for the entire company. Icahn initially proposed buying only 58 percent of the company while increasing its debt load, a proposal the special committee regarded as fraught with risk. The special committee ultimately concluded that Icahn was nearly $4 billion short of the cash needed to finance his proposed $12 per share special dividend, and recommended the Dell/ Silver Lake buyout.

Ultimately, the fate of the company was decided in Delaware's Court of Chancery. Icahn sued in August, seeking an expedited hearing and an order seeking to block Dell's planned shareholder vote approving the buyout. But in a conference on Aug. 16, Chancellor Leo Strine, Jr., rejected Icahn's demands. He found that Icahn had not mounted any credible challenge to the independence of the Dell special committee and had not shown any violation of the directors' fiduciary duties.

Strine therefore denied the request for an expedited hearing and refused to interfere with the committee's scheduling of the shareholder vote. Icahn threw in the towel shortly afterwards, and Michael Dell's final offer ($13.75 a share plus a 13 cent per share special dividend) was accepted by the shareholders.

It remains to see if Michael Dell's plan to transform Dell, Inc. from a PC maker to an enterprise software company can succeed. But his going-private transaction, supported by an independent, energetic special committee, already has and serves as an example of how corporations and their boards of directors can navigate the murky waters of related party transactions.

Private Equity Backed Going-private Transactions

On September 12, 2013, shareholders of the PC maker Dell Inc. approved the company's $24.9 billion sale to its founder and chief executive, Michael Dell, and the private equity firm Silver Lake. But taking the company that bears his name private was not an easy task for Mr. Dell. A group of shareholders, led by the active investor Carl C. Icahn, opposed the deal, forcing Mr. Dell and Silver Lake to raise their bid, though only slightly. Fierce controversy over voting rules and appraisal rights also took place before the completion of the transaction.

As Dell's management buyout suggests, going-private deals are often a rather complex endeavour. Nevertheless, struggling corporations, especially those with undervalued stock, may still be attractive for private equity firms willing to make the effort to purchase and restructure them for a future sale at profit. With more than 400 companies listed and its main stock index, IBOVESPA, 25% lower than it was at its peak in 2008, the Brazilian stock market might offer good opportunities for private equity firms – as well as some challenges.

As most Brazilian corporations still have a concentrated ownership structure, the first step a fund must take in order to carry out a going-private transaction in Brazil is to negotiate a contract with the target's controlling shareholder or group.

If this contract implies a sale of control for purposes of article 254-A of the Brazilian Corporations Act, the fund must make a tender offer to acquire all the target's minority shareholders common shares for at least 80% of the price it agreed to pay for the controlling shareholders' shares. In the sequence, if there are still outstanding shares, the fund shall then make the tender offer set forth in article 4, § 4 of the Brazilian Corporations Act to acquire all minority shareholders' shares – although all shares of the same class must be offered the same price, different prices can be offered to shares of different classes. The fund may ask the CVM (the Brazilian SEC), for an authorization to merge both article 254-A and article 4, § 4 tender offers. Actually, even if the fund does not ask, the CVM will likely impose such a merger.

If the contract does not imply a sale of control, an article 254-A tender offer is not required. Not being the controlling shareholder, the fund is not allowed to make the article 4, § 4 tender offer. In this case, the contract should arrange for the controlling shareholder to carry out such going-private tender offer.

The going-private transaction is deemed approved if shareholders holding 2/3 of the outstanding shares either expressly agree with it or accept the article 4, § 4 tender offer. Shares held by "no-show" shareholders are not considered outstanding shares, making the approval easier. Those that do not accept the tender offer remain as minority shareholders. However, once the offer is closed, if less than 5% of the company stock remain outstanding, minority shareholders may be squeezed out, receiving the same price per share paid to the ones that previously accepted the tender offer.

To prevent the risk of continuing to have minority shareholders after going private – a risk private equity funds almost certainly will want to avoid –, it is advisable to set out upfront that the offer will be conditioned on the acceptance of shareholders holding at least 95% of the target's shares.

The article 4, § 4 tender offer price (or prices) must be "fair" and supported by a valuation report of the company filed with the CVM. Shareholders individually or collectively holding 10% or more of minority shareholders' shares may request a special minority shareholders meeting to vote on whether to challenge the valuation report and appoint a new appraiser. Such challenge must be justified.

If minority shareholders commission a new valuation report and it assesses a lower or equal value for the company, then the tender offer goes through with its original price. In this case, shareholders that voted for such new valuation must pay for it, which reduces the risk of moral hazard. On the other hand, if the value appointed in the new valuation report is higher than that in the first one, the offer or must either change the price (or prices) of the offer to make it compatible with the new valuation or withdraw the offer.

It is difficult to forecast how long a going-private transaction takes to be completed. In the cases of Amil and Redecard, two leading Brazilian corporations that went private recently, it took about seven to eight months between the disclosure of the intention of going private and the final cancellation of their public company registration with the CVM.

With careful planning and close attention to legal formalities – which is important to try to mitigate hurdles similar to those faced by Mr. Dell in his recent buyout –, going-private transactions could present interesting opportunities for the PE&VC industry, especially in a moment in which the Brazilian stock market is far from its historical peak.

Take a Company Private

It is quite likely that a smaller business that has gone public will find that the cost and liability associated with doing so is too great, and so wants to take the company private. When a company deregisters its equity securities, this is called *going private*. A company can go private under one of the following two circumstances:

- There are no more than 300 shareholders of record
- There are no more than 500 shareholders of record and the company has not exceeded $10 million of assets as of the end of the last three fiscal years

Note that under the 2012 Jumpstart Our Business Startups (JOBS) Act, the criterion for having 500 shareholders and a $10 million asset cap has increased to 2,000 shareholders or 500 unaccredited investors – in regard to being forced to file reports with the SEC. Presumably, the same requirements work in reverse to make it easier to go private.

A *shareholder of record* is a person or entity listed in the shareholder records of a business as owning its stock. A brokerage can be the shareholder of record on behalf of its clients. Thus, it is possible to have many more actual shareholders than is indicated by the number of shareholders of record.

For either of the two preceding circumstances, going private involves filing the very simple Form 15 with the SEC. Only the approval of the board of directors is required to go private; there is no shareholder vote. In addition, if a company's shares are listed on a stock exchange, the exchange should be notified. The type of notification varies by exchange.

If senior management is at all uncertain about a company's ability to continue as a public company, it should try to keep the number of shareholders as low as possible. This means not handing out a few extra shares to employees, or issuing warrants, or any other action that will result in a scattering of a small number of shares amongst a large number of new shareholders.

If there are too many shareholders, the company will have to find a way to reduce the number, such as through a stock buyback program or a reverse stock split. It then documents its intentions in the much more elaborate Schedule 13e-3, which it files with the SEC. Schedule 13e-3 requires a discussion of the purposes of the stock buyback or reverse split, any alternatives considered by the company, and whether the transaction is unfair to unaffiliated shareholders.

The SEC views going private transactions with considerable suspicion, on the grounds that they must be one-sided transactions in favour of those buying existing shares. Consequently, expect the SEC to review and comment on the Schedule 13e-3, possibly several times, which can result in a multi-month delay between filing the form and taking any of the actions noted in it.

Once the company then takes steps to reduce the number of shareholders that were outlined in the Schedule 13e-3, it can file a Form 15 and take itself private.

A company that is trying to go private must be careful not to undertake share repurchases in a manner that would be construed as a tender offer, since the filing of a tender offer requires substantial documentation. A repurchase is considered a tender offer if most of the following conditions are present:

- There is active and widespread solicitation of shareholders for their shares
- The solicitation is made for a substantial percentage of company stock
- The offer to purchase is for a premium over the current market rate
- The terms of the offer are firm, rather than negotiable
- The offer is contingent upon the tendering of a fixed number of shares
- The offer is open only for a limited period of time
- The offeree is subjected to pressure to sell stock
- There is publicity concerning the repurchase program

Thus, the avoidance of a tender offer may mandate occasional stock repurchases in small numbers over a period of time, where contacts are made with individual shareholders. To avoid the condition regarding a substantial percentage of company stock, consider only buying back the shares of odd lot shareholders, which should constitute a very small proportion of total shares outstanding. It is best to involve the company's securities attorneys in this process, to mitigate the risk of having a formal tender offer.

Much of this discussion has been about ways to avoid the filing requirements associated with going private. However, there is a risk of shareholder lawsuits if a company goes private without a formal tender offer to buy back shares, since it will be very difficult for shareholders to liquidate their holdings once the company has gone private. Thus, the risk of lawsuits must be weighed against the ease of using a Form 15 filing to go private.

The Going Private Transaction

Holdings, a Delaware corporation, was formed March 4, 2003 and had no operations prior to July 29, 2003 when it acquired all of the outstanding common stock and stock options of EXCO Resources, Inc. (EXCO, Resources, we) (the going private transaction). Prior to July 29, 2003, EXCO was a public company whose common stock was traded on the NASDAQ National Market (NASDAQ). For the period from March 4, 2003 (date of inception) and after the acquisition of EXCO on July 29, 2003, through October 3, 2005, the date of the Equity Buyout, Holdings and EXCO are collectively referred to herein as the Company. On July 29, 2003, pursuant to an Agreement and Plan of Merger, ER Acquisition, Inc., a Texas corporation, and wholly-owned subsidiary of Holdings merged into Resources. Prior to July 29, 2003 EXCO's financial statements are referred to as Public Predecessor and subsequent to that date through October 3, 2005, the date of the Equity Buyout, they are referred to as Private Predecessor and include purchase accounting adjustments related to this change in control.

Holdings was formed by the chairman and chief executive officer, Douglas H. Miller, and his buying group for the purpose of entering into the merger agreement. The holders of EXCO's common stock, other than Holdings and its subsidiaries, received cash of $18.00 per share. The buyout of EXCO was funded with borrowings from EXCO's existing credit facilities of approximately $53.6 million and approximately $172.0 million of Holdings' equity. The equity capital for Holdings was provided by:

- Cerberus Capital Management, L.P., or Cerberus, an investment management firm—$106.5 million in cash;
- other institutional investors—$34.3 million in cash;
- certain members of EXCO's management—$10.5 million in cash and the contribution of EXCO shares; and
- other institutional and other investors—$20.7 million in cash and the contribution of EXCO shares.

Upon completion of the merger transaction, EXCO's common stock was delisted from trading on the NASDAQ or any other exchange and EXCO's common stock registration pursuant to Section 12(g)(4) of the Securities Exchange Act of 1934 was terminated.

The total purchase price for EXCO was $353.5 million representing the purchase of all outstanding common stock and stock options including the amounts contributed to Holdings by management and key employees and other investors, and liabilities assumed as detailed below and was allocated as follows (in thousands):

Purchase price calculations:			
Payments for tendered shares including options	$	195,327	
Value of EXCO shares contributed by management		8,429	
Value of EXCO shares contributed by other investors		17,966	
Assumption of debt		130,003	
Merger related costs		1,819	
Total EXCO acquisition costs	$	353,544	
Allocation of purchase price:			
Oil and natural gas properties—proved	$	358,111	
Oil and natural gas properties—unproved		9,967	
Goodwill		51,120	
Other property and equipment and other assets		3,678	
Current assets		36,705	
Deferred income taxes(1)		(50,733	)
Accounts payable and accrued expenses		(37,757	)
Asset retirement obligations		(15,744	)
Fair value of oil and natural gas derivatives		(1,803	)
Total allocation	$	353,544	

Represents deferred income taxes recorded at the date of the merger due to differences between the book basis and the tax basis of assets. For book purposes, we had a step-up in basis related to purchase accounting while our existing tax basis carried over.

As a result of the change in control, generally accepted accounting principles (GAAP) requires the acquisition by Holdings to be accounted for as a purchase transaction in accordance with Statement of Financial Accounting Standards (SFAS) No. 141, "Business Combinations." Accordingly, the financial statements for periods subsequent to July 28, 2003, reflect Holdings' stepped-up basis resulting from the acquisition.

The aggregate purchase price was allocated to the underlying assets and liabilities based upon the respective estimated fair values at July 29, 2003 (date of acquisition). Carryover basis accounting applies for tax purposes. All financial information presented prior to July 29, 2003 represents the Public Predecessor basis of accounting.

The purchase price allocation resulted in $51.1 million of goodwill, $24.2 million in the EXCO operating segment and $26.9 million in the Canadian geographic operating segment (reflected on the consolidated balance sheet at December 31, 2004 as Assets of discontinued operations).

Taking a Public Company Private – An Overview

In recent years an increasing number of small to mid-sized pubic companies have elected to go private for reasons including:

(i) eliminating legal, accounting and public relations costs associated with being a public company,

(ii) focusing on long term company objectives rather than being dictated by the short term results driven culture fostered by quarter to quarter reporting,

(iii) reducing the potential for securities litigation against the company, its directors and officers and well as director and officer liability under SOX,

(iv) reducing the disclosure of sensitive business information associated with SEC reporting requirements, and

(v) allowing additional corporate governance flexibility.

In going-private transactions, a controlling shareholder typically acquires the shares of minority shareholders in a public company for cash, debt or stock thereby reducing the company's shareholder base sufficiently to permit the company to elect to terminate its status as a public company. Under SEC rules, a company may elect to go private when it is owned, directly or indirectly, by fewer than 300 persons. Going-private transactions take a variety of forms but typically are:

(i) accomplished by a merger, tender offer or reverse stock split,

(ii) spearheaded by the company's senior management, and

(iii) financed by third party debt and/or equity financers.

The form chosen for the transaction in any particular case depends on need for outside financing, the composition of the shareholder base and the likelihood of a competing bid for the company, among other factors.

Tender Offer

A tender offer is the structure of choice when the proponents of the going-private transactions do not own a controlling interest in the company. In order to take acquire a controlling interest in a company, proponents of going private offer to purchase shares held by certain or all of the shareholders on an individual basis. Under Delaware law a controlling interest is obtained when an acquirer owns at least 90%. As a result, tender offers are commonly conditioned on the acquirer obtaining this threshold ownership mark which allows the acquirer to perform a short form merger or reverse stock split to obtain the remaining outstanding shares. If the board of directors has assisted the acquirer in the course of the tender offer, the company is generally required to form a special committee that advises the shareholders to tender. Acquirers often favour tender offers since independent court appraisal of their share value is not available to shareholders who accept a tender offer.

Merger

State laws generally provide for two types of mergers: long and short form mergers. In long form mergers, an acquirer negotiates and executes a merger agreement with the company's board of directors and, if approved by a vote of the company's shareholders, the company mergers with an entity formed by the acquirer and shares of the company's stock are converted into the rights to assert appraisal rights or receive the merger consideration. A long form merger generally leaves the surviving company with one shareholder, a subsidiary of the acquirer. Short form mergers allow an acquirer who has more than 90% of the company's stock to merge without a vote of shareholders. Minority shareholders receive cash or debt in exchange for their shares subject to appraisal rights under applicable state law.

"Entire Fairness" Standard

Ordinarily the decisions of a company's board of directors are governed by the "business judgment rule" in determining whether it has fulfilled its fiduciary duty to shareholders to act in good faith, informed manner, without self dealing or direct self interest. In interested transactions, such as going private transactions, where directors are also members of the buyout group, Delaware courts have applied a more rigorous "entire fairness" standard. The standard requires the acquirer in a going private transaction to prove the elements of "fair dealing" and "fair price". Fair dealing relates to the process by which the transaction was approved by examining factors such as the timing of the transaction, how it was initiated, structured and negotiated and how director and shareholder approval was obtained. Fair price involves an economic analysis of value received by shareholders.

The burden of proving the entire fairness of a given transaction is normally placed on the acquirer. In order to avoid conflicts of interest and shift the burden of proof to the challenger of a given transaction it is now standard practice for a company's board to appoint a special committee of independent directors to negotiate an arm's length transaction in the best interest of shareholders. For a special committee to operate independently and for the company to obtain the benefit of burden shifting "particular consideration must be given to the evidence of whether the special committee was truly independent, fully informed, and had the freedom to negotiate at arm's length." The role of the special committee is to negotiate the best deal for shareholders, and therefore it should retain its own legal and financial advisers and should not be influenced by the actions of insiders. Although the burden of proof can be shifted by utilising a special committee, the entire fairness of the private transaction must still be demonstrated.

The appointment of a special committee is standard practice in long form mergers since they require board and shareholder approval. Tender offers do not automatically trigger the entire fairness test but Delaware courts have required that offers conducted by controlling shareholders must include certain terms to ensure that they are non-coercive.

SEC Scrutiny

Viewing them as inherently one-sided, the SEC requires extensive disclosure and closely scrutinizes going-private transactions. Schedule 13E-3 requires disclosures and certifications regarding the following items:

- The purpose of the transaction
- Whether alternatives were considered and why they were rejected
- Reasons for the structure of the transaction
- Identity of persons filing, including affiliates engaged in the transaction
- Description of the relationship of the buyers of the company and their roles in the transaction
- All expenses relating to the transaction

- Why the transaction is being undertaken at this time
- Why the company or affiliate taking the company private believes the transaction is fair
- All reports, opinions and appraisals relating to the value of the transaction
- Extensive audited financial information

Keys to a Successful Going Private Transaction include the following:

- Appoint an independent and diligent Special Committee of the Board with broad authorization to negotiate an arm's length transaction that is conducted in a fair and transparent manner
- Retain independent legal counsel and financial advisers to the Special Committee
- Keep detailed minutes of the Board of the Special Committee meeting relating to the transaction, and a detailed record of all negotiation, deliberation and proceedings relating to the consummation of the transaction
- Agree on a price that is "demonstrably fair"

Chapter 4

Introduction to Real Options

Definition of 'Real Option'

An alternative or choice that becomes available with a business investment opportunity. Real options can include opportunities to expand and cease projects if certain conditions arise, amongst other options. They are referred to as "real" because they usually pertain to tangible assets such as capital equipment, rather than financial instruments. Taking into account real options can greatly affect the valuation of potential investments. Oftentimes, however, valuation methods, such as NPV, do not include the benefits that real options provide.

What are Real Options?

Real options capture the value of managerial flexibility to adapt decisions in response to unexpected market developments. Companies create shareholder value by identifying, managing and exercising real options associated with their investment portfolio. The real options method applies financial options theory to quantify the value of management flexibility in a world of uncertainty. If used as a conceptual tool, it allows management to characterize and communicate the strategic value of an investment project.

Traditional methods (e.g. net present value) fail to accurately capture the economic value of investments in an environment of widespread uncertainty and rapid change. The real options method represents the new state-of-the-art technique for the valuation and management of strategic investments. The real option method enables corporate decision-makers to leverage uncertainty and limit downside risk.

Real Options Theory

Real Options Theory is an important new framework in the theory of investment decision. The standard theory it modifies is the Expect Net Present Value theory of investment decision. According to NPV theory the future cash flows of an investment project are estimated and if there is uncertainty about those cash flow the expected value determined. The expected cash flows are discounted at the cost of capital for the corporation and the results summed. If the NPV is positive the project is worthwhile and should be pursued. If it is negative the project should be turned down. If the NPV is zero it does not matter to the corporation whether the project is accepted or rejected.

Where NPV theory is difficient and where Real Options theory fills the gap is where subsequent decisions can modify the project once it is undertaken. NPV makes no provision for this flexibility of the project and consequently undervalues its benefits. In the auction of petroleum explaration contracts it was commonplace for the highest bids to exceed the net present value calculation. This is because the successful bidder knew that once some initial drilling was done the company could, on the basis of that information, stop the exploration or expand the exploration.

Real Options Theory is related to decision tree analysis which in turn is related to Richard Bellman's Dynamic Programming. What Real Options Theory adds to the past methods of optimal sequential decision-making is the formal theory of the valuation of options, which was pioneered by Fischer Black, Myron Scholes and Robert C. Merton.

Uncovering Real Options

Taking an options-based approach is not simply a matter of using a new set of valuation equations and models. It requires a new way of framing strategic decisions. The questions become less, What will we gain by moving from point A to point B? and more, If we begin down the path from point A to point B, what options will open for us and where will we gain by having those options? The first step in reorienting strategic thinking, then, is to identify the real options that exist in investment decisions.

Uncovering real options can be tough. Unlike financial options, real options are not precisely defined or neatly packaged. But they do exist in almost every business decision, and they tend to take a limited number of forms. By understanding these forms, managers can become better able to spot the options in their own decisions. The following are hypothetical examples of the most common types of real options:

Timing Options. Sales of Low: fat ice cream are surging. Operating at full capacity, the Healthy Cow Creamery is considering whether to expand its plant. Launching the expansion would require a big up-front investment, and the company's managers can't be sure that the sales boom will persist. They have the option of delaying the investment until they learn more about the strength of demand. It may be that the risk avoided by waiting to invest has a greater value than the sales that might be forfeited by postponing construction.

Growth Options: Friend-to-Friend, a company that sells cosmetics through a network of independent salespeople, is trying to decide whether to enter the vast Chinese market. The initial investment to build a manufacturing and sales organisation would be large, but it may lead to the opportunity to sell a whole range of products through an established sales network. The investment would thus create growth options that have value above and beyond the returns generated by the initial operations.

Staging Options: The top management team at International Widget is reviewing a proposal from the senior vice president of operations to install a new manufacturing system. The proposal calls for a full, multimillion-dollar rollout at all factories over the next two years. But the business benefits of the project remain uncertain. The company has the option to invest in the new system in stages rather than all at once. The conclusion of each stage ill in turn provide further options — for continuing, for delaying, or for abandoning the effort. All these options add value to the proposed project.

Exit Options: Molecular Sciences has a patent for a promising new chemical product, but it's worried about the size of the market opportunity, and it's unsure whether the manufacturing process will meet government regulations regarding toxic chemicals. If the company does begin an effort to commercialize the product, though, it will have the option to abandon the project if demand doesn't materialize or if the environmental liability appears too large. The exit option increases the value of the project because it reduces the size of the investment at risk.

Flexibility Options: Cell, Incorporated needs to decide how to best manufacture its latest cellular telephone. Demand for the new product is uncertain, although forecasts indicate that sales will be spread across two continents. A traditional manufacturing analysis indicates that a single plant would be much cheaper to build and operate than two plants on two continents. But the analysis fails to take into account the flexibility of option that would be created by building two plants - the option to shift production from continent to continent in response to shifts in demand, exchange rates, or production costs. If the value of the option outweighs the cost saved by building just one plant, then Cell should invest in two plants and carry the excess capacity.

Operating Options: Bright Light Software has long contracted with other companies to produce and package its CD-ROMs Its sales have grown rapidly in recent years, however, and now the company is trying to decide whether it makes sense to build its own plant. If it goes ahead, it would gain a number of operating options. It would, for example, have the option to shut down the operations during times of weak demand and the option to run additional shifts during times of high demand. The value of these options adds to the value of the plant.

Learning Options: Hollywood Partners is planning to release three movies in the midst of the Christmas season. Before the films actually open, the studio's executives can't tell which one will be the biggest hit, so they can't be sure how to best allocate their marketing and advertising dollars.

But they have an important learning option. They can release each movie on a limited number of screens in selected cities and then refine their marketing plans based on what they learn. They can, for example, roll out the most popular movie nationwide and give it a large advertising budget while putting the other films into more limited release.

The Real Options Discipline

The goal of strategy is clear - to make investment decisions that lead to greater shareholder value. But when it comes to actually achieving that goal, things get fuzzy. In volatile markets, where prices and demand are always in flux, it's hard to predict how a particular investment will ultimately influence a company's value. Senior executives spend a lot of time structuring their decisions, tracing out possible implications, assigning probabilities, and assessing risk.

Rarely, though, does everyone agree about how an investment will play out. Different managers draw on different experiences and have different perspectives, which lead them to different conclusions. It's hard to sort out whose answers are the right answers.

In fact, there is only one right answer: the answer of the financial markets. The markets are the final arbiters of an investment's value, and the markets are adept at calculating uncertainty on value. By applying the discipline of the markets, managers can avoid basing important decisions on subjective judgments about the future. They can incorporate the market's objective measure of value under uncertainty into their own strategic choices.

When does a decision become disciplined? Discipline, in our view, has three components:

- The decision is structured, or framed, in terms of the options it creates.
- All the relevant information value and risk available in the financial markets is taken into account.
- Financial-market transactions are used to acquire options or otherwise mitigate risk whenever that's economically justified.

Applying market discipline changes the way managers make decisions, and it changes the decisions themselves. All kinds of companies have the opportunity to draw on financial markets' techniques, benchmarks and information. They can discipline their decisions and align them with the investment decisions of the markets. They can close the gap between strategy and shareholder value.

Real Options

The real options approach is the extension of options theory to the management of real assets. The real option tools enhance the traditional approaches to capital budgeting and valuation.

In a world of uncertainty, companies have the flexibility to defer a project to adjust its scale (expand, contract, or abandon), and to extend or shorten the life of the project in response to technological and economic developments over time. These opportunities and flexibilities can be valued using the pricing methods of financial put and call options.

The real option tools enhance the traditional approaches to capital budgeting and valuation. Real options are not publicly traded and replicable like financial options but it is possible to use the pricing method of financial options to understand them and calculate their values.

Real options analysis GENERALIZES the traditional valuation methods such as Net Present Value (NPV) or Discounted Cash Flows (DCF) to take into account the values of the different options associated with the investment.

Put differently, the traditional NPV and DCF valuation methods are special cases of the real options valuation method.

What's "Wrong" with Net Present Value or Discounted Cash Flow Rules?

NPV or DCF is based on one or all of the following assumptions:

- The investment is an all or nothing, now or never, project.
- The project is held *passively*. A SINGLE EXPECTED cash flow forecast is used in the NPV analysis.

All the possible future cash flows and their probabilities, for any given time, are "collapsed" into a single EXPECTED cash flow.

This ignores the fact that managers can take advantage of futures developments.

Managers can *add value* to the project by responding to developing circumstances – making the most of opportunities when conditions turn out to be "good" or reducing losses when conditions turn out to be "bad."

- The expected cash flows are discounted using a CONSTANT risk-adjusted discount rate.

This is because the risk is assumed to be constant over the life of the project.

Real options analysis GENERALIZES the NPV (DCF) rule by taking into account the values of the different options and opportunities associated with the investment.

For Example

- The company has the option to delay the investment to a later date.
- The company has the flexibility to scale (expand, contract or abandon) the project at future dates after some uncertainty is resolved.
- The project risk, internal (technological, project specific) risk and external (market or systematic) risk change over time. (Think of developing a new drug. At the beginning, the critical factor is the ability to develop the drug. Then, after a successful drug is developed, market conditions tend to become the bigger factor.)

Opportunities and flexibilities can be valued using the pricing methods of financial put and call options. The real options approach is the extension of options theory to the management of real assets. The real option tools enhance the traditional approaches to capital budgeting and valuation. Real options are not publicly traded and replicable like financial options but it is possible to use the pricing method of financial options to understand them and calculate their values.

Real options analysis provides a framework and a decision-making process:

- Getting together people from different units to examine how to take advantage of uncertainty; become aware of the costs and benefits of doing or not doing things, build flexibility and take advantage of opportunities over time.
- The option to make decisions gradually and sequentially as the project develops over time.
- Develop efficient dynamic relations with customers and suppliers.
- Improve the functioning and management of the company.
  1. Embracing uncertainty – Limited losses (limited to initial investment) versus substantial potential gains.
  2. Embracing TIME - Time is on your side.

Just the process of taking time to think about, and be more prepared for, some of the future choices adds value, even when we do not use "real options values."

Real options analysis provides a MARKET-BASED, objective, discipline to quantify and value uncertain situations and opportunities.

It provides valuation models (of risky cash flows) that can be "sold" to managers, financial analysts and shareholders.

Real option analysis = Dynamic decision-tree analysis with "certified" financial techniques.

Option pricing theory also provides a way to examine how sensitive our present values are to the different factors affecting our cash flows.

Examples of Real Options

THE TIMING OPTION - The Value Of Waiting To Invest.

Scaling Options: options to expand or contract the abandonment option

Sequential (Or Compound) Options.

RAINBOW OPTIONS - Options that involve several sources of uncertainty.

Switching Options – Options to switch between different modes of operation at a cost.

A Very Important Flaw: The Human Factor

Real option analysis typically ignores the psychological, political and organisational considerations.

For example, we assume that if the optimal (financial) decision is to abandon a "favourite" project – management will indeed abandon it.

If the net present value is flawed, why is it being used so much?

- Managers are familiar with it and are comfortable using it.

Making people abandon "old habits" and replacing them with new and improved methods takes time.

- There are many situations where the difference between the net present value answer and the real options answer is quite small.

There are projects where the net present value is so high, it is clear even without adding the value of future options that we should adopt it.

Conversely, there are projects with a large negative net present value, where no amount of flexibility provided by options can save it.

Real Options and the Financial Markets

Although not a new concept, strategic options - the future opportunities that are created by today's investments - have recently attracted considerable attention in both the strategy and decision science literatures.

For example, Ron Howard, one of the pioneers of modern decision science, commented in 1994 "the prerogative to recognise and create options is too frequently overlooked in the framing and structuring of decision problems. This is a failure to recognise the sequential nature of most decision situations."

Financial economists, who have laboured for the most part independently of strategists and decision scientists, have struggled to make the broad sweep of option thinking conform to the rigors of financial option valuation.

When attempting to apply financial option models to real assets, academics and practioners immediately run up against a problem: some of the most significant sources of uncertainty that affect the value of strategic options are not "priced" in the financial markets. For many, the confusion on this issue sometimes gives the appearance that real options is nothing more than window dressing on concepts already explored in other fields.

We would like to propose that real options be defined as the subset of strategic options in which the exercise decision is largely triggered by market-priced risk, a risk that is captured in the value of a traded security. For example, oil price fluctuations are a market-priced risk because they are captured in the value of oil futures contracts. Risks not captured in the price fluctuations of traded securities are known as private risks.

Assets with market-priced risk are associated with a wider set of opportunities because one can always acquire, reduce or reshape the risk through a position in traded securities.

Our definition of real options may appear a bit fuzzy, but this is intentional. Securities markets are changing rapidly. What is private risk today may well be securitized in the future. Witness recent developments like telecommunications bandwidth trading, the creation of weather derivatives, and the wave of IPOs of young firms without profits. Each reflects the forces of securitization, the pricing of additional risk and return in the public arena.

Securitization also has the effect of deepening existing markets, creating liquidity, and lowering transactions costs. Despite this, there will be instances in which the difference between a real option and a strategic option will become blurred. A key question for real options - one that arises from the presence of private risk in most applications - is the extent to which hybrid models are aligned with the pricing of risk in the financial markets.

Three Reasons Why Real Options Doesn't Apply to Pharmaceutical Drug Development

Pharmaceutical drug development is often represented as a sequence of options. We think that decision analysis is a better tool for project valuation in this industry.

First, over two-thirds of drugs are sold in countries with managed healthcare expenditures. These government programs have the effect of separating consumer drug spending from price signals, and so neither quantity nor price is sensitive to industry or macro conditions. There are country-specific risks associated with managed care - such as the recent decision by Germany to cut payments for prescription drugs by half - but these are private risks, uncorrelated with other economic indicators.

Pharmaceutical stocks themselves are not good proxies for project risk as they are actually portfolios of drug projects. The private risk of each project is naturally diversified away at the portfolio level and pharma stocks have lower stock price volatility (about 25% annually) than most major industries. Also, the information revelations that move pharma companies' stock prices will be fairly different than the revelations that would cause revisions in the value of a single drug project.

A second reason that this application does not lend itself to real options is that there is an enormous amount of private risk that affects decisions in all stages of development. For example, in examining proprietary data for one of the blockbuster drugs of the past decade, we found that one year before launch the range of uncertainty about the present value of sales was ± 100%.

The reason? The drug maker did not yet know the wording the regulatory body would allow on the label. The wording can dramatically enlarge or restrict the market potential for the drug.

Other private risk that significantly affects value includes uncertainty about safety, efficacy, dosage, formulation, side-effects and so on. The effect of these private risks for development decisions is larger than the effect of fluctuations in the market-priced risk, even if the latter was well-established.

The third reason we don't believe real options applies to drug development arises from the type of information that is gathered in each phase. In the latter phases the expected value of the drug is hugely positive, and drugs are seldom abandoned for economic reason. From Phase III (large-scale human trials) on, there are no significant options - just points of sudden death. Before Phase III, information-gathering investments are designed to rapidly seek the most valuable product performance and positioning in a multi-dimensional white space.

While the early phases of pharmaceutical drug development have some of the features of a strategic option - in the sense that today's investment creates a set of future choices - the real options toolkit seems largely irrelevant to decisions in pharmaceutical drug development. The industry has been using decision analysis to quantify its strategic options, which is an appropriate tool for searching out value and assessing the value of information. We don't see any pressing need for change.

The Craft of Framing Real Options in the Real World: Four Examples

Framing is the act of setting up the application, of drawing out the analogy at the level of inputs and decision between the expansion option and the financial option. As these quick examples illustrate, there is a bit of a craft to the application of real options in the real world.

The value of the payoff at Yahoo! During the turmoil of 2000 and 2001, Yahoo! significantly revised expectations. Its advertising-based business model was not working in the downturn of 2001, and a new business model was not yet in sight. Yahoo!'s stock price fell more quickly and more deeply than did Amazon's, because without a clear business model, Yahoo! lost the value of both its steady business (captured by a discounted cash flow analysis) and its upside potential (the payoff to any expansion options.)

The blended volatility at Omni Media. Omni Media (Martha Stewart's company) wants to be a mature, nationwide content company. The firm creates content for Internet, print, and television. What determines the volatility of the payoff to an expansion option for Omni Media? A mix of Internet, content, and traditional publishing business models. The appropriate volatility captures the mix of risks from the online and offline worlds. Using volatility estimates from traditional publishing may omit the Internet components. Conversely, using volatility estimates from Internet-only companies neglects that mature business will have relatively low volatility. Judgment, and a sensitivity analysis, will be required.

The option trigger in cable companies. In April 1999 Laura Martin, cable and media equity analyst at Credit Suisse First Boston, issued a report using real options to value the assets of cable companies. At the time, cable companies across the United States were upgrading the connection to customers' homes to a 750 MHz capacity. Only 650 MHz had identified uses, and the remainder was "dark fibre." Using a DCF model, Martin valued the projected free cash flow of the cable companies she covered. After adjusting for debt, the DCF estimate of stock price equaled the trading price.

In a pioneering analysis, she went on to value the dark fibre as an expansion option: When the right deal came along, the cable companies would open up another channel. The expansion option simply increased the business-as-usual possibilities.

The driver of the exercise decision is the arrival of an attractive deal for the channel, which is largely unrelated to the value of the payoff. The real options analogy is only an approximation. But when Martin's report was released, cable company stock prices increased 10 percent to 15 percent, and market values of cable companies exceeded

DCF values for the remainder of 1999. As this example shows, while the analogy was not airtight, the equity report made the expansion option visible, and its value was capitalized into cable company value thereafter.

The value decay in online pet stores. In 1999 venture capitalists funded six very similar companies with hundreds of millions of dollars, each racing for market share in the online pet store market. The pet companies felt the pressure-it seemed that with each passing month, potential market share slipped away to competitors. Viewed from an options angle, the payoff value was decaying.

It is straightforward to quantify the effect of value decay on the expansion option. A sixth variable, the rate of value decay, is added to the input list. With the adjustment, the future outcome of S remains uncertain, but the new variable introduces a downward drift to the fluctuations, gently lowering the range of future outcomes. Value decay is very costly to option value.

The implication was that investors grossly overestimated the value in online pet stores at the time of their funding. The implication for the management teams was that there was a reason to rush for market share. With value decay, waiting leads to a lower and lower payoff.

Real Options Valuation

Real Options Valuation, also often termed real options analysis, (ROV or ROA) applies option valuation techniques to capital budgeting decisions. A real option itself, is the right — but not the obligation — to undertake certain business initiatives, such as deferring, abandoning, expanding, staging, or contracting a capital investment project.

For example, the opportunity to invest in the expansion of a firm's factory, or alternatively to sell the factory, is a real call or put option, respectively. Real options are generally distinguished from conventional financial options in that they are not typically traded as securities, and do not usually involve decisions on an underlying asset that is traded as a financial security. A further distinction is that option holders here, i.e. management, can directly influence the value of the option's underlying project; whereas this is not a consideration as regards the underlying security of a financial option.

Real options analysis, as a discipline, extends from its application in corporate finance, to decision making under uncertainty in general, adapting the techniques developed for financial options to "real-life" decisions. For example, R&D managers can use Real Options Valuation to help them allocate their R&D budget among diverse projects; a non business example might be the decision to join the work force, or rather, to forgo several years of income to attend graduate school.

It, thus, forces decision makers to be explicit about the assumptions underlying their projections, and for this reason ROV is increasingly employed as a tool in business strategy formulation.

Types of Real Option

Investment

This simple example shows the relevance of the real option to delay investment and wait for further information, and is adapted from "Investment Example"..

Consider a firm that has the option to invest in a new factory. It can invest this year or next year. The question is: when should the firm invest? If the firm invests this year, it has an income stream earlier. But, if it invests next year, the firm obtains further information about the state of the economy, which can prevent it from investing with losses.

The firm knows its discounted cash flows if it invests this year: 5M. If it invests next year, the discounted cash flows are 6M with a 66.7% probability, and 3M€ with a 33.3% probability. Assuming a risk neutral rate of 10%, future discounted cash flows are, in present terms, 5.45M and 2.73M, respectively.

The investment cost is 4M. If the firm invests next year, the present value of the investment cost is 3.63M.

Following the net present value rule for investment, the firm should invest this year because the discounted cash flows(5M) are greater than the investment costs (4M) by 1M. Yet, if the firm waits for next year, it only invests if discounted cash flows do not decrease. If discounted cash flows decrease to 3M€, then investment is no longer profitable. If, they grow to 6M, then the firm invests. This implies that the firm invests next year with a 66.7% probability and earns 5.45M - 3.63M if it does invest.

Thus the value to invest next year is 1.21M. Given that the value to invest next year exceeds the value to invest this year, the firm should wait for further information to prevent losses. This simple example shows how the net present value may lead the firm to take unnecessary risk, which could be prevented by real options valuation.

Staged Investment

Staged investments are quite often in the pharmaceutical, mineral, and oil industries. In this example, it is studied a staged investment abroad in which a firm decides whether to open one or two stores in a foreign country. This is adapted from "Staged Investment Example"..

The firm does not how well its stores are accepted in a foreign country. If their stores have high demand, the discounted cash flows per store are 10M. If their stores have low demand, the discounted cash flows per store are 5M. Assuming that the probability of both events is 50%, the expected discounted cash flows per store is 7.5M. It is also known that if the store's demand is independent of the store: if one store has high demand, the other also has high demand. The risk neutral rate is 10%. The investment cost per store is 8M.

Should the firm invest in one store, two stores, or not invest? The net present value suggests the firm should not invest: the net present value is -0.5M per store. But is it the best alternative? Following real options valuation, it is not: the firm has the real option to open one store this year, wait a year to know its demand, and invest in the new store next year if demand is high.

By opening one store, the firm knows that the probability of high demand is 50%. The potential value gain to expand next year is thus 50%*(10M-8M)/1.1 = 0.91M. The value to open one store this year is 7.5M - 8M = -0.5. Thus the value of the real option to invest in one store, wait a year, and invest next year is 0.41M. Given this, the firm should opt by opening one store. This simple example shows that a negative net present value does not imply that the firm should not invest.

The flexibility available to management – i.e. the actual "real options" – generically, will relate to project size, project timing, and the operation of the project once established. In all cases, any (non-recoverable) upfront expenditure related to this flexibility is the option premium. Real options are also commonly applied to stock valuation.

Options Relating to Project Size

Where the project's scope is uncertain, flexibility as to the size of the relevant facilities is valuable, and constitutes optionality.

- Option to expand: Here the project is built with capacity in excess of the expected level of output so that it can produce at higher rate if needed. Management then has the option (but not the obligation) to expand – i.e. exercise the option – should conditions turn out to be favourable. A project with the option to expand will cost more to establish, the excess being the option premium, but is worth more than the same without the possibility of expansion. This is equivalent to a call option.

- Option to contract : The project is engineered such that output can be contracted in future should conditions turn out to be unfavourable.

  Forgoing these future expenditures constitutes option exercise. This is the equivalent to a put option, and again, the excess upfront expenditure is the option premium.

- Option to expand or contract: Here the project is designed such that its operation can be dynamically turned on and off. Management may shut down part or all of the operation when conditions are unfavourable (a put option), and may restart operations when conditions improve (a call option). A flexible manufacturing system (FMS) is a good example of this type of option. This option is also known as a Switching option.

Options Relating to Project Life and Timing

Where there is uncertainty as to when, and how, business or other conditions will eventuate, flexibility as to the timing of the relevant project(s) is valuable, and constitutes optionality. Growth options are perhaps the most generic in this category – these entail the option to exercise only those projects that appear to be profitable at the time of initiation.

- Initiation or deferment options: Here management has flexibility as to when to start a project. For example, in natural resource exploration a firm can delay mining a deposit until market conditions are favourable. This constitutes an American styled call option.
- Option to abandon: Management may have the option to cease a project during its life, and, possibly, to realise its salvage value. Here, when the present value of the remaining cash flows falls below the liquidation value, the asset may be sold, and this act is effectively the exercising of a put option. This option is also known as a Termination option. Abandonment options are American styled.
- Sequencing options: This option is related to the initiation option above, although entails flexibility as to the timing of more than one inter-related projects: the analysis here is as to whether it

is advantageous to implement these sequentially or in parallel. Here, observing the outcomes relating to the first project, the firm can resolve some of the uncertainty relating to the venture overall. Once resolved, management has the option to proceed or not with the development of the other projects. If taken in parallel, management would have already spent the resources and the value of the option not to spend them is lost. The sequencing of projects is an important issue in corporate strategy. Related here is also the notion of Intraproject vs. Interproject options.

Options Relating to Project Operation

Management may have flexibility relating to the product produced and /or the process used in manufacture. This flexibility constitutes optionality.

- Output mix options: The option to produce different outputs from the same facility is known as an output mix option or product flexibility. These options are particularly valuable in industries where demand is volatile or where quantities demanded in total for a particular good are typically low, and management would wish to change to a different product quickly if required.
- Input mix options: An input mix option – process flexibility – allows management to use different inputs to produce the same output as appropriate. For example, a farmer will value the option to switch between various feed sources, preferring to use the cheapest acceptable alternative. An electric utility, for example, may have the option to switch between various fuel sources to produce electricity, and therefore a flexible plant, although more expensive may actually be more valuable.
- Operating scale options: Management may have the option to change the output rate per unit of time or to change the total length of production run time, for example in response to market conditions. These options are also known as Intensity options.

Valuation

Given the above, it is clear that there is an analogy between real options and financial options, and we would therefore expect options-based modelling and analysis to be applied here. At the same time, it is nevertheless important to understand why the more standard valuation techniques may not be applicable for ROV.

Applicability of Standard Techniques

ROV is often contrasted with more standard techniques of capital budgeting, such as discounted cash flow (DCF) analysis / net present value (NPV). Under this "standard" NPV approach, future expected cash flows are present valued under the empirical probability measure at a discount rate that reflects the embedded risk in the project. Here, only the expected cash flows are considered, and the "flexibility" to alter corporate strategy in view of actual market realisations is "ignored".

The NPV framework (implicitly) assumes that management is "passive" with regard to their Capital Investment once committed. Some analysts account for this uncertainty by adjusting the discount rate, e.g. by increasing the cost of capital, or the cash flows, e.g. using certainty equivalents, or applying (subjective) "haircuts" to the forecast numbers, or via probability-weighting as in rNPV. Even when employed, however, these latter methods do not normally properly account for changes in risk over the project's lifecycle and hence fail to appropriately adapt the risk adjustment.

By contrast, ROV assumes that management is "active" and can "continuously" respond to market changes. Real options consider each and every scenario and indicate the best corporate action in any of these contingent events. Because management adapts to each negative outcome by decreasing its exposure and to positive scenarios by scaling up, the firm benefits from uncertainty in the underlying market, achieving a lower variability of profits than under the commitment/ NPV stance. The contingent nature of future profits in real option models is captured by employing the techniques developed for financial options in the literature on contingent claims analysis. Here the approach, known as risk-neutral valuation, consists in adjusting the probability distribution for risk consideration, while discounting at the risk-free rate. This technique is also known as the certainty-equivalent or martingale approach, and uses a risk-neutral measure.

Given these different treatments, the real options value of a project is typically higher than the NPV – and the difference will be most marked in projects with major flexibility, contingency, and volatility. (As for financial options higher volatility of the underlying leads to higher value).

Options Based Valuation

Although there is much similarity between the modelling of real options and financial options, ROV is distinguished from the latter, in that it takes into account uncertainty about the future evolution of the parameters that determine the value of the project, *coupled with* management's ability to respond to the evolution of these parameters.

It is the combined effect of these that makes ROV technically more challenging than its alternatives.

"First, you must figure out the full range of possible values for the underlying asset.... This involves estimating what the asset's value would be if it existed today and forecasting to see the full set of possible future values... [These] calculations provide you with numbers for all the possible future values of the option at the various points where a decision is needed on whether to continue with the project... "

When valuing the real option, the analyst must therefore consider the inputs to the valuation, the valuation method employed, and whether any technical limitations may apply.

Valuation Inputs

Given the similarity in valuation approach, the inputs required for modelling the real option corresponds, generically, to those required for a financial option valuation. The specific application, though, is as follows:

- The option's underlying is the project in question – it is modelled in terms of:
- Spot price: the starting or current value of the project is required: this is usually based on management's "best guess" as to the gross value of the project's cash flows and resultant NPV;
- Volatility: a measure for uncertainty as to the change in value over time is required:
- the volatility in project value is generally used, usually derived via monte carlo simulation; sometimes the volatility of the first period's cash flows are preferred.
- some analysts substitute a listed security as a proxy, using either its price volatility (historical volatility), or, if options exist on this security, their implied volatility.
- Dividends generated by the underlying asset: As part of a project, the dividend equates to any income which could be derived from real assets and paid to the owner. These reduce the appreciation of the asset.

- Option characteristics:
- Strike price: this corresponds to any (non-recoverable) investment outlays, typically the prospective costs of the project. In general, management would proceed (i.e. the option would be in the money) given that the present value of expected cash flows exceeds this amount;
- Option term: the time during which management may decide to act, or not act, corresponds to the life of the option. As above, examples include the time to expiry of a patent, or of the mineral rights for a new mine. Note though that given the flexibility related to timing as described, caution must be applied here.
- Option style and option exercise. Management's ability to respond to changes in value is modelled at each decision point as a series of options, as above these may comprise, *i.a.*:
- the option to contract the project (an American styled put option);
- the option to abandon the project (also an American put);
- the option to expand or extend the project (both American styled call options);
- switching options, composite options or rainbow options which may also apply to the project.

Valuation Methods

The valuation methods usually employed, likewise, are adapted from techniques developed for valuing financial options. Note though that, in general, while most "real" problems allow for American style exercise at any point (many points) in the project's life and are impacted by multiple underlying variables, the standard methods are limited either with regard to dimensionality, to early exercise, or to both.

In selecting a model, therefore, analysts must make a trade off between these considerations; The model must also be flexible enough to allow for the relevant decision rule to be coded appropriately at each decision point.

- Closed form, Black–Scholes-like solutions are sometimes employed. These are applicable only for European styled options or perpetual American options. Note that this application of Black–Scholes, assumes constant — i.e. deterministic — costs: in cases where the project's costs, like its revenue, are also assumed stochastic, then Margrabe's formula can (should) be applied instead, here valuing the option to "exchange" expenses for revenue.

- The most commonly employed methods are binomial lattices. These are more widely used given that most real options are American styled. Additionally, and particularly, lattice-based models allow for flexibility as to exercise, where the relevant, and differing, rules may be encoded at each node. Note that lattices cannot readily handle high-dimensional problems; treating the project's costs as stochastic would add (at least) one dimension to the lattice, increasing the number of ending-nodes by the square.
- Specialised Monte Carlo Methods have also been developed and are increasingly, and especially, applied to high-dimensional problems. Note that for American styled real options, this application is somewhat more complex; although recent research combines a least squares approach with simulation, allowing for the valuation of real options which are both multidimensional and American styled.
- When the Real Option can be modelled using a partial differential equation, then Finite difference methods for option pricing are sometimes applied. Although many of the early ROV articles discussed this method, its use is relatively uncommon today—particularly amongst practitioners—due to the required mathematical sophistication; these too cannot readily be used for high-dimensional problems.

Various other methods, aimed mainly at practitioners, have been developed for real option valuation. These typically use cash-flow scenarios for the projection of the future pay-off distribution, and are not based on restricting assumptions similar to those that underlie the closed form (or even numeric) solutions discussed. The most recent additions include the Datar–Mathews method and the fuzzy pay-off method.

Limitations

The relevance of Real options, even as a thought framework, may be limited due to market, organisational and / or technical considerations. When the framework is employed, therefore, the analyst must first ensure that ROV is relevant to the project in question. These considerations are as below.

Market Characteristics

As discussed above, the market and environment underlying the project must be one where "change is most evident", and the "source, trends and evolution" in product demand and supply, create the "flexibility, contingency, and volatility" which result in optionality. Without this, the NPV framework would be more relevant.

Organisational Considerations

Real options are "particularly important for businesses with a few key characteristics", and may be less relevant otherwise. In overview:

1. Corporate strategy has to be adaptive to contingent events. Some corporations face organisational rigidities and are unable to react to market changes; in this case, the NPV approach is appropriate.
2. Practically, the business must be positioned such that it has appropriate information flow, and opportunities to act. This will often be a market leader and / or a firm enjoying economies of scale and scope.
3. Management must understand options, be able to identify and create them, and appropriately exercise them. (This contrasts with business leaders focused on maintaining the status quo and / or near-term accounting earnings.)
4. The financial position of the business must be such that it has the ability to fund the project as, and when, required (i.e. issue shares, absorb further debt and / or use internally generated cash flow). Management must also have appropriate access to this capital.

Technical Considerations

Limitations as to the use of these models arise due to the contrast between Real Options and financial options, for which these were originally developed. The main difference is that the underlying is often not tradable – e.g. the factory owner cannot easily sell the factory upon which he has the option.

Additionally, the real option itself may also not be tradeable – e.g. the factory owner cannot sell the right to extend his factory to another party, only he can make this decision (some real options, however, can be sold, e.g., ownership of a vacant lot of land is a real option to develop that land in the future). Even where a market exists – for the underlying or for the option – in most cases there is limited (or no) market liquidity.

Finally, even if the firm can actively adapt to market changes, it remains to determine the right paradigm to discount future claims

The Difficulties

1. As above, data issues arise as far as estimating key model inputs. Here, since the value or price of the underlying cannot be (directly) observed, there will always be some (much) uncertainty as to its value (i.e. spot price) and volatility (further complicated by uncertainty as to management's actions in the future).
2. It is often difficult to capture the rules relating to exercise, and consequent actions by management: Some real options are proprietary (owned or exercisable by a single individual or a company) while others are shared (can be exercised by many parties). Further, a project may have a portfolio of embedded real options, some of which may be mutually exclusive.
3. Theoretical difficulties, which are more serious, may also arise.
   - Option pricing models are built on rational pricing logic. Here, essentially:
     (a) it is presupposed that one can create a "hedged portfolio" comprising one option and "delta" shares of the underlying.
     (b) Arbitrage arguments then allow for the option's price to be estimated today;
     (c) When hedging of this sort is possible, since delta hedging and risk neutral pricing are *mathematically* identical, then risk neutral valuation may be applied, as is the case with most option pricing models.
     (d) Under ROV however, the option and (usually) its underlying are clearly not traded, and forming a hedging portfolio would be difficult, if not impossible.
   - Standard option models:
     (a) Assume that the risk characteristics of the underlying do not change over the life of the option, usually expressed via a constant volatility assumption.
     (b) Hence a standard, risk free rate may be applied as the discount rate at each decision point, allowing for risk neutral valuation.

   Under ROV, however:

     (a) managements' actions actually change the risk characteristics of the project in question, and hence

(b) the Required rate of return could differ depending on what state was realised, and a premium over risk free would be required, invalidating (technically) the risk neutrality assumption.

These issues are addressed via several interrelated assumptions:

1. As discussed above, the data issues are usually addressed using a simulation of the project, or a listed proxy. Various new methods also address these issues.
2. Also as above, specific exercise rules can often be accommodated by coding these in a bespoke binomial tree:.
3. The theoretical issues:
   - To use standard option pricing models here, despite the difficulties relating to rational pricing, practitioners adopt the "fiction" that the real option and the underlying project are both traded (the so called, Marketed Asset Disclaimer (MAD) approach). Although this is a strong assumption, it is pointed out that, interestingly, a similar fiction in fact underpins standard NPV / DCF valuation (and using simulation as above).
   - To address the fact that changing characteristics invalidate the use of a constant discount rate, some analysts use the "replicating portfolio approach", as opposed to Risk neutral valuation, and modify their models correspondingly. Under this approach, we "replicate" the cash flows on the option by holding a risk free bond and the underlying in the correct proportions. Then, since the value of the option and the portfolio will be identical in the future, they may be equated today, and *no* discounting is required.

History

Whereas business managers have been making capital investment decisions for centuries, the term "real option" is relatively new, and was coined by Professor Stewart Myers of the MIT Sloan School of Management in 1977. It is interesting to note though, that in 1930, Irving Fisher wrote explicitly of the "options" available to a business owner (*The Theory of Interest*, II.VIII). The description of such opportunities as "real options", however, followed on the development of analytical techniques for financial options, such as Black–Scholes in 1973. As such, the term "real option" is closely tied to these option methods.

Real options are today an active field of academic research. Professor Lenos Trigeorgis has been a leading name for many years, publishing several influential books and academic articles. Other pioneering academics in the field include Professors Eduardo Schwartz, Gonzalo Cortazar, Michael Brennan, Han Smit, Avinash Dixit and Robert Pindyck (the latter two, authoring the pioneering text in the discipline). An academic conference on real options is organised yearly (Annual International Conference on Real Options).

Amongst others, the concept was "popularized" by Michael J. Mauboussin, then chief U.S. investment strategist for Credit Suisse First Boston. He uses real options to explain the gap between how the stock market prices some businesses and the "intrinsic value" for those businesses. Trigeorgis also has broadened exposure to real options through layman articles in publications such as The Wall Street Journal. This popularization is such that ROV is now a standard offering in postgraduate finance degrees, and often, even in MBA curricula at many Business Schools.

Recently, real options have been employed in business strategy, both for valuation purposes and as a conceptual framework. The idea of treating strategic investments as options was popularized by Timothy Luehrman in two HBR articles: "In financial terms, a business strategy is much more like a series of options, than a series of static cash flows". Investment opportunities are plotted in an "option space" with dimensions "volatility" & value-to-cost ("NPVq").

Luehrman also co-authored with William Teichner a Harvard Business School case study, *Arundel Partners: The Sequel Project,* in 1992, which may have been the first business school case study to teach ROV. Interestingly, and reflecting the "mainstreaming" of ROV, Professor Robert C. Merton discussed the essential points of Arundel in his Nobel Prize Lecture in 1997. Arundel involves a group of investors that is considering acquiring the sequel rights to a portfolio of yet-to-be released feature films.

In particular, the investors must determine the value of the sequel rights before any of the first films are produced. Here, the investors face two main choices. They can produce an original movie and sequel at the same time *or* they can wait to decide on a sequel after the original film is released. The second approach, he states, provides the option *not* to make a sequel in the event the original movie is not successful. This real option has economic worth and can be valued monetarily using an option-pricing model.

Identifying Real Options

In many project evaluation settings, the firm has one or more options to make strategic changes to the project during its life. For example, a natural resource company may decide to suspend extraction of gold at its mine if the price of gold falls below the extraction cost. Conversely, a company with the right to mine in a particular area may decide to begin operations if the price rises above the cost of extraction. This occurred during the Gulf war when a number of oil fields in Texas and Southern California (where the deposits are such that the cost of extraction is relatively high) began operations when the price of oil rose.

These strategic options, which are known as real options, are typically ignored in standard discounted cash flow (DCF) analysis where a single expected present value is computed. These real options, however, can significantly increase the value of a project by eliminating unfavourable outcomes. Consider the following stylized example to illustrate the value of an option to abandon a project during its life.

Types of Real Options

Input Mix Options or Process Flexibility: The option to use different inputs to produce the same output is known as an input mix option or process flexibility. These options are particularly important in agricultural settings. For example, a beef producer will value the option to switch between various feed sources, preferring to use the cheapest acceptable alternative.

These options are also valuable in the utility industry. An electric utility, for example, may have the option to switch between various fuel sources to produce electricity. In particular, consider an electric utility that has the choice of building a coal-fired plant or a plant that burns either coal or gas.

Naive implementation of discounted cash flow analysis might suggest that the coal-fired plant be constructed since it is considerably cheaper. Whereas the dual plant costs more, it provides greater flexibility. Management has the ability to select which fuel to use and can switch back and forth depending on energy conditions and the relative prices of coal and gas. The value of this operating option should be taken into account.

Output Mix Options or Product Flexibility

The option to produce different outputs from the same facility is known as an output mix option or product flexibility. These options are particularly valuable in industries where goods are typically bought in small batches or where demand is volatile. For example, consider a toy manufacturer's ability to cease producing a style of toy that has become unfashionable and quickly begin producing a popular new style of toy.

Abandonment or Termination Options

Whereas traditional capital budgeting analysis assumes that a project will operate in each year of its lifetime, the firm may have the option to cease a project during its life. This option is known as an abandonment or termination option. Abandonment options, which are the right to sell the cash flows over the remainder of the project's life for some salvage value, are like American put options.

When the present value of the remaining cash flows falls below the liquidation value, the asset may be sold. Abandonment is effectively the exercising of a put option. These options are particularly important for large capital intensive projects such as nuclear plants, airlines, and railroads. They are also important for projects involving new products where their acceptance in the market is uncertain.

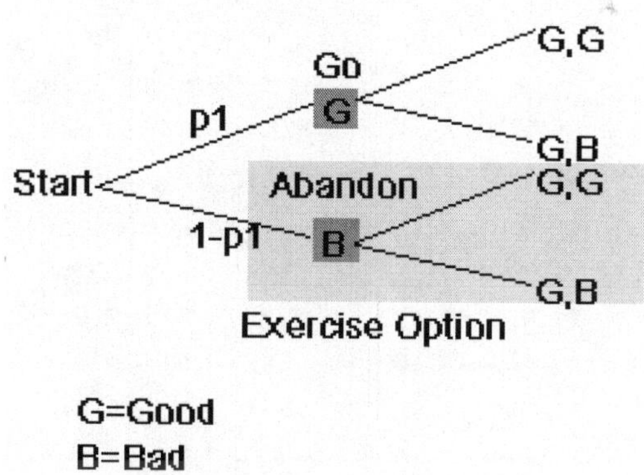

Temporary-Stop or Shutdown Options

For projects with production facilities, it may not be optimal to operate a plant for a given period if revenues will not cover variable costs. If the price of oil falls below the cost of extraction, for example, it may be optimal to temporarily shut down the oil well until the oil price recovers. This type of option is known as a temporary-stop or shutdown options. Shutdown options are also valuable in farming (where they may be exercised if the cost of fertilizing, watering and harvesting exceeds the sale price of the product) and real-estate development (where they may be exercised if the cost of construction exceeds rent revenues).

Explicit recognition of this type of flexibility is critical when choosing among alternative production technologies with different ratios of variable-to-fixed costs.

Intensity or Operating Scale Options

Intensity or operating scale options involve the flexibility to expand or contract the scale of the project. For example, management may have the option to change the output rate per unit of time or to change the total length of production run time.

In order to obtain the option to expand production if demand increases suddenly, a firm may build production capacity in excess of the expected level of output.

In this case, management has the right, but not the obligation to expand, and will exercise the option only if project conditions turn out to be favourable. Whereas the excess capacity will have an initial cost, the project with the option to expand is worth more than the project without the possibility of expansion, in which case the extra cost may be justified.

Also, a firm may build a plant whose physical life exceeds the expected duration of use, thereby providing the firm with the option of producing more by extending the life of the project.

Conversely, many projects can be engineered in such a way that output can be contracted in future. For example, many projects can be modularized. Forgoing future expenditures by contracting a project is equivalent to exercising a put option. Since this put option has value, a project with an option to contract is worth more than a project without the possibility of contraction.

Also, a firm may choose to construct a plant with high maintenance costs relative to construction costs. Management thereby gains the flexibility to reduce the life of the plant and contract the scale of project by reducing expenditures on maintenance in the future.

Option to Expand

Build production capacity in excess of expected level of output (so it can produce at higher rate if needed). Management has the right (not the obligation to expand). If project conditions turn out to be favourable, management will exercise this option.

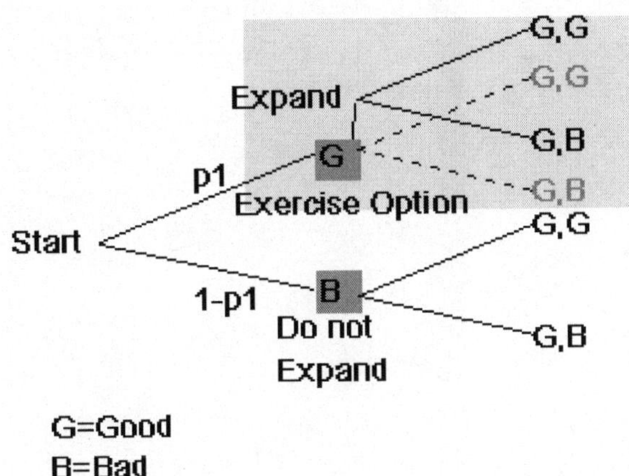

A project with option to expand is worth more than project without possibility of expansion

Option to Contract

This is the equivalent to a put option. Many projects can be engineered in such a way that output can be contracted in future. Example—modularization of project.

Forgoing future expenditures is equivalent to exercising the put option.

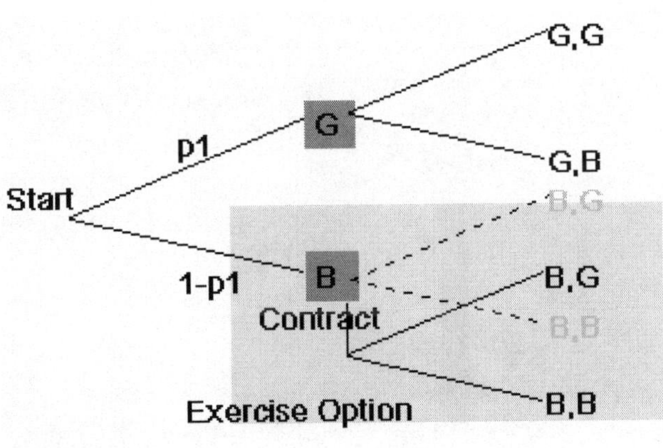

Figure: *Option to Contract*

A project with an option to contract is worth more than project without possibility of contraction.

Option to Expand or Contract (Switching Option).

This is the most general situation. It is equivalent to the firm having a portfolio of call and put options.

Restarting operations when project currently shut down is a call option. Shutting down is a put option.

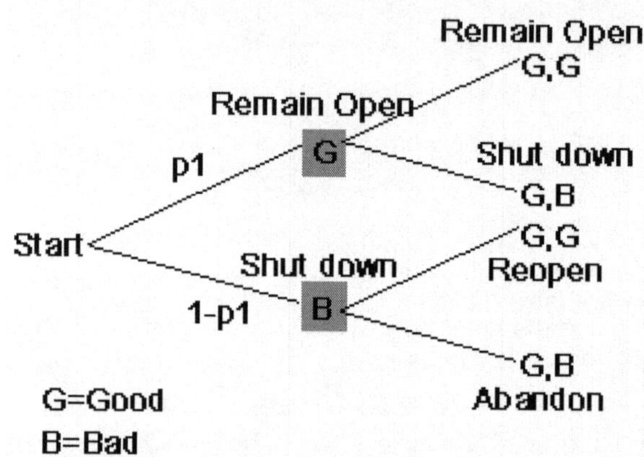

A project whose operation can be dynamically turned on and off (or switched to two distinct locations) is worth more than the same project without the flexibility to switch.

A flexible manufacturing system (FMS) is a good example of this type of option.

Other Examples include the Following: Choose a plant with high maintenance costs relative to construction costs. Management gains the flexibility to reduce the life of the plant and contract the scale of project by reducing expenditures on maintenance.

Build plant whose physical life exceeds the expected duration of use (thereby providing the firm with the option of producing more by extending the life of project).

Initiation or Deferment Options

The option to choose when to start a project is an initiation or deferment option. For example, the purchaser of an off-shore lease can choose when, if at all, to develop property. Initiation options are particularly valuable in natural resource exploration where a firm can delay mining a deposit until market conditions are favourable.

If natural resource companies were committed to producing all resources discovered, they would never explore in areas where the estimated extraction cost exceeded the expected future price at which the resource could be sold.

For example, a purchaser of an off-shore lease can choose when, if at all, to develop property. This option has significant value.

If the U.S. government required immediate development of leases:

- Prices paid for leases would decline
- Some leases would not be purchased at all.

This is also true for exploration in general. If natural resource companies were committed to produce all resources discovered, then they would never explore in areas where the estimated extraction cost exceeded the expected future price at which the resource could be sold.

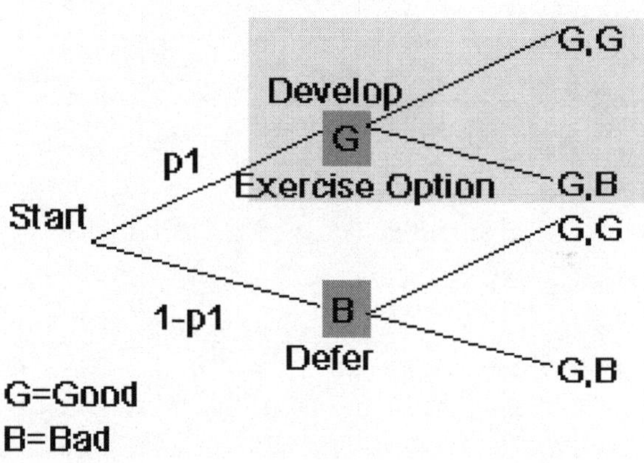

Sequencing Options

The sequencing of projects is an important issue in corporate strategy. For example, successful marketing of consumer products often requires *brand name* recognition or *brand equity*.

Suppose a firm is evaluating projects to produce a number of consumer products. It may be advantageous to implement the projects sequentially rather than in parallel.

Pursuing the development of a single product, the firm can resolve some of the uncertainty surrounding its ability to establish brand equity. Once resolved, management has the option to proceed or not with the development of the other projects.

If taken in parallel, management would have already spent the resources and the value of the option not to spend them is lost.

Intraproject vs. Interproject Options

Interproject options arise when the development of one project creates options that attach to other projects. Sequencing options, for example, are interproject options because the sequencing of projects creates options subsequent projects as the direct result of undertaking the initial project.

Traditional capital budgeting analysis will miss this option because projects evaluated on stand-alone basis. Ignoring interproject options can lead to significant undervaluation of projects. The obvious example is research and development expenditure.

The real value in R&D is in the options that are created to undertake other projects. Interproject options are created whenever management makes an investment that places the firm in a position to use new technology to enter a different industry.

Growth Options

The value of the firm can exceed the market value of the projects currently in place because the firm may have the opportunity to undertake positive NPV projects in the future. Standard capital budgeting techniques involve establishing the present value of these projects based on anticipated implementation dates.

However, this implicitly assumes that the firm is committed to go ahead with the projects. Since management need not make such a commitment, they retain the option to exercise only those projects that appear to be profitable at the time of initiation.

The value of these options should be considered in valuing the firm. Growth options are particularly valuable in infrastructure-based or strategic industries.

For example, in the high-tech and software industries (where there are significant first-mover advantages) valuable growth options can be obtained through R&D expenditure and by creating strategic links with other industry players — even though these activities may appear to be negative NPV investments when viewed in isolation.

Shadow Costs

Standard valuation techniques may overvalue some projects by failing to recognise the losses in flexibility to the firm that result from implementation.

The acceptance of one project may eliminate options that attach to other projects. These shadow costs should be considered in project evaluation. For example, building a plant in a particular city eliminates the options to expand the capacity of plants in nearby cities.

Financial Flexibility:

Choice of capital structure can affect value of project. Like operating flexibility, financial flexibility can be measured by the value of the financial options made available to the firm by its choice of capital structure. Interaction between financial and operating options can be strong — especially for long-term investment projects with a lot of uncertainty.

The option valuation framework is particularly useful to the corporate strategist because it provides an integrative analysis of both operating and financial options associated with the combined investment and financing decisions.

Example: Oil Extraction

Valuation of Heavy Oil Asset. Deferral options are critical. In addition, production could be phased in over time. Conventional NPV will significantly undervalue these assets. Two operating options are important: The option to defer and the option of deferring expansion program.

Example: Precious Metal Mining

Four silver production sites, each with different layout and extraction technologies.

The price of silver has been very volatile. To value firm based upon forecasts of silver prices (traditional NPV approach) could grossly underestimate the value.

Value is enhanced by:

(i) Operational flexibilities and

(ii) Switching options (shut down, reopening, abandonment).

Insight can be gained into the opening-up and shutting-down decision.

If the mine is already open, it might be optimal to keep it open even when the marginal revenue from a ton of output falls below the marginal cost of extraction. Intuitively, the fixed cost of closing an operation might be needlessly incurred if the price rose in the future.

The logic is just the opposite for the closing-down decision. Due to the cost of reopening the mine, the optimal decision might be to keep it closed until the commodity price rises substantially above the marginal cost of production.

Example: Pharmaceutical R&D

A drug company needed to value a new drug research and development project. There were four development phases:

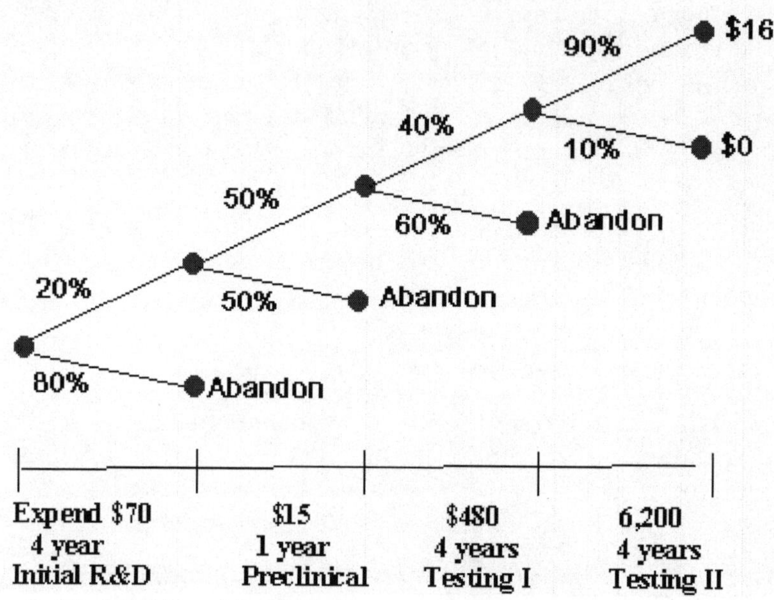

1. Initial R&D with 20% chance of success
2. Preclinical testing, with 50% chance of success
3. Testing I, with 40% chance of success
4. Testing II, with a 90% chance of success.

Chapter 5

Knowledge and Uncertainty

The Uncertainty of Knowledge

"Human beings of all societies in all periods of history believe that their ideas on the nature of the real world are the most secure, and that their ideas on religion, ethics and justice are the most enlightened. Like us, they think that final knowledge is at last within reach. Like us, they pity the people in earlier ages for not knowing the true facts. Unfailingly, human beings pity their ancestors for being so ignorant and forget that their descendants will pity them for the same reason."

E. Harrison, who penned the above, sees knowledge as perpetually uncertain and always changing. Scientists will always be surprised, he says, and scientific laws are never final. He concludes:

> *"I feel liberated by this philosophy. I find comfort in the thought that the creative mind fashions the world in which we live. For it means that the mind and reality are more profound than we normally suppose."*

Knowledge, Uncertainty and Trust

The development and application of knowledge and moral values play crucial roles in society. Empirically-based knowledge and expertise, as well as conceptions of the good life and the just society, contribute to the creation of identity and social change. The application of knowledge and moral values can bring about greater security and control, and enable mastery of practice. However, new knowledge and new moral values can also increase uncertainty and make established practice problematic.

The relationship between knowledge, justice, insecurity/ uncertainty and confidence will be a recurring theme in the research team's studies: how do people seek to improve practice by applying different forms of knowledge? Uncertainty and risk are managed by networks of experts and decision-makers, as well as the media, interest groups and the general public. The team will look at how these endeavours maintain public confidence or lead to new development opportunities. This includes both innovative and normative endeavours. How are human knowledge, communication and interaction oriented towards achieving certain values?

The team will focus on empirical manifestations of the dynamics between knowledge, normativity, uncertainty and confidence in the following themes:

1) "The general public, politics and expertise". This theme will address issues such as how to generate understanding of risk and subsequent forms of action in national and international political or knowledge forums, and will include analyses of their social and political consequences. It will also look at how forms of knowledge and legitimacy differ between experts and laymen, and between citizens and their political representatives in a global society.
2) "Organisation and working life". The focus will be on questions such as: what impact do measurement techniques such as quality assessments or evaluations have on practice in organisations/institutions and working life in a broader sense? And what are the effects of professional expertise and lay-knowledge on those involved in trying to optimise processes in the public and private sectors, as well as in the leisure sector?
3) "Lifestyle, health, body". The focus here will be on dilemmas, risks and opportunities associated with critical situations or individuals' attempts to improve their life situations with regard to, e.g. career or health. Other issues concern the forms of knowledge, technology, practice and interventions that are currently used or that could be developed in connection with improving lifestyles or counteracting lifestyle-related diseases.
4) "Science and scientific institutions" will deal with how sociology casts a critical light on the theoretical and methodological basis for both scientific and everyday knowledge-generating activities. It will also investigate how historical, social and cultural factors influence development and practice within scientific institutions (including universities).

The research group applies perspectives of sociology of knowledge and culture in investigating knowledge-creating and norm-setting institutions such as science, technology or media, and how actors seek to optimize their different forms of practices, bodies and identities.

What is Measurement and Uncertainty?

Measurement is fundamental to science. While measurement might sometimes seem obvious, students can harbor basic misconceptions about measurement that prevent them from understanding science concepts. In particular, students often don't always understand what conclusions can or cannot be reached based on the degree of uncertainty of measurements they make. These misunderstandings can affect their ability to acquire knowledge during hands-on, inquiry-based learning.

The goal of this module is to provide science educators clearly written, effective material to teach introductory level students the fundamentals of effective measurement, and describe how to integrate these ideas into science teaching. This module provides instructional material appropriate for high school and introductory college students that is conceptually consistent with the methods of measurement taught at more advanced levels and used in industry. In addition, this module shows how to adapt lab activities so that they are consistent with this approach.

Recognition of uncertainty is a characteristic of the scientific method and can be viewed from different aspects – mathematical, philosophical and statistical. Important decisions are made, in government and business, in the light of uncertain scientific advice, yet the methods by which different scientific disciplines assess and communicate uncertainty are rarely compared. A cross-fertilization of ideas for how to represent and communicate uncertainty could have enormous benefits on our understanding of everything from economics to health issues or climate change.

Recent public debate about climate change has undoubtedly demonstrated that uncertainty in science needs to be more effectively explained. Despite a growing number of suggestions that the science of climate change is becoming more uncertain, weather and climate scientists have, in fact, pioneered techniques to assess uncertainty in the evolution of complex nonlinear systems and our understanding is growing more confident. However, we are not yet fully exploiting the inherent value of our knowledge of uncertainty in communicating with business, government, the media and the public.

Uncertainty is a complex and broadly defined phenomenon, with many possible categorisations and disciplinary approaches. A simple but useful distinction is between uncertainty about what might happen in the sense of chance, randomness or essential unpredictability, and uncertainty about facts due to lack of knowledge or even ignorance.

Randomness occurs naturally in games of chance or in the fundamental laws of physics as described in the axioms of quantum mechanics. But even within classical physics, with its deterministic and precisely known laws, Ed Lorenz's prototype model of chaos shows that for many nonlinear systems long-term prediction is impossible. More importantly, perhaps, Lorenz illustrates the rather generic notion that whilst initial uncertainty can sometimes be relatively unimportant, on other occasions it can rapidly destroy the accuracy of a prediction. This is where weather and climate change scientists may be in a position to pioneer techniques to predict and better communicate uncertainty in the evolution of complex nonlinear systems.

Uncertainty in the sense of inadequacy of our knowledge is present, for example, in current problems in cosmology, a unique science beset by special types of uncertainty. The emergence of a "dark universe", so far unexplained, and the question of whether our universe is part of a much larger multiverse, raise basic questions about uncertainties in our understanding of fundamental theories of physics.

Probabilistic approaches in policy making could be a more preferable way of sharing information compared to the traditional cautious focus on "worst case" scenarios. For example, in recent government predictions of a flu pandemic, worst case scenarios were used for both policy making and public communication, leading to wide criticism of decisions made when the worst case did not materialise.

While some may view probabilistic predictions as too complex for the public to understand, basic understanding may not be the key issue; the public understands that a horse rated as 2-1 on is not a racing certainty to win, but can distinguish it from a 100-1 outsider. If a more uniform approach to probabilistic prediction could be taken across a range of public-facing scientific disciplines, then acceptance of this approach by the public may be more widespread.

For example, if the public were more exposed to weather prediction as a probabilistic forecast problem, this in turn might help dispel the false dichotomy of viewing the climate change problem either in terms of "belief" or "scepticism".

Important political and business decisions are nevertheless made in the light of uncertain scientific input. Predictions which have properly quantified estimates of uncertainty make for better decision making than over-confident predictions with no estimate of uncertainty. But decisions can only be made if one can value the different probabilistic alternatives. In many business situations this may be a relatively simple economic matter. In other cases it is less straightforward. How do we value the sustainable existence of the Amazonian rainforest, or of the African Sahel? Estimating value, in this generalised sense, is clearly an extremely challenging issue for all of us. One of the consequences of the development of methodologies to estimate uncertainty is that it forces us to confront these difficult issues.

The problem of handling uncertainty is common across all disciplines, even if the language used varies markedly with discipline. Science may need to work more closely with the social science community on this. Case studies where uncertainties have been assessed, both quantitatively and qualitatively, and yet decisions made in the face of these uncertainties, will help all scientists looking to estimate and communicate uncertainty.

Choice Under Risk and Uncertainty

Randomness in Economic Theory

Surprisingly, risk and uncertainty have a rather short history in economics. The *formal* incorporation of risk and uncertainty into economic theory was only accomplished in 1944, when John von Neumannand Oskar Morgenstern published their *Theory of Games and Economic Behaviour* - although the exceptional effort of Frank P. Ramsey (1926) must be mentioned as an antecedent. Indeed, the very *idea* that risk and uncertainty might be relevant for economic analysis was only really suggested in 1921, by Frank H. Knight in his formidable treatise, *Risk, Uncertainty and Profit.* What makes this lateness even more surprising is that not only could early economists count several prominent statistical theorists among their ranks (notably Francis Y. Edgeworth and John Maynard Keynes), but that the very concept of marginal utility, the foundation stone of Neoclassical economics, was introduced by Daniel Bernoulli (1738) in the context of choice under risk.

Previous to Frank H. Knight's 1921 treatise, only a handful of economists, notably Carl Menger (1871), Irving Fisher (1906) and Francis Y. Edgeworth (1908), even deigned to acknowledge the potential modifications risk and uncertainty might make to economic theory. It was in Knight's treatise that for effectively the first time the case was made for the economic importance of these concepts. Indeed, he linked profits, entrepreneurship and the very existence of the free enterprise system to risk and uncertainty. After Knight, economists finally began to take it into account: John Hicks (1931), John Maynard Keynes (1936, 1937), Michal Kalecki (1937), Helen Makower and Jacob Marschak (1938), George J. Stigler (1939), Gerhard Tintner (1941), A.G. Hart (1942) and Oskar Lange (1944), appealed to risk or uncertainty to explain things like profits, investment decisions, demand for liquid assets, the financing, size and structure of firms, production flexibility, inventory holdings, etc.

As Arrow's (1951) survey of the state of affairs illustrates, it was a growing field with severe growing pains and much confusion. The great barrier in a lot of this early work was in making precise what it means for "uncertainty" or "risk" to affect economic decisions. How do agents evaluate ventures whose payoffs are random? How exactly does increasing or decreasing uncertainty consequently lead to changes in behaviour? These questions were crucial, but with several fundamental concepts left formally undefined, appeals risk and uncertainty were largely of a heuristic and unsystematic nature.

The great missing ingredient was the formalization of the notion of "choice" in risky or uncertain situations. Already Hicks (1931), Marschak (1938) and Tintner (1941) had a sense that people should form preferences over distributions, but how does one separate the element of attitudes towards risk or uncertainty from pure preferences over outcomes? Alternative hypotheses included ordering random ventures via their means, variances, etc., but no precise or satisfactory means were offered up. Ocassionally, they took some quite bizarre turns: for instance, Arthur C. Pigou attempted to measure a "fundamental unit of uncertainty-bearing" by defining it as "the exposure of a ï½£ to a given scheme of uncertainty, or ... to a succession of like schemes of uncertainty during a year ... by a man of representative temperament and with representative knowledge.".

Surprisingly, Daniel Bernoulli's (1738) notion of expected utility which decomposed the valuation of a risky venture as the sum of utilities from outcomes weighted by the probabilities of outcomes, was generally not appealed to by these early economists. Part of the problem was that it did not seem sensible for rational agents to maximize expected utility and not something else. Specifically, Bernoulli's assumption of diminishing marginal utility seemed to imply that, in a gamble, a gain would increase utility less than a decline would reduce it. Consequently, many concluded, the willingness to take on risk must be "irrational", and thus the issue of choice under risk or uncertainty was viewed suspiciously, or at least considered to be outside the realm of an economic theory which assumed rational actors.

The great task of John von Neumann and Oskar Morgenstern (1944) was to lay a rational foundation for decision-making under risk according to expected utility rules. Once this was done, the floodgates opened - albeit, even then, only slowly. The novelty of using the axiomatic method - combining sparse explanation with often obtuse axioms - ensured that most economists of the time would find their contribution inaccessible and bewildering. Indeed, there was substantial confusion regarding the structure and meaning of the von Neumann-Morgenstern expected utility hypothesis itself. Restatements and re-axiomatizations by Jacob Marschak (1950), Paul Samuelson (1952) and I.N. Herstein and J. Milnor (1953) did much to improve the situation.

A second revolution occurred soon afterwards. The expected utility hypothesis was given a celebrated subjectivist twist by Leonard J. Savage in his classic *Foundations of Statistics* (1954). Inspired by the work of Frank P. Ramsey (1926) and Bruno de Finetti (1931, 1937), Savage derived the expected utility hypothesis without imposing objective probabilities but rather by allowing subjective probabilities to be determined jointly. Savage's brilliant performance was followed up by F.J. Anscombe and R.J. Aumann (1963). In some regards, the Savage-Anscome-Aumann "subjective" approach to expected utility has been considered more "general" than the older von Neumann-Morgenstern concept.

Another "subjectivist" revolution was initiated with the "state-preference" approach to uncertainty of Kenneth J. Arrow (1953) and Gerard Debreu (1959). Although not necessarily "opposed" to the expected utility hypothesis, the state-preference approach does not involve the assignment of mathematical probabilities, whether objective or subjective, although it often might be useful to do so. The structure of the state-preference approach is more amenable to Walrasian general equilibrium theory where "payoffs" are not merely money amounts but actual bundles of goods. It became particularly popular after useful applications were pursued by Jack Hirshleifer (1965, 1966), Peter Diamond (1967) and Roy Radner (1968, 1972) and has since become the dominant method of incorporating uncertainty in general equilibrium contexts.

The comparative properties of the expected utility hypothesis when payoffs are univariate (i.e. "money") were further examined and developed in the post-war period. The concept of "risk aversion" was analyzed by Milton Friedman and Leonard J. Savage (1948) and Harry Markowitz (1952) and measurements of risk aversion developed by John W. Pratt (1964) and Kenneth J. Arrow (1965) and later refined by Stephen Ross (1981). Menachem Yaari (1968) and Richard Kihlstrom and L. Mirman (1974) pursued definitions of risk-aversion in multi-variate contexts. Measurements of "riskiness" were suggested by Michael Rothschild and Joseph E. Stiglitz (1970, 1971), Peter Diamond and J.E. Stiglitz (1974) and others. These have been particularly useful in many economic applications.

There have also always been disputants. George L.S. Shackle (1949), Maurice Allais (1953) and Daniel Ellsberg (1961) were among the first to challenge the expected utility decomposition of choice under risk or uncertainty and to suggest substantial modifications. Influential experimental studies, such as those by Daniel Kahneman and Amos Tversky (e.g. 1979), have reinforced the need to rethink much of the theory. Towards this end, in recent years, many attempts have been made to reaxiomatize the theory of choice under uncertainty, with weighted expected utility, rank-dependent expected utility, non-linear expected utility, regret theory, non-additive expected utility and state-dependent preferences.

Risk, Uncertainty and Expected Utility

Much has been made of Frank H. Knight's famous distinction between "risk" and "uncertainty". In Knight's interpretation, "*risk*" refers to situations where the decision-maker can assign mathematical probabilities to the randomness which he is faced with. In contrast, Knight's "*uncertainty*" refers to situations when this randomness "cannot" be expressed in terms of specific mathematical probabilities. As John Maynard Keynes was later to express it:

"By `uncertain' knowledge, let me explain, I do not mean merely to distinguish what is known for certain from what is only probable. The game of roulette is not subject, in this sense, to uncertainty...The sense in which I am using the term is that in which the prospect of a European war is uncertain, or the price of copper and the rate of interest twenty years hence...About these matters there is no scientific basis on which to form any calculable probability whatever. We simply do not know." (J.M. Keynes, 1937)

Nonetheless, many economists dispute this distinction, arguing that Knightian risk and uncertainty are one and the same thing. For instance, they argue that in Knightian uncertainty, the problem is that the agent *does not* assign probabilities, and not that she actually *cannot*, i.e. that uncertainty is really an epistemological and not an ontological problem, a problem of "knowledge" of the relevant probabilities, not of their "existence". Going in the other direction, some economists argue that there are actually no probabilities out there to be "known" because probabilities are really only "beliefs". In other words, probabilities are merely subjectively-assigned expressions of beliefs and have no necessary connection to the true randomness of the world (if it is random at all!).

Nonetheless, some economists, particularly Post Keynesians such as G.L.S. Shackle and Paul Davidson have argued that Knight's distinction is crucial. In particular, they argue that Knightian "uncertainty" may be the only relevant form of randomness for economics - especially when that is tied up with the issue of time and information. In contrast, situations of Knightian "risk" are only possible in some very contrived and controlled scenarios when the alternatives are clear and experiments can conceivably be repeated — such as in established gambling halls.

Knightian risk, they argue, has no connection to the murkier randomness of the "real world" that economic decision-makers usually face: where the situation is usually a unique and unprecedented one and the alternatives are not really all known or understood. In these situations, mathematical probability assignments usually cannot be made. Thus, decision rules in the face of uncertainty ought to be considered different from conventional expected utility.

The "risk versus uncertainty" debate is long-running and far from resolved at present. As a result, we shall attempt to avoid considering it with any degree of depth here. What we shall refer throughout as "uncertainty" does not correspond to its Knightian definition. Instead, we will use the term with more fluidity in analyzing modern theories of choice in random situations. However, some form of the Knightian distinction may still be useful, in that it permits us to roughly divide theories between those which use the assignment of mathematical probabilities and those which do not make such assignments. In this manner, the expected utility theory with objective probabilities of von Neumann and Morgenstern (1944) is clearly one of "risk", whereas the state-preference approach of Arrow (1953) and Debreu(1959). in which there are no assignments of probabilities whatsoever is (perhaps less obviously) one of "uncertainty". However, the intermediate theory of Savage (1954), which yields expected utility with subjective probabilities, is not clearly in one camp or another: on the one hand, the very assignment of numerical probabilities - even if subjective - implies that it represents choice under "risk"; on the other hand, these probabilities are merely expressions of what is ultimately amorphous belief and thus may seem more like "uncertainty".

In the first section, we shall concentrate on the expected utility hypothesis with objective probabilities of von Neumann and Morgenstern (1944). We shall consider Savage's theory after that and the Arrow-Debreu approach later on. As we have noted, there are other approaches to choice under uncertainty, but these three are the most developed and prominent ones and thus we shall concentrate on them.

Excellent surveys of uncertainty theory include Peter C. Fishburn and Edi Karni and David Schmeidler at a relatively advanced level and Jack Hirshleifer and John G. Riley (1979, 1992), Jean-Jacques Laffont (1989) and Mark Machina (1987) at a more accessible level. The remarkable little classic of David M. Kreps (1988) is especially recommended for its excellent exposition and intuition. The older text by R.D. Luce and H. Raiffa (1957) may also be still worth consulting. The volume edited by Peter Diamond and Michel Rothschild (1978) reproduces several classical articles. Finally, the relevant entries in *The New Palgrave*, several of them conveniently collected and reprinted in a distinct volume (Eatwell, Milgate and Newman, 1990), are highly recommended. For surveys focused more on applications of uncertainty theory.

Sources of Knowledge

We claim to know a lot of facts, for example, that fire is hot, that George Washington was the first U.S. president, and, in the case of Heaven's Gate believers, that superior aliens are roaming the galaxy. Our knowledge claims vary dramatically, and frequently we claim to know something that we really don't know. One way of understanding the concept of knowledge is to look at the different ways in which we acquire knowledge.

Philosophers have traditionally maintained that there are two types of knowledge from two entirely different sources. First, there is knowledge through experience: seeing something, hearing about something, feeling something. This goes by the Latin term *a posteriori* which literally means knowledge that is *posterior* to – or after experience. Second, there is knowledge that does not come from experience, but perhaps instead is intuitively supplied from reason itself, such as logical and mathematical truths. This is called *a priori* knowledge, which, from Latin, literally means knowledge that is *prior* to experience.

Experiential Knowledge. Experiential (*a posteriori*) knowledge is of many types, the most obvious of which involves *perception*. Each of our five senses is like a door to the outside world; when we throw them open, we are flooded with an endless variety of sights, sounds, textures, smells and tastes. When I look at a cow in front of me and say "I know that it is brown," the source of this knowledge rests upon my visual perception of the brown cow. While perception is perhaps the dominant source of experiential knowledge, it immediately raises a critical question: when I look at a cow, do I perceive the actual cow itself, or just a mental copy of it that is processed through my visual system?

A theory called *direct realism* holds that we see that actual cow itself. This is what we ordinarily assume when we open our eyes and perceive anything around us: I perceive the real table, chair, car, or whatever. We have a natural confidence in our senses, and we simply assume that what we see is what is actually there. But, according to a rival theory called *indirect realism*, this could not possibly be true, since there are countless instances where we know that the actual objects do not match what we perceive. Objects appear to get larger as I move closer to the object, while the object itself clearly remains the same size.

There are optical illusions, such as a stick which appears bent when in water; there are mirages, such as the appearance of water puddles on hot roads. According to indirect realism, then, I do not see the actual cow itself when I look at it, but only a copy or visual representation of it, almost as if I am viewing the cow on a television screen. There is, then, a big gap between what the cow itself and the image of it that appears to me, and for all I know the real cow may be vastly different than how it is represented. Thus, as much as we rely on perception to gain knowledge, uncertainty is built into the very act of perception.

A second source of experiential knowledge is *introspection*, which involves directly experiencing our own mental states. Introspection is like a sixth sense that looks into the most intimate parts of our minds, which allows us to inspect how we are feeling and how our thoughts are operating. If I go to my doctor complaining of an aching back, she'll ask me to describe my pain. Through introspection I then might report, "Well, it's a sharp pain that starts right here and stops right here." The doctor herself cannot directly experience what I do and must rely on my introspective description. Like perception, introspection is not always reliable. When surveying my mental states, I may easily misdescribe feelings, such as mistaking a feeling of disappointment for a feeling of frustration. Other mental states seem to defy any clear descriptions at all, such as feelings of love or happiness.

A third source of experiential knowledge is *memory*. My memory is like a recording device that captures events that I experience more or less in the order that they occur. I remember my trip to the doctor and the pain that I described to her at the time. This recollection itself constitutes a new experience. Again, experiential knowledge through memory is not always reliable. For example, I might wrongly recollect that there's pizza in the refrigerator, completely forgetting that I ate it all last night. Also, sometimes overbearing people like police investigators can make us think that we remember something that never happened. And then there's the phenomenon of *deja vu*, the feeling that we've encountered something before when we really haven't.

A fourth source of experiential knowledge is the *testimony* of other people. Take, for example, my knowledge that George Washington was the first U.S. president. Since Washington died centuries before I was born, I couldn't know this through direct perception. Instead, I rely on the statements in history books. The authors of those books, in turn, rely on accounts from earlier records, and eventually it traces back to the direct experience of eyewitnesses who personally knew George Washington. A large portion of our knowledge rests on testimony – facts about people we've never seen our places we've never been to. While it's convenient for us to trust the testimony of others, there is often a high likelihood of error. This is particularly so with word-of-mouth testimonies: talk is cheap, and we're often sloppy in the accounts that we convey to others. Testimonies from written sources are usually more reliable than oral sources, but much depends on the integrity of the author, publisher, and the methods of fact-gathering. With oral or written sources, the longer the chain of testimony is, the greater the chance is of error creeping in.

Perception, introspection, memory, and testimony: these are the four main ways of acquiring knowledge through experience. Did we leave any out? There are a few contenders, one of which is *extrasensory perception*, or ESP. For example, you might telepathically access my mind and know what I'm thinking. Or, through clairvoyance, you might be aware of an event taking place far away without seeing it or hearing about it. If ESP actually worked, we might indeed classify it among the other sources of experiential knowledge. But does it? Typical studies into ESP involve subjects guessing symbols on cards that are hidden from view. If the subject does better than a chance percentage, this is presumed to be evidence of ESP. However, the most scientifically rigorous experiments of this sort have failed to produce anything better than a chance percentage. While we regularly hear rumors of people having ESP, we have little reason to take them seriously. The safe route, then, would be to leave ESP off the list of sources of experiential knowledge.

Consider next religious experiences. Believers sometimes say that they receive prophecies from God, or are guided by him, or know something through faith. Christian theologian John Calvin even spoke of a sense of the divine that we all have, which informs us that God exists. Might any of this count as experiential knowledge? The question is a complex one considering the wide range of religious experiences that believers report. Let's narrow the question to two representative types: knowledge through faith and prophetic knowledge. Regarding faith, as typically understood, faith involves belief without evidence, such as faith that God exists, or that the bodies of the dead will be resurrected in the future, or that our souls will be reincarnated in different bodies.

These faith beliefs may important for in our personal religious lives, but there is a problem when we to claim to *know* something through faith. One of the chief requirements for something to count as "knowledge" is that there is evidence to support it—as we'll see more clearly in the next section. But since faith is belief without evidence then, technically speaking faith wouldn't qualify as knowledge. Prophetic knowledge faces the same challenge as ESP: are prophecies any more successful than educated guesses? Imagine an experiment that we might conduct in which half of the subjects were prophets, and the other half non-prophets. We then asked both groups to make predictions about the upcoming year; at the end of the year we then checked the results. How would the prophets do? The odds are slim that we could even conduct the experiment since prophets would say that they can't prophesize on demand: it's a unique and unpredictable revelatory experience. They might also say that their revelations from God are not the sort of things that can be confirmed in the newspaper. If prophetic experiences are genuine sources of knowledge, the burden of proof seems to be on the believer. In the mean time, it would be premature to include it among the normal sources of experiential knowledge.

***Non-Experiential Knowledge*:** Turning next to non-experiential (*a priori*) knowledge, this source of information is much more difficult to describe. Some philosophers depict it as knowledge that flows from human reason itself, unpolluted by experience. We presumably gain access to this knowledge through rational insight. Usual examples of non-experiential knowledge are mathematics and logic. Take, for example, 2+2=4. Indeed, I might learn from experience that two apples plus two more apples will give me four apples. Nevertheless, I can grasp the concept itself without relying on any apples; I can also expand on the notion in ways that I could never experience, such as with the equation 2,000,000 + 2,000,000 = 4,000,000. Logic is similar; take for example the following argument:

All men are mortal.

Socrates is a man.

Therefore, Socrates is mortal.

When we strip this argument of all its empirical parts – men, morality, Socrates – the following structure is revealed:

All X are Y

Z is an X

Therefore Z is a Y

This logical structure is something that we know independently of experience. In addition to math and logic, there are other truths that we know non-experientially, such as these:

- All bachelors are unmarried men.
- A sister is a female sibling.
- Red is a colour.

In each of the above cases, the truth depends entirely on the concepts within these statements. In the first, "unmarried men" is part of the definition of "bachelor"; the statement is thus true by definition, irrespective of our experiences.

Two concepts have been important in fleshing out the notion of non-experiential knowledge. First is *necessity*: non-experiential truths are necessary in that they could never be false, regardless of how differently the world was constructed. 2+2 would equal 4 in every conceivable science fiction scenario of the universe. Even if no human being ever existed, it would still be true that "All bachelors are unmarried men" based on the meaning of the words themselves. Experiential knowledge, though, is different in that it is *contingent,* as opposed to necessary: it could be false if the world had unfolded differently. Take the statement "George Washington was the first U.S.

president," which is an item of experiential knowledge. It is of course true as things stand now. But we can imagine a thousand different things that might have prevented Washington from becoming president. What if he was sent to an orphanage for chopping down the family cherry tree? What if he choked to death on his wooden teeth prior to his inauguration? The truth of all experiential knowledge hinges on the precise construction of the world as it currently is.

The other concept embedded in the notion of non-experiential knowledge is that of an *analytic statement*: a statement that becomes self-contradictory if we deny it. Take, for example, the statement "All bachelors are unmarried men." Its denial would be this:

It is not the case that all bachelors are unmarried men. This is clearly self-contradictory since it would be like claiming that there exists some bachelor who is married, which is impossible. Many traditional philosophers have held that non-experiential knowledge is analytic in the above sense. Denying math or logic would produce a self-contradiction. Experiential knowledge, on the other hand, is *synthetic*: denying it won't produce a self-contradiction. Take again the statement "George Washington was the first U.S. president," which we know is true from experience. Its denial would be this:

It is not the case that George Washington was the first U.S. president. While this statement is false as things actually stand, it isn't self-contradictory since, if the world had unfolded differently, the U.S. might well have had a different first president.

Rationalism and Empiricism. An important philosophical war took place in the 17th and 18th centuries between two schools of thought. Most briefly, first there were *rationalists* from continental Europe who were critical of sense experience and felt that genuine knowledge was acquired non-experientially through reason. The leaders on this side were René Descartes, Benedict Spinoza, and Gottfried Leibniz. Second there were *empiricists* from the British Isles who felt that non-experiential reasoning would give us nothing, and experience was the only path to knowledge. John Locke, George Berkeley and David Hume were the leaders on this side. The war finally ended when Immanuel Kant proposed a compromise: true knowledge depends on a mixture of experiential and non-experiential knowledge. We need both, Kant argued, otherwise our whole mental system will not operate properly.

Let's return to the rationalist position, particularly the version championed by Descartes. Sense experience, he argued, is seriously flawed and cannot be the source of important ideas that we have. Take, for example, the idea of a triangle. Look around the world and you'll never see a perfect triangle, whether it's a shape that we draw on a piece of paper or the side of a pyramid in Egypt. On close inspection, they'll all have irregular lines.

The fact remains, though, that we do have conceptions of perfectly-shaped triangles. Rationalism, according to Descartes, offers the best explanation of how we get those perfect ideas. There are two central components to the rationalist position: innate ideas and deductive reasoning. *Innate ideas*, according to Descartes, are concepts that we have from birth that serve as a foundation for all of our other ideas. While they are inborn, we only become aware of them later in life – when we reach the "age of reason" as one philosopher called it.

Innate ideas are in a special class of their own: we know them with absolute certainty, and it's impossible for us to acquire them through experience. While rationalists were reluctant to offer a complete list of innate ideas, the most important ones include the ideas of God, infinity, substance and causality. Regarding *deductive reasoning*, Descartes held that from our innate ideas we deduce other ideas. It's like in geometry where we begin with foundational concepts of points and lines, and deduce elaborate propositions from these about all kinds of geometrical shapes.

Descartes was in fact inspired by the deductive method of geometry and maintained that we deduce ideas in the same way. Through deduction, the certainty that we have of innate ideas transfers to the other ideas that we derive from these. Mistakes creep in only when our deductions become so long that they rest on memory. All knowledge, he argued, including scientific knowledge, proceeds from innate ideas and deductive demonstration.

Turn now to empiricism, particularly Locke's version. Locke's first task was to challenge the theory of innate ideas: none of our concepts, he argued, are inborn. Our mind is from birth like a blank sheet of paper, and it is only through experience that we write anything on it. One problem with innate ideas is that we can explain the origin of each one of them through experience. The idea of God, for example, is not innate as Descartes supposed, but comes from our perceptions of the world around us. There's thus no reason to put forward the theory of innate ideas when experience explains these notions just fine. Locke also found fault with the rationalist position that we don't become aware of innate ideas until later in life. It's not clear how such ideas can linger in our minds for so many years before we can be conscious of them. And by that time our minds have been flooded with experience, and a late-blooming innate idea wouldn't contribute anything to our knowledge of the world. Empiricists also challenged the rationalists' emphasis on deductive demonstration. We don't expand our knowledge by deducing new concepts from foundational ones, as mathematicians do. Geometry is the wrong role model to follow.

Instead, we acquire new knowledge through *induction*, such as making generalizations from our experiences. I hit ten light bulbs with a hammer and each breaks; I generalize from this that all similar light bulbs that I hit with a hammer will also break. We first perceive, then we generalize. We perceive some more, then generalize some more. That's how we push knowledge forward.

And then comes along Kant, the great mediator in the rationalism-empiricism debate. Kant was sympathetic with empiricism but thought that it suffered from a serious problem: it doesn't offer a good explanation for how we acquire non-experiential knowledge, such as mathematics and logic. Complex mathematical formulas in particular could not come from sense perception. There is a quality of self-evidence and certainty that they have, which fallible experience could never produce. Kant's solution was not to resurrect the old theory of innate ideas. Instead, he argued that there are innate organising structures in our minds that automatically systematize our raw experiences – sort of like a skeleton that gives shape to flesh.

For example, as I watch someone hit a light bulb with a hammer, raw sensory information rushes in through my eyes. My mind immediately reconstructs this information into a three-dimensional image and puts it on a timeline. My mind then imposes other organisational schemes on the sensory information. It makes me see the hammer and light bulb as separate things, rather than just a single blob of stuff. It then makes me see the hammer as the *cause* of the light bulb breaking. My experience of the world, then, is a fusion of innate structures and raw experience. The innate part is a concession to rationalism, and the experience part a concession to empiricism.

Rationalism and empiricism in their original forms are outdated theories today, in part because of Kant's insights. Nevertheless, they still are useful for depicting two fundamentally different ways in which we assess the sources of knowledge. Rationalism will continue to be attractive whenever we have knowledge that cannot be easily explained by experience. Empiricism will be attractive whenever the claims of innateness look fishy.

The Definition of Knowledge

Throughout our discussion of knowledge so far, certain concepts have appeared again and again. There's the question of the *truth* of a claim. There is also the matter of our personal *belief* conviction for a claim. There are also issues about the evidence or *justification* that we have for a claim. Tradition has it that these are the three key elements to knowledge: truth, belief and justification. For example, when I say "I know that Paris is the capital of France", this means

It is *true* that Paris is the capital of France.

I *believe* that Paris is the capital of France.

I am *justified* in believing that Paris is the capital of France.

For short, contemporary philosophers call this definition of knowledge *justified true belief* – often abbreviating it "JTB". The crucial point about this definition is that all three components *must* be present: if any one of the three is absent, then it doesn't count as knowledge.

Justified True Belief. To better understand the JTB definition of knowledge, let's go through each of the three elements. First is that the statement must be *true.* I can't claim to know that Elvis Presley is alive, for example, if he is in fact dead. Knowledge goes beyond my personal feelings on the matter and involves the truth of things as they actually are. Some critics of the JTB definition of knowledge question whether truth is always necessary in our claim to know something. For example, based on the available evidence of the time, scientists in the middle ages claimed to know that the earth was flat. Even though we understand now that it isn't, at the time they had knowledge of something that was false. Didn't they? In response, it may have been reasonable for scientists back then to believe the world was flat, but they really didn't *know* that it was. Their knowledge claims were premature in spite of how strong their convictions were. This is a trap that we fall into all the time. While talking with someone I may say insistently, "I *know* that Joe's car is blue!" When it turns out that Joe's car is in fact red, I have to apologize for overstating my conviction. Truth, then, is an indispensable component of knowledge.

Second, I must *believe* the statement in order to know it. For example, it's true that Elvis Presley is dead, and there is enormous evidence to back this up. But if I still believe that he is alive, I couldn't sincerely say that I *know* that he is dead. Part of the concept of knowledge involves our personal belief convictions about some fact, irrespective of what the truth of the matter is. Critics of the JTB definition of knowledge sometimes think that belief isn't always required for our claims to know something. For example, I might say "I know I'm growing old, but I don't believe it!" In this case, I have knowledge of a particular fact without believing that fact. In response, if I say the previous sentence, what I actually mean is that I'm not capable of imagining myself getting old or I haven't yet emotionally accepted that fact. I just make my point more dramatically by saying "I don't believe it!" Instead I really do believe it, but I don't like it.

Third, I must be *justified* in believing the statement insofar as there must be good evidence in support of it. Suppose that I randomly pick a card out of a deck without seeing it. I believe it is the Queen of Hearts, and it actually is that card. In this case I couldn't claim to *know* that I've picked the Queen of Hearts; I've only made a lucky guess. Critics question whether evidence is really needed for knowledge. For example, a store owner might say "I know that my employees are stealing from me, but I can't prove it!" Here the store owner has knowledge of a particular fact without any evidence for it. In response, the store owner is really saying that he strongly believes that his employees are stealing from him, but doesn't have enough evidence to press charges. Evidence, then, is indeed an integral part of knowledge.

The Gettier Problem. For centuries philosophers took it for granted that knowledge consists of justified true belief. In 1963 a young philosophy professor named Edmund Gettier published a three-page paper challenging this traditional view. He argued that there are some situations in which we have justified true belief, but which do not count as knowledge. This was dubbed "The Gettier Problem" and discussions of it quickly dominated philosophical accounts of knowledge. Gettier's actual illustrations of the problem are rather complex, but a more simple one makes the same point.

Suppose that a ball in front of me appears to be red. First, I *believe* it is red. Second, I'm *justified* in this belief since that's how the ball appears to me. Third, it's also *true* that the ball is red. I thus have a justified true belief that the ball is red. However, it turns out that the ball is illuminated by a red light which casts a red tint over it – a fact that I'm unaware of. Although the ball in reality is red, under the light it would appear red to me even if the ball was a different colour. Consequently, I can't claim to *know* that the ball is red even though I have a justified true belief that it is. I was fooled by the effects of the red light, but made a lucky guess anyway. Again, the point of this counterexample is to show that some instances of justified true belief do not count as genuine knowledge. This suggests that the traditional JTB definition of knowledge is seriously flawed.

What can we do to rescue the JTB account of knowledge from the Gettier problem? A common response is to add a stipulation to the definition of knowledge that would weed out counterexamples like the red ball. Most of the Gettier-type counterexamples involve a case of mistaken identity. In our current example, I mistake the appearance of a red-illuminated ball for an actual red ball. Perhaps, then, we can stipulate that knowledge is justified true belief except in cases of mistaken identity. More precisely, we can add a fourth condition to the definition of knowledge in this way:

I Know that the Ball is Red When,

(1) It is *true* that the ball is red;

(2) I *believe* that the ball is red;

(3) I am *justified* in my belief that the ball is red;

(4) There is no additional fact that would make my belief unjustified (for example, a fact about a red light).

According to the above, my belief about the red ball would not count as knowledge since it wouldn't pass the fourth condition. That is, there is indeed an additional fact regarding the red light that would make my initial belief about the ball unjustified. That additional fact undermines — or defeats – my original justification. We've thus saved the JTB definition of knowledge, although cluttering it a little with a fourth condition. This strategy is called the *no-defeater theory* (also called the *indefeasibility theory*). A problem with this strategy, though, is that there are possible counter examples even to this – that is, situations in which we have *undefeated* justified true belief that don't count as true knowledge. This, in fact, is a problem with most proposed solutions to the Gettier problem: if we get creative enough, we will likely find a new counter example that defies the solution.

Truth, Justification and Relativism

Truth and justification, we've seen, are two of the key components of knowledge. They are also concepts that need some explanation themselves. Let's first look at the notion of truth.

Theories of Truth. The concept of truth has many possible meanings. We talk about having *true* friends, owning a *true* work of art, or someone being a *true* genius. In all of these cases the word "true" means genuine or authentic. In philosophy, though, the notion of truth is restricted to statements or beliefs about the world – such as the statement that "My car is white" or "Paris is the capital of France". While we all have gut feelings about what it means for a statement to be true, philosophers have been particularly keen on arriving at a precise definition of truth. Here's one suggestion from a classic song:

"What is truth?" you ask and insist,
"Correspondence to things that exist?"
The answer, you fool, requires no sleuth:
Whatever I say is the truth.
Want proof of the truth? I say so! So there!
Purveyors of falsehood beware:
I'm sick of your lies, and, truth be told,
I am the truth, behold!

The above account of truth is clearly satirical since no one would seriously grant that the truth of all statements is grounded in the assertions of one individual person. But what are the more serious alternatives for definitions of truth? As usual in philosophy, there's much disagreement about what the correct definition is. We will consider the three leading candidates here.

The first and most famous definition of truth is the *correspondence theory*: a statement is true if it corresponds to fact or reality. This is the most commonsensical way of looking at the notion of truth and is how standard dictionaries define the concept. A true statement simply reflects the way things really are. Take the statement "My car is white." This statement is true if it conforms to how the world actually is, specifically whether my car is in fact painted white. As compelling as the correspondence theory of truth seems, skeptics immediately see one major flaw with it: we don't have access to the world of facts. In spite of my best efforts to discover the way things really are, I'm at the mercy of my five senses, which, we've seen, are unreliable. While my senses tell me that my car is white, the colour receptors in my eyes may not be working properly and my car may be a shade of yellow. For that matter, I may be living in a world of hallucinations and don't even own a car. The sad fact is I can never reach beyond my perceptions and see the world as it really is.

With trivial issues, such as the truth concerning the colour of my car, I may be willing to simply pretend that I have direct access to the world of facts and blindly trust my senses. This may serve my immediate needs perfectly well. It isn't so easy to pretend, though, when I investigate the truth of more serious statements, such as whether "Bill murdered Charlie." Even if I have a mountain of evidence that implicates Bill, such as fingerprints and eyewitness testimony, it's impossible for me to turn back the hands of time and directly access the scene of Charlie's murder. I only have hints about what the reality is. Similarly, if I'm investigating the truth of the statement "God exists," I can't directly access the reality of an infinitely powerful deity, even if God did exist and stood right in front of me. The best I would have is some imperfect evidence that the mysterious being standing before me was indeed God. Thus, the correspondence theory would not permit us to say either that "It is true that Bill murdered Charlie" or "It is true that God exists."

A second famous definition of truth is the *coherence theory*, which aims to address the shortcomings of the correspondence theory. According to the coherence theory, a statement is true if it coheres with a larger set of beliefs. Rather than attempting to match up our statements with the actual world of facts, we instead try to see if our statements mesh with a larger web of beliefs that support them. For example, the statement "my car is white" is true if it coheres with a collection of other beliefs such as "many cars are painted white," "I perceive that my car is white," and "other people invariably report that my car is white." With the coherence theory, we avoid skeptical obstacles such as the unreliability of our senses and the possibility that we are hallucinating. What matters is our web of beliefs, which we all have access to — in contrast with a hidden world of facts that is blurred by the limits of our sensory perceptions. We also can even investigate statements such as "It is true that Bill murdered Charlie" or "It is true that God exists." What matters here is whether these statements consistently fit with other beliefs that we have — beliefs about the pieces of evidence against Bill and beliefs about the evidence regarding a divine being.

Unfortunately the coherence theory faces serious criticisms, the most important of which is that it is relativistic. That is, it grounds truth in the changeable beliefs of human beings, rather than in an unchanging external reality. According to the coherence theory, the standard for all truth is the larger web of beliefs that people hold – beliefs about white cars, criminal evidence, evidence for God's existence, and countless other issues. The problem is that belief systems come and go. Take beliefs about criminal evidence as just one example. Many cultures throughout history based criminal convictions on the evidence of supernatural omens: prophetic visions, the flight path of birds, patterns in the guts of sacrificed animals. That was their belief system which they relied on. In other cultures the testimony of one eye witness is sufficient to prove guilt. In our culture today we have fingerprints,

DNA samples and psychological profiles which all contribute to our belief system about criminal guilt. The statement "Bill murdered Charlie" could cohere with some belief systems, but not with others. We typically think about truth as being absolute: either Bill murdered Charlie or he didn't. If truth hinges on a changeable belief system, though, truth is no longer absolute.

The problems with the correspondence and coherence theories are so serious that many contemporary philosophers have abandoned both. In fact some philosophers have even abandoned the concept of "truth" as being completely unnecessary. This brings us to our third theory, the *deflationary theory of truth*: to assert that a statement is true is just to assert the statement itself. Compare these two statements:

- *My car is white.*
- *It is true that my car is white.*

What is the difference between the two? Nothing of substance. The phrase "it is true that" seems to be just repeating something that is already assumed in the phrase "my car is white." In that sense, I am being redundant if I use the phrase "it is true that." At times it may be rhetorically helpful to use the phrase "it is true that" in an effort to convince someone of my belief. Suppose you say to me "I don't believe that your car is white." I might respond by saying, "You're wrong: it's absolutely true that my car is white". Again, I've not added anything of substance by injecting the notion of truth into my response; I've just stood up to you more forcefully. In short, according to the deflationary theory, the quest for a clear conception of truth—such as correspondence or coherence—will not succeed because it is ultimately a quest for something that doesn't really exist.

But the deflationary theory also faces problems, one of which is that the notion of truth is built into our normal expectations of what we assert. When I say that "my car is white" you have an expectation that what I'm saying is true. Occasionally I do say something that is false, but when that happens we all recognise that I'm doing something that is incorrect. The normal expectation, then, is that my assertion will be truthful. And this creates a problem for the deflationary theory: by eliminating the notion of truth, it cannot adequately account for our normal expectation of truthfulness.

Theories of Justification. Of the three components of knowledge, justification is the one that has attracted the most attention among contemporary philosophers. For centuries most philosophers followed a theory of justification called *foundationalism*. On this view, our justified beliefs are arranged like bricks in a wall, with the lower ones supporting the upper ones. These lowest bricks are called "basic beliefs", and the ones they support are "non-basic" beliefs. Take this example:

- My car is white (non-basic belief)

This belief rests upon some supporting ground-level basic beliefs, including these:

- *I recognise the car in front of me as my car (basic belief)*
- I remember what white things look like (basic belief)
- The car in front of me looks white (basic belief)

There are two distinct elements to this foundationalist theory of justification. First, our ground-level basic beliefs are self-evident, or self-justifying, and thus require no further justification. When we have such beliefs, we cannot be mistaken about them, we cannot doubt them, and we cannot be corrected in our beliefs about them. For example, if I am perceiving the colour white, then my belief that I am perceiving white is self-evident in this way. Even if I am hallucinating at the moment, my *belief* that I am perceiving the colour white cannot be called into question.

The second element of foundationalism is that justification transfers up from my foundational basic beliefs to those non-basic beliefs that rest upon them. Think of it like the mortar between bricks that begins at the very bottom level, locks them solid, and moves upwards to lock the higher bricks into place. For example, if I have the three basic beliefs about my car and whiteness listed above, then I am justified in inferring the non-basic belief that "my car is white."

While foundationalism holds a respected place in the history of philosophy, it faces a major problem: it is not clear that there really are any self-evident basic beliefs that form the foundation of other beliefs. Foundationalists themselves have mixed views about what exactly our lowest-level foundational beliefs are. Descartes, for example, argued that there is only one single brick at the foundation of my wall of beliefs, namely, my belief that I exist. Every other belief I have rests on this. Locke, on the other hand, held that our most foundational beliefs are simple perceptions such as blue, round, sweet, smooth, pleasure, motion. These combine together to make more complex ideas. Contemporary philosophers resist both Descartes' and Locke's depiction of our most foundational beliefs. Some offer examples such as "I see a rock" (a basic belief about one's perception), "I ate cornflakes this morning" (a basic belief about one's memory), or "That person is happy" (a basic belief about another person's mental state). But even these are questionable since they seem to rely on beliefs or perceptions that are more ground-level. If there really are ground-level foundational beliefs that are self-evident or self-justifying, you'd think that philosophers would have agreed along time ago about exactly which ones they are. But there is no such agreement.

An alternative to foundationalism is *coherentism*: justification is structured like a *web* where the strength of any given area depends on the strength of the surrounding areas. Thus, my belief that my car is white is justified by a web of related beliefs, such as these:

- I recognise the car in front of me as my car
- I remember what white things look like
- The car in front of me looks white

These, though are not foundational, but instead depend on another web of beliefs related to them, which includes these:

- I remember purchasing my car
- People seem to agree that I use the term "white" properly
- Nothing is abnormally colouring my vision, such as a pair of sun glasses

Each of these, in turn, rests on an ever-widening web of related beliefs. At no point do we reach a bottom-level foundation to these beliefs; the justification of each belief rests on the support it receives from the surrounding web of beliefs that relates to it. Coherentism is closely associated with the coherence theory of truth. With truth we determine that a proposition is true if it coheres with a larger web of beliefs. With justification, we determine that a belief is justified if it is supported by a larger web of beliefs.

To use another metaphor, it is similar to how each entry in the dictionary consists of words that the dictionary also defines. It is a self-contained system of definitions that isn't reliant on foundational notions outside of itself. Coherentism's similarities with the coherence theory of truth make it vulnerable to the same fundamental charge of relativism: not everyone's belief system is the same, so a particular belief might find justification within your larger web of beliefs, but not within mine.

Your belief system might justify the belief that "Bill killed Charlie," that "God exists," or that "abortion is immoral," while my belief system might not justify any of these. We'd like to think that justification is a bit more universal and not dependent on the peculiarities of a particular person's belief system.

Given the liabilities of both foundationalism and coherentism, many contemporary philosophers hold a third position called reliabilism: justified beliefs are those that are the result of a reliable *process*, such as a reliable memory process or a reliable perception process. It's like how we depend on a reliable clock to tell us what time it is. As long as we have confidence in the clock mechanism itself, then that's all we need in order to trust the time that it tells us. We don't have to inspect the internal gears of the clock and see how they relate to the movement of the clock's hands. Similarly, to justify my beliefs, I don't need to inspect how each belief connects with surrounding beliefs that are beneath them or next to them; I just trust the reliability of my mental process that gives me the belief. If my memory process is on the whole reliable, then I'm justified in my belief that I ate cornflakes this morning for breakfast. If my perceptual process is on the whole reliable, then I'm justified in my belief that my car is white. That is, I am justified in believing that my care is white since I'm not delusional or mentally impaired in any other way that might compromise the reliability of my perceptions. What matters is the reliability of the larger processes upon which my beliefs rest, not my other beliefs that border them.

According to reliabilism, the fault with both foundationalism and coherentism is that they rely too much on introspection: presumably, with our mind's eye, we can see the strength of our specific beliefs and how they gain support from other beliefs that are connected to them (either like bricks in a wall or strands in a web). But, says the reliabilist, this approach places too much confidence in our ability to internally witness the connections between our specific beliefs. Introspection, we've seen, is notoriously unreliable, and our standards of justification should not depend on what our mysterious mind's eye internally perceives, but, instead, upon more external standards and mental processes that we know are reliable through our life experiences. I am justified in believing that I ate cornflakes for breakfast because that's what I remember, and I trust my memory since it is a reliable process of supplying me with information about the past.

Reliabilism is an appealing theory since it dispenses with the untrustworthy mechanism of introspection and has us place our confidence in our normally reliable mental processes. In ordinary situations, such as justifying that my car is white, reliabilism may work just fine. But in extraordinary situations, such as police investigations, mental health examinations, investigative reporting, historical documentation, and theological or political debates, a simple appeal to the reliability of our mental processes may not be good enough. We may be forced into investigating how our convictions rest upon other beliefs, and those upon still more beliefs. It thus may not be that easy to set aside either foundationalist or coherentist approaches to justification.

What's so Bad about Relativism? Twice so far the issue of relativism has raised its ugly head, and how we assess theories of truth and justification hinges greatly on how we feel about relativism. The relativist position in general is that knowledge is always dependent upon some particular conceptual framework (that is, a web of beliefs), and that framework is not uniquely privileged over rival frameworks. The most famous classical statement of relativism was articulated by the Greek philosopher Protagoras (*c.* 490–*c.* 420 BCE), who said that "Man is the measure of all things." His point was that human beings are the standard of all truths, and it's a futile task to search for fixed standards of knowledge beyond our various and ever-flexible conceptual frameworks. Knowledge in medieval England depended on the conceptual framework of that place and time. Knowledge for us today depends on our specific conceptual frameworks throughout the world and throughout our wide variety of social environments.

Our initial reactions to relativism are usually negative. "The truth is the truth," I might say, "and it shouldn't make any difference what my individual conceptual framework is. Some conceptual frameworks are simply wrong, and others may be a little closer to the truth." But is relativism really so bad that it warrants this negative reaction?

The first step to answering this question is to recognise that there are different types of relativism, some of which may be less sinister than others. The most innocent and universally accepted type is *etiquette relativism*, the view that correct standards of protocol and good manners depend on one's culture. When I meet people for the first time, should I bow to them or shake hands? If I make the wrong decision, I might offend that person, rather than befriend them. Clearly, that depends on the social environment that you're in, and it makes no sense to seek for an absolute standard that applies in all situations. Etiquette by its very nature is relative. There is also little controversy regarding *aesthetic relativism*, the view that artistic judgments depend on the conceptual framework of the viewer. We commonly feel that there is no absolute right and wrong when it comes to art, and it's largely a matter of opinion. I might enjoy velvet paintings of dogs playing cards, while that might offend your aesthetic sensibilities. In many cases, *perceptual relativism* is also no big issue: one's sensory perceptions depend on the perceiver. Something might appear red to me but green to you. There are people known as "supertasters" who experience flavours with far greater intensity than the average person, so much so that they need to restrict themselves to food that you or I would find bland. How we perceive sensations depends on our physiology, which we readily acknowledge may differ from person to person.

The types of relativism that we often resist, though, are those connected specifically with the two components of knowledge that we've discussed above, namely, truth and justification. *Truth relativism* is the view that truth depends upon one's conceptual framework. This amounts to a denial of the correspondence theory of truth and acknowledges our inability to access an objective and independent reality. *Justification relativism* is the view that what counts as evidence for our beliefs depends upon one's conceptual framework. This is a denial of foundationalism and an acknowledgement of coherentism. The German philosopher Friedrich Nietzsche (1844-1900) boldly embraced truth and justification relativism, as we see here:

> Positivism stops at phenomena and says, "These are only facts and nothing more." In opposition to this I would say: No, facts are precisely what is lacking, all that exists consists of *interpretations*. We cannot establish any fact "in itself": it may even be nonsense to desire to do such a thing. . . . To the extent to which knowledge has any sense at all, the world is knowable: but it may be interpreted differently, it has not one sense behind it, but hundreds of senses. "Perspectivity." [*Will to Power*, 481]

For Nietzsche, then, there are many perspectives from which the world can be interpreted when we make judgments. Some justification relativists even go so far as to deny the universal nature of so-called laws of logic; even these, they maintain, are grounded in mere social conventions.

A standard criticism of truth and justification relativism is that it leads to absurd consequences that no rational person would accept. By surrendering to relativism, we abandon any stable notion of reality and place ourselves at the mercy of cultural biases, fanatical social groups, and power hungry tyrants who are more than happy to twist our conceptual frameworks to their benefits. Everything, then, becomes a matter of customs that are imposed on us, even in matters of science. Scottish philosopher James Beattie (1768–1790) makes this point in a fictional story where he describes a crazy scientist who attempts to put relativism into practice:

[The scientist] was watching a hencoop full of chickens, and feeding them with various kinds of food, in order, as he told me "that they might [give birth to live offspring and] ... lay no more eggs," which seemed to him to be a very bad custom. . . . "I have also," continued he, "under my care some young children, whom I am teaching to believe that two and two are equal to six, and a whole less than one of its parts; that ingratitude is a virtue, and honesty a vice; that a rose is one of the ugliest, and a toad one of the most beautiful objects in nature." [James Beattie, "The Castle of Skepticism"]

According to Beattie, if we took the relativist's position seriously, we'd be forced to accept absurd views like "it is just a matter of custom that chickens lay eggs," or that "it's possible that 2+2=6." Thus, even if we acknowledge a certain level of relativism with etiquette, aesthetics and perception, we need to draw the line when it comes to standards of truth and justification.

How might the relativist respond to this criticism? One approach is to hold that not all conceptual schemes are on equal footing, and some indeed are better than others. Nietzsche argues that there are competing perspectives of the world, and the winner is the one whose conceptual framework succeeds the best:

It is our needs that interpret the world; our instincts and their impulses for and against. Every instinct is a sort of thirst for power; each has its point of view, which it would gladly impose upon all the other instincts as their norm. [*Will to Power*, 481]

Nietzsche presents the conflict as a kind of power struggle among competing conceptual frameworks, where the winner takes all. A more gentle approach, though, would be to hold that the winner is the one that best assists us in our life's activities and allows us to thrive. If people today held that "it is just a matter of custom that chickens lay eggs," or "it is possible that 2+2=6", their underlying conceptual framework would not enable them to succeed very well in the world. For that matter, such a conceptual framework would not have allowed people to thrive very well in medieval England or any other pre-modern period of human history.

While there may be an underlying objective reality that molds our conceptual frameworks in successful ways, that possibility is irrelevant since, according to the relativist, we could never know such an objective reality even if it existed. What we *do* know is how our conceptual frameworks enable us to succeed in the world, and that's the real litmus test for truth and justification.

Thus, with many ordinary life beliefs, relativist theories of truth and justification work reasonably well, without leading us down the path to absurd consequences. What, though, of more scientific theories? In medieval times people thought mental illness was caused by demon possession; today we think that it is caused by physiological brain disorders. The medieval theory worked well in its own day; does that mean that it was true back then – supported by its own web of beliefs – but not now? In scientific matters, people feel uncomfortable with relativism and instead believe that our knowledge of physics, chemistry and biology has a fixed and objective reference point.

Risk, Uncertainty and Profit

We must now consider more concretely and in detail the effects of uncertainty on the general form of organisation of economic life. The best method seems to be to take up a society in which uncertainty is absent, imagine uncertainty introduced, and try to ascertain what changes will take place in its structure. We therefore return to the argument of chapter IV in which the mechanics of exchange and competition were studied with uncertainty (and progress) absent. The same method will be followed, beginning with the problem in as simple a form as possible and studying the effects of different factors separately, analyzing the complexity of real life "synthetically" by building it up in imagination out of its elements.

To secure the minimum degree of uncertainty and at the same time keep the discussion as close to reality as possible, it is necessary to exercise some care in defining the assumptions with which we are working. The most obvious initial requirement is to eliminate the factors of social progress from consideration and consider first a static society. But this postulate calls for discrimination in handling. In an *absolutely* unchanging social life there would, as we have repeatedly observed, be no uncertainty whatever, and our analysis in chapter IV proceeded on this assumption.

Such conditions are thoroughly incompatible with the most fundamental facts of the world in which we live, but their study serves the analytic purpose of isolating the effects of uncertainty. For different kinds of change and different degrees of change are real facts, and it will therefore involve less abstraction to study hypothetical conditions under which change is restricted to the most fundamental and ineradicable kind and amount. Societies may be and have been nearly *unprogressive,* and the obvious simplification to make is therefore the elimination of progressive change.

After abstracting all the elements of general progressive change enumerated in chapter V a large amount of uncertainty will be left in human life, due to changes of the character of *fluctuations* which cannot be thought away without violence to material possibility. Strictly accurate formulation of conditions involving a realistic minimum of uncertainty cannot be made, but are not necessary; it is sufficient to indicate in a rough way the situation we propose to discuss. Several factors affect the amount of uncertainty to be recognised, and have to be taken into account. The first to be noted is the time length of the production process, for the longer it is, the more uncertainty will naturally be involved.

Of very great importance also is the general level of economic life. The lower wants of man, those having in the greatest degree the nature of necessities, are the most stable and predictable. The higher up the scale we go, the larger the proportion of the æsthetic element and of social suggestion there is involved in motivation, the greater becomes the uncertainty connected with foreseeing wants and satisfying them. On the production side, on the other hand, most manufacturing processes are more controllable and calculable as to outcome than are agricultural operations under usual conditions. We must notice also the development of science and of the technique of social organisation. Greater ability to forecast the future and greater power to control the course of events manifestly reduce uncertainty, and of still greater importance is the status of the various devices noted in the last chapter for reducing uncertainty by consolidation.

All these perplexities about which some more or less definite assumption must be made can be disposed of by being as realistic as possible. Let us say simply that we are talking about the United States in the early years of the twentieth century, but with abstraction made of progressive changes. That is, we assume a population static in numbers and composition and without the mania of change and advance which characterizes modern life. Inventions and improvements in technology and organisation are to be eliminated, leaving the general situation as we know it today to remain stationary. Similarly in regard to the saving of new capital, development of new natural resources, redistribution of population over the soil or redistribution of ownership of goods, education, etc., among the people.

But we shall not assume that men are omniscient and immortal or perfectly rational and free from caprice as individuals. We shall neglect natural catastrophes, epidemics, wars, etc., but take for granted the "usual" uncertainties of the weather and the like, along with the "normal" vicissitudes of mortal life, and uncertainties of human choice.

Returning now to the kind of social organisation described in chapter IV, let us inquire as to what will be the effects of introducing the minimum degree of uncertainty into the situation. The essential features of the hypothetical society as thus far constructed need to be kept clearly in mind. Acting as individuals under absolute freedom but without collusion, men are supposed to have organised economic life with primary and secondary division of labour, the use of capital, etc., developed to the point familiar in present-day America.

The principal fact which calls for exercise of the imagination is the internal organisation of the productive groups or establishments. With uncertainty entirely absent, every individual being in possession of perfect knowledge of the situation, there would be no occasion for anything of the nature of responsible management or control of productive activity. Even marketing operations in any realistic sense would not be found. The flow of raw materials and productive services through productive processes to the consumer would be entirely automatic.

We do not need to strain the imagination by supposing supernatural powers of prescience on the part of men. We can think of the adjustment as the result of a long process of experimentation, worked out by trial-and-error methods alone. If the conditions of life and the people themselves were entirely unchanging a definite organisation would result, perfect in the sense that no one would be under an incentive to change. So in the organisation of the productive groups, it is not necessary to imagine every worker doing exactly the right thing at the right time in a sort of "pre-established harmony" with the work of others. There might be managers, superintendents, etc., for the purpose of coordinating the activities of individuals. But under conditions of perfect knowledge and certainty such functionaries would be labourers merely, performing a purely routine function, without responsibility of any sort, on a level with men engaged in mechanical operations.

With the introduction of uncertainty—the fact of ignorance and necessity of acting upon opinion rather than knowledge—into this Eden-like situation, its character is completely changed. With uncertainty absent, man's energies are devoted altogether to doing things; it is doubtful whether intelligence itself would exist in such a situation; in a world so built that perfect knowledge was theoretically possible, it seems likely that all organic readjustments would become mechanical, all organisms automata. With uncertainty present, doing things, the actual execution of activity, becomes in a real sense a secondary part of life; the primary problem or function is deciding what to do and how to do it. The two most important characteristics of social organisation brought about by the fact of uncertainty have already been noticed. In the first place, goods are produced for a market, on the basis of an entirely impersonal prediction of wants, not for the satisfaction of the wants of the producers themselves. The producer takes the responsibility of forecasting the consumers' wants. In the second place, the work of forecasting and at the same time a large part of the technological direction and control of production are still further concentrated upon a very narrow class of the producers, and we meet with a new economic functionary, the entrepreneur.

When uncertainty is present and the task of deciding what to do and how to do it takes the ascendancy over that of execution, the internal organisation of the productive groups is no longer a matter of indifference or a mechanical detail. Centralization of this deciding and controlling function is imperative, a process of "cephalization," such as has taken place in the evolution of organic life, is inevitable, and for the same reasons as in the case of biological evolution. Let us consider this process and the circumstances which condition it. The order of attack on the problem is suggested by the classification worked out in chapter VII of the elements in uncertainty in regard to which men may in large measure differ independently.

In the first place, occupations differ in respect to the kind and amount of knowledge and judgment required for their successful direction as well as in the kind of abilities and tastes adapted to the routine operations. Productive groups or establishments now compete for managerial capacity as well as skill, and a considerable rearrangement of personnel is the natural result. The final adjustment will place each producer in the place where his particular combination of the two kinds of attributes seems to be most effective.

But a more important change is the tendency of the groups themselves to specialise, finding the individuals with the greatest managerial capacity of the requisite kinds and placing them in charge of the work of the group, submitting the activities of the other members to their direction and control. It need hardly be mentioned explicitly that the organisation of industry depends on the fundamental fact that the intelligence of one person can be made to direct in a general way the routine manual and mental operations of others. It will also be taken into account that men differ in their powers of effective control over other men as well as in intellectual capacity to decide what should be done. In addition, there must come into play the diversity among men in degree of confidence in their judgment and powers and in disposition to act on their opinions, to "venture."

This fact is responsible for the most fundamental change of all in the form of organisation, the system under which the confident and venturesome "assume the risk" or "insure" the doubtful and timid by guaranteeing to the latter a specified income in return for an assignment of the actual results.

Uncertainty thus exerts a fourfold tendency to select men and specialise functions:

(1) an adaptation of men to occupations on the basis of kind of knowledge and judgment;

(2) a similar selection on the basis of degree of foresight, for some lines of activity call for this endowment in a very different degree from others;

(3) a specialisation within productive groups, the individuals with superior managerial ability (foresight and capacity of ruling others) being placed in control of the group and the others working under their direction; and

(4) those with confidence in their judgment and disposition to "back it up" in action specialise in risk-taking.

The close relations obtaining among these tendencies will be manifest. We have not separated confidence and venturesomeness at all, since they act along parallel lines and are little more than phases of the same faculty—just as courage and the tendency to minimize danger are proverbially commingled in all fields, though they are separable in thought. In addition the tendencies numbered (3) and (4) operate together.

With human nature as we know it would be impracticable or very unusual for one man to guarantee to another a definite result of the latter's actions without being given power to direct his work. And on the other hand the second party would not place himself under the direction of the first without such a guaranty. The result is a "double contract" of the type famous in the history of the evasion of usury laws. It seems evident also that the system would not work at all if good judgment were not in fact generally associated with confidence in one's judgment on the part both of himself and others. That is, men's judgment of their own judgment and of others' judgment as to both kind and grade must in the large be much more right than wrong.

The result of this manifold specialisation of function is *enterprise and the wage system of industry.* Its existence in the world is a direct result of the fact of uncertainty; our task in the remainder of this study is to examine this phenomenon in detail in its various phases and divers relations with the economic activities of man and the structure of society. It is not necessary or inevitable, not the only conceivable form of organisation, but under certain conditions has certain advantages, and is capable of development in different degrees.

The essence of enterprise is the specialisation of the function of *responsible direction* of economic life, the neglected feature of which is the inseparability of these *two* elements, *responsibility* and *control.* Under the enterprise system, a special social class, the business men, direct economic activity; they are in the strict sense the producers, while the great mass of the population merely furnish them with productive services, placing their persons and their property at the disposal of this class; the entrepreneurs *also* guarantee to those who furnish productive services a fixed remuneration. Accurately to define these functions and trace them through the social structure will be a long task, for the specialisation is never complete; but at the end of it we shall find that in a free society the two are essentially inseparable. Any degree of effective exercise of judgment, or making decisions, is in a free society coupled with a corresponding degree of uncertainty-bearing, of taking the responsibility for those decisions.

With the specialisation of function goes also a differentiation of reward. The produce of society is similarly divided into *two kinds of income,* and two only, contractual income, which is essentially *rent,* as economic theory has described incomes, and residual income or *profit.* But the differentiation of contractual income, like that of profit, is never complete; neither variety is ever met with in a pure form, and every real income contains elements of both rent and profit. And with uncertainty present (the condition of the differentiation itself) it is not possible even to determine just how much of any income is of one kind and how much of the other; but a partial separation can be made, and the causal distinction between the two kinds is sharp and clear.

We may imagine a society in which uncertainty is absent transformed on the introduction of uncertainty into an enterprise organisation. The readjustments will be carried out by the same trial-and-error methods under the same motives, the effort of each individual to better himself, which we have already described. The ideal or limiting condition constantly in view would still be the equalization of all available alternatives of conduct by each individual through the distribution of efforts and of expenditure of the proceeds of effort among the lines open. Under the new system labour and property services actually come into the market, become commodities and are bought and sold. They are thus brought into the comparative value scale and reduced to homogeneity in price terms with the fund of values made up of the direct means of want satisfaction.

Another feature of the new adjustment is that a condition of perfect equilibrium is no longer possible. Since productive arrangements are made on the basis of anticipations and the results actually achieved do not coincide with these as a usual thing, the oscillations will not settle down to zero. For all changes made by individuals relate to the established value scale and this price-system will be subject to fluctuations due to unforeseen causes; consequently individual changes in arrangements will continue indefinitely to take place. The experiments by which alone the value of human judgment is determined involve a proportion of failures or errors, are never complete, and in view of human mortality have constantly to be recommenced at the beginning.

We turn now to consider in broad outline the two types of individual income implied in the enterprise system of organisation, contractual income and profit. We shall try as hitherto to explain events by placing ourselves in the actual positions of the men acting or making decisions and interpreting their acts in terms of ordinary human motives. The setting of the problem is a free competitive situation in which all men and material agents are competing for employment, including all men at the time engaged as entrepreneurs, while all entrepreneurs are competing for productive services and at the same time all men are competing for positions as entrepreneurs. The essential fact in understanding the reaction to this situation is that men are acting, competing, on the basis of what they *think* of the *future*. To simplify the picture and make it concrete we shall as before assume that there exists some sort of grouping of men and things under the control of other men as entrepreneurs (a random grouping will do as a start) and those entrepreneurs and others are in competition as above stated.

The production-distribution system is worked out through offers and counter-offers, made on the basis of anticipations, of two kinds. The labourer asks what he thinks the entrepreneur will be able to pay, and in any case will not accept less than he can get from some other entrepreneur, or by turning entrepreneur himself. In the same way the entrepreneur offers to any labourer what he thinks he must in order to secure his services, and in any case not more than he thinks the labourer will actually be worth to him, keeping in mind what he can get by turning labourer himself. The whole calculation is in the future; past and even present conditions operate only as grounds of prediction as to what may be anticipated.

Since in a free market there can be but one price on any commodity, a general wage rate must result from this competitive bidding. The rate established may be described as the socially or competitively anticipated value of the labourer's product, using the term "product" in the sense of specific contribution, as already explained. It is not the opinion of the future held by either party to an employment bargain which determines the rate; these opinions merely set maximum and minimum limits outside of which the agreement cannot take place. The mechanism of price adjustment is the same as in any other market. There is always an established uniform rate, which is kept constantly at the point which equates the supply and demand.

If at any moment there are more bidders willing to employ at a higher rate than there are employees willing to accept the established rate, the rate will rise accordingly, and similarly if there is a balance of opinion in the opposite direction. The final decision by any individual as to what to do is based on a comparison of a momentarily existing price with a subjective judgment of significance of the commodity. The judgment in this case relates to the indirect significance derived from a twofold estimate of the future, involving both technological and price uncertainties.

The employer in deciding whether to offer the current wage, and the employee in deciding whether to accept it, must estimate the technical or physically measured product (specific contribution) of the labour and the price to be expected for that product when it comes upon the market. The estimation may involve two sorts of calculation or estimate of probability. The venture itself may be of the nature of a gamble, involving a large proportion of inherently unpredictable factors. In such a case the decision depends upon an "estimate" of an "objective probability" of success, or of a series of such probabilities corresponding to various degrees of success or failure. And normally, in the case of intelligent men, account will be taken of the probable "true value" of the estimates in the case of all estimated factors.

The meaning of the term "social" or "competitive" anticipation will now be clear. The question in the mind of either party to an employment agreement relates simply to the fact of a difference between the current standard of remuneration for the services being bargained for and his own estimate of their worth, discounted by probability allowances. The magnitude of the difference is altogether immaterial. The prospective employer may know absolutely that the service has a value to him ever so much greater than the price he is paying, but he will have to pay only the competitively established rate, and his purchase will affect this rate no more than if he were ever so hesitant about the bargain, just so he makes it. It is the general estimate of the magnitudes involved, in the sense of a "marginal" demand price, which fixes the actual current rate.

In many respects the nature of the organisation we are now dealing with is the same as that described in chapter IV, with uncertainty and progress absent. The value of a labourer or piece of material equipment to a particular productive group is determined by the specific physical contribution to output under the principle of diminishing returns with increase in the proportion of that kind of agency in the combination, and on the price of this contribution under the principle of diminishing utility with increase in the proportion of productive energy devoted to making the particular product turned out by the establishment in question. But the facts upon which the working-out of the organisation depends can no longer be objectively determined with accuracy by experiment; all the data in the case must be *estimated,* subject to a larger or smaller margin of error, and this fact causes differences more fundamental than the resemblances in the two situations. The function of making these estimates and of "guaranteeing" their value to the other participating members of the group falls to the responsible entrepreneur in each establishment, producing a new type of activity and a new type of income entirely unknown in a society where uncertainty is absent.

Even in the hypothetical situation dealt with in chapter IV there would be likely to be a concentration of certain control and coordinating functions in a separate person or group of persons in each productive group. But the duties of such persons would be of a routine character merely, in no significant respect different from those of any other operatives; they would be labourers among labourers and their incomes would be wages like other wages. When, however, the managerial function comes to require the exercise of judgment involving *liability to error,* and when in consequence the assumption of *responsibility* for the correctness of his opinions becomes a condition prerequisite to getting the other members of the group to submit to the manager's direction, the nature of the function is revolutionized; the manager becomes an entrepreneur. He may, and typically will, to be sure, continue to perform the old mechanical routine functions and to receive the old wages; but in addition he makes responsible decisions, and his income will normally contain in addition to wages a pure *differential* element designated as "profit" by the economic theorist. This profit is simply the difference between the market price of the productive agencies he employs; the amount which the competition of other entrepreneurs forces him to guarantee to them as a condition of securing their services, and the amount which he finally realises from the disposition of the product which under his direction they turn out.

The character of the entrepreneur's income is evidently complex, and the relations of its component elements subtle. It contains an element which is ordinary contractual income, received on the ground of routine services performed by the entrepreneur personally for the business (wages) or earned by property which belongs to him (rent or capital return). And the differential element is again complex, for it is clear that there is an element of calculation and an element of luck in it. An adequate examination and analysis of this phenomenon requires time and careful thinking.

The background of the problem should now be clear: the uncertainty of all life and conduct which call for the exercise of judgment in business, the economy of division of labour which compels men to work in groups and to delegate the function of control as other functions are specialised, the facts of human nature which make it necessary for one who directs the activities of others to assume responsibility for the results of the operations, and finally the competitive situation which pits the judgment of each entrepreneur against that of the extant business world in adjusting the contractual incomes which he must pay before he gets anything for himself.

The first step in attacking the problem is to inquire into the meaning of entrepreneur ability and its conditions of demand and supply. In regard to the first main division of the entrepreneur's income, the ordinary wage for the routine services of labour and property furnished to the business, no comment is necessary. This return is merely the competitive rate of pay for the grade of ability or kind of property in question. To be sure, it may not be possible in practice to say exactly what this rate is. Not merely is perfect standardization of things and services unattainable under the fluctuating conditions of real life, but in addition the conditions of the entrepreneur specialisation may well bring it about that the same things are not done under closely comparable conditions by entrepreneurs and non-entrepreneurs. Hence the separation between the pure wage or rent element and the elements arising out of uncertainty cannot generally be made with complete accuracy. The serious difficulty comes with the attempt to deal with the relation between judgment and luck in determining that part of the entrepreneur's income which is associated with the performance of his peculiar twofold function of

(a) exercising responsible control and

(b) securing the owners of productive services against uncertainty and fluctuation in their incomes.

Clearly this special income is also connected with a sort of effort and sacrifice and into the nature and conditions of supply and demand of the capacities and dispositions for these efforts and sacrifices it must be pertinent to inquire.

It is unquestionable that the entrepreneur's activities effect an enormous saving to society, vastly increasing the efficiency of economic production. Large-scale operations, highly organised industry, and minute division of labour would be impossible without specialisation of the managerial function, and human nature being as it is, the guaranteeing function must apparently go along with that of control; indeed, in the ultimate sense of control the two are not even theoretically separable.

Thus there would be a large saving even outside of any question of the superior abilities of certain individuals over other individuals for the performance of this function. And there is still another gain of large magnitude through the reduction of uncertainty by the principle of consolidation, which also is independent of the personal attributes of the entrepreneur. But these economies, due to the system as such, and not to activities of the individuals performing a special function, accrue to society; no cause can be discovered in this connection alone which would give rise to a special distributive share.

As to the actual comparative magnitude of the various elements of gain secured through the enterprise system it would be rash to guess, but certainly a very large real gain is secured through the selection of managers having superior fitness for the work. Now it is of supreme importance that such selection is possible only because and in so far as such fitness can be identified in advance of its demonstration in each particular case.

The prospective entrepreneur himself has an opinion of his own suitability, in so far as he forms an estimate of the true value of his prognostications and policies. Other persons may or may not agree with his opinion of himself. A man may actually get into the position of entrepreneur in several ways. If he has property or known personal productive powers of a technological sort he may assume the functions of entrepreneur without convincing any one outside himself of any special fitness to exercise them. As long as his own resources safeguard the interests of the persons to whom he agrees to pay contractual incomes these persons need not worry about the correctness of the judgments on which the entrepreneur's policies are based. If he cannot make such guarantees he must, of course, convince either the persons with whom he makes wage or rent bargains or some outside party who will underwrite the guarantees for him.

The effect of this transfer of the guarantee function on the nature of entrepreneurship is a subtle question and will be taken up presently. It might even conceivably happen, in the third place, that a person not judging himself especially fit to control industrial policies would get into the place of entrepreneur, if other persons have a sufficiently high opinion of his abilities and trustworthiness. This case is more complicated still and its treatment must also be deferred. Discussion of divided entrepreneurship will lead naturally to the problem of the hired manager, most difficult of all. Let us consider first the simple case of unique and undivided exercise of the function, the control and uncertainty-bearing being all concentrated in the same individual, under the assumption that outsiders whether employed by him or not have neither opinions upon nor interest in the question of his competence. It will further simplify the problem if we begin by assuming that this is the only type of entrepreneurship in our society.

First, a further word as to the character of the process by which the entrepreneur's income is fixed. It may be distinguished from the contractual returns received for services not involving the exercise of judgment, and which are paid by the entrepreneur, by pointing out that the latter are *imputed,* while his own income is *residual.* That is, in a sense, the entrepreneur's income is not "determined" at all; it is "what is left" after the others are "determined." The competition of entrepreneurs bidding in the market for the productive services in existence in the society "fix" prices upon these; the entrepreneur's income is not fixed, but consists of whatever remains over after the fixed incomes are paid. Hence we must examine the entrepreneur's income indirectly, by inquiring into the forces which determine the fixed incomes, in relation to the whole product of an enterprise or of society.

Assuming perfect competition in the market for productive services, the contractual incomes are fixed for every entrepreneur by the competitive or marginal anticipations of entrepreneurs as a group in relation to the supply of each kind of agency in existence.

Whether any particular individual becomes an entrepreneur or not depends on his believing (strongly enough to act upon the conviction) that he can make productive services yield more than the price fixed upon them by what other persons think they can make them yield (with the same provision that the belief must lead to action).

After any individual has become an entrepreneur, the amount of his income depends on his success in producing the anticipated excess, and in this sense is a matter of the correctness of his judgment. But it is clear that his success is equally a matter of:

(a) the failure of the judgment, or

(b) an inferiority in capacity, on the part of his competitors.

The two factors of (a) capacity and (b) judgment of one's capacity are inseparably connected, and business capacity is again compounded of judgment (of factors external to the person judging) and executive capacity.

Moreover, there is in the exercise of the best judgment and highest capacity an inevitable margin of error. A successful outcome in any particular case cannot be attributed entirely to judgment and capacity even taken together. The best men would fail in a certain proportion of cases and the worst perhaps succeed in a certain proportion. The results of one trial or of a small number of trials can at most establish a certain presumption in favour of the view that ability has or has not been shown. A dependable estimate of ability can only come from a considerable number of trials.

Even then there are differences in kind of ability, as well as degree. And in business management no two instances, perhaps, are ever very closely alike, in any objective, describable sense. It is one of the mysteries of the workings of mind that we are able to form estimates of "general ability" which have any value, but the fact that we do is of course indisputable.

Still further, the venture itself may be a gamble, as we have repeatedly pointed out. Most decisions calling for the exercise of judgment in business or responsible life in any field involve factors not subject to estimate and which no one makes any pretense of estimating. The judgment itself is a judgment of the probability of a certain outcome, of the proportion of successes which would be achieved if the venture could be repeated a large number of times. The allowance for luck is therefore twofold. It requires a large number of trials to show the real probabilities in regard to which judgment is exercised in any given kind of case as well as to distinguish between intrinsic quality in the judgment and mere accident.

And bearing in mind again the extreme crudeness of the classification of instances at best, the marvel grows that we are able to live as intelligently as we do. Let us now attempt to state the principles determining entrepreneur income more accurately and in the form of laws of demand and supply.

The demand for a productive service depends upon the steepness of the curve of diminishing returns from increasing amounts of other kinds of services applied to the first. In the familiar case of land, the more rapidly the returns from increased applications of labour and capital applied to a given plot of land fall off, the higher will be the rent on land. Now there is evidently a law of diminishing returns governing the combination of productive services with entrepreneurs. It is based on the fact already stated of limitation in the space range of foresight and executive capacity.

The greater the magnitude of operations which any single individual attempts to direct the less effective in general he will be—"beyond a certain point," as in other cases of the law. The demand for entrepreneurs, again, like that for any productive agency, depends directly upon the supply of other agencies.

The supply of entrepreneurs involves the factors of:

(a) ability, with the various elements therein included,

(b) willingness,

(c) power to give satisfactory guarantees, and

(d) the coincidence of these factors.

If society as a whole secures a high quality of management for its enterprises it will be through a coincidence of ability with willingness, or of all three factors, as well as through an abundant supply of the elements separately. Willingness plus power to give guarantees, not backed up by ability, will evidently lead to a dissipation of resources, while ability without the other two factors will be merely wasted. To find men capable of managing business efficiently and secure to them the positions of responsible control is perhaps the most important single problem of economic organisation on the efficiency side.

The supply of entrepreneur qualities in society is one of the chief factors in determining the number and size of its productive units. It is a common and perhaps justifiable opinion that most of the other factors tend toward greater economy with increasing size in the establishment, and that the chief limitation on size is the capacity of the leadership. If this is true the ability to handle large enterprises successfully, when it is met with, must tend to secure very large rewards.

The income of *any particular entrepreneur* will in general tend to be larger:

(1) as he himself has ability, and good luck; but

(2) perhaps more important, as there is in the society a scarcity of self-confidence combined with the power to make effective guarantees to employees.

The abundance or scarcity of mere ability to manage business successfully exerts relatively little influence on profit; the main thing is the rashness or timidity of entrepreneurs (actual and potential) as a class in bidding up the prices of productive services.

Entrepreneur income, being residual, is determined by the demand for these other services, which demand is a matter of the self-confidence of entrepreneurs as a class, rather than upon a demand for entrepreneur services in a direct sense. We must see at once that it is perfectly possible for entrepreneurs as a class to sustain a net loss, which would merely have to be made up out of their earnings in some other capacity. This would be the natural result in a population combining low ability with high "courage."

On the other hand, if men generally judge their own abilities well, the *general rate* of profit will probably be low, whether ability itself is low or high, but much more variable and fluctuating for a low level of real capacity. The condition for large profits is a narrowly limited supply of high-grade ability with a low general level of initiative as well as ability.

The analysis of profit is much simplified for students of political economy by the fact that the conventional distribution has placed such (misguided) emphasis on the concept of residual income, notably, of course, in the treatment of rent. Yet it will not do to press the parallel too far, for there is this important difference: Rent—and as every one now understands, any other share as well—is residual after the *products* of the other shares are deducted (product being the marginal contribution of a single unit multiplied by the number of units). But profit (under the simplified conditions we are now dealing with) is the residue after deduction of the *payment* for the other agencies, determined by the *marginal bid* of entrepreneurs as a class for all agencies as aggregates. The residue in the latter case is not a product residue, but a margin of error in calculation on the part of the non-entrepreneurs and entrepreneurs who do not force the successful entrepreneurs to pay as much for productive services as they could be forced to pay.

As the argument is quite complicated, it will be well to recapitulate. We have assumed in this first approximation that each man in society knows his own powers as entrepreneur, but that men know nothing about each other in this capacity. The division of social income between profits and contractual income then depends on the supply of entrepreneur ability in the society and the rapidity of diminishing returns from (other factors applied to) it, the size of the profit share increasing as the supply of ability is small and as the returns diminish more rapidly.

If men are poor judges of their own powers as well as ignorant of those of other men, the size of the profit share depends on whether they tend on the whole to overestimate or underestimate the prospects of business operations, being larger if they underestimate. These statements abstract from the question of possession of means to guarantee the fixed incomes which they contract to pay; limitations in this respect act as limitations on the supply of entrepreneur ability. If entrepreneur ability is of such high quality that it practically is not subject to diminishing returns, the competition among even a very few such men will raise the rate of contractual returns and lower the residual share, if they know their own powers. If they do not, the size of their profits will again depend on their "optimism," varying inversely with the latter.

A man's knowledge of his own powers involves knowledge of the amount of uncertainty he deals with in trusting his own judgment, which, if the scale of operations is large enough, means the absence of uncertainty in the effective sense, if the knowledge is complete. Even if judgment itself subject to error is exercised in regard to the real probabilities in an intrinsic gambling situation, we have for the uncertainty in the situation as a whole an objective probability with predictable results for a large number of cases. The presence of true profit, therefore, depends on an absolute uncertainty in the estimation of the value of judgment, or on the absence of the requisite organisation for combining a sufficient number of instances to secure certainty through consolidation. With men in complete ignorance of the powers of judgment of other men it is hard to see how such organisation could be effected. Yet so elusive is the mechanism by which we know our world, so great the capacity of mind for seizing upon indirect methods of increasing certainty, that a further sweeping reservation must be made. If men, ignorant of other men's powers, know that these other men themselves know their own powers, the results of general knowledge of all men's powers may be secured; and this is true even if such knowledge is (as it is in fact) very imperfectly or not at all communicable.

If those who furnish productive services for a contractual remuneration know that those who bid for the services know what they are worth to themselves, the bidders, or if each bidder knows this to be true of the others, the latter will be forced to pay all that they are willing to pay, which is to say all that they can pay. To be sure, competition under such conditions would be likely to take on the character of a poker game, a bluffing contest. But it must be admitted that actual wage bargains are in no slight degree of this character.

The case of European exploiters among primitive peoples illustrates the possibility of large profits to be made by a small number of men who know what they are doing among a large number who do not. But if they compete among themselves there must come a time, if their number increases, when they will force prices to their competitive level without any action on the part of the exploited masses more shrewd than that of accepting a larger offer in preference to a smaller one.

The number of competitors required to bring about this result depends upon the steepness of the curve of diminishing returns from entrepreneurship, upon the limitation of the scope of enterprise one man can deal with effectively. And the idea of scope must be extended to include the variety of situations to be dealt with. The question of diminishing returns from entrepreneurship is really a matter of the amount of uncertainty present. To imagine that one man could adequately manage a business enterprise of indefinite size and complexity is to imagine a situation in which effective uncertainty is entirely absent.

The entire foregoing argument has dealt with a simplified situation inasmuch as the members of our society have been assumed to know something about the true value, each of his own judgment and ability to control events in accordance with it, but to know these things about each other only as the other man's own opinion of himself is manifested in his dispositions to act. In fact men form judgments of other men on the basis of watching their performances over a period of time, and in addition form impressions having some claim to validity from mere personal appearance, conversation, etc. Such knowledge of others is one of the most important factors in our efforts to live together intelligently in organised society. It is the most difficult to discuss scientifically of all the data connected with the practical bearings of knowledge and uncertainty.

Estimates of the worth of other men's opinions and capabilities probably form by far the largest part of the data on which any individual makes decisions in his own life, at least in the sphere of economic activity where such activity is highly organised. Such estimates function as an indirect indication of what we may expect to happen in any set of conditions; we know and give ourselves credit for knowing nothing of value about the problem itself, but we know what is the belief of other men whose judgment we respect and which we accept in place of an opinion of our own.

The degree of confidence which we feel in our own situation is simply the degree of confidence we feel in the value of the judgment of the "authority" whose pronouncement we accept as the best information available on the merits of the case.

To be sure, the mode of formation of these opinions of others' opinions is complex and obscure, and is rarely free from all passing of judgment on the case itself independently. There is a mutual reinforcement; we have *some* ideas of our own in the premises, and these agree with the views of some authority. We often if not in general believe what we do because the authority believes it, but to some extent we believe in the authority because he holds the view to which we were already inclined.

In large measure we even believe in ourselves because and in the measure that we think others believe in us, though, on the other hand, again, . . . But it is enough to indicate the complexity of the relations between our own and others' opinions without attempting to set all these relations out in logical statements. The importance of indirect knowledge of fact through knowledge of others' knowledge is the point we wish to emphasize.

Correspondingly, the uncertainty of the knowledge on the basis of which we act is in large measure the margin of error in our estimates of the authorities whom we elect to follow. The uncertainties of business are predominantly of this character, and the genus calls for particularly careful study. Our discussion hitherto has assumed pure and undivided entrepreneurship, which would follow from the impossibility of knowledge by one person of another person's capabilities.

In the absence of such knowledge it is clear that no one would put his resources under the direction of another without a valid guarantee of the payment agreed upon, and no one could become an entrepreneur who was not in a position to make such guarantees without assistance, it being equally clear that no one would make such a guarantee for another. That is, entrepreneurship would be completely specialised in a pure form, responsibility and control completely associated.

When men have knowledge, or opinions on which they are willing to act, of other men's capacities for the entrepreneur function, all this is changed; entrepreneurship is no longer a simple and sharply isolated function. This is, of course, the state of affairs in real life, and it is this partially specialised and more or less distributed entrepreneurship which merits most careful consideration. Several forms of organisation distribution of the function call for notice.

The simplest division of entrepreneurship which we can think of is the separation of the two elements of control and guarantee and their performance by different individuals. This is a natural arrangement; for it must often happen that entrepreneur ability will not be associated with a situation on the part of its possessor enabling him to make satisfactory guarantees of the contractual incomes promised. Under such circumstances it may be mutually profitable for him to enter into agreement with some one in a position to underwrite his employment contracts, but not himself possessed of the ability or disposition to undertake the direction of enterprises.

The form of this partnership and conditions of division of the profit may be highly various. As a matter of fact we know that it commonly takes the shape of a new wage bargain, the guarantor hiring the director in much the same way as the latter hires the productive services which he organised and controls. This transfer of function involves a transformation in character also which must be considered at length, and will be taken up in the next chapter.

Let us note here that it is usually impracticable to separate all the guaranteeing responsibility from the control of the enterprise. It is rare that a hired entrepreneur receives a contractual income as his only interest in the business. He is usually a part owner, or at least his salary is so adjusted as to make it clear that his continuance in the position is contingent upon its prosperity under his direction.

An effect of the evaluation of ability nearly as important as the transformation in entrepreneurship with its partial transfer to another individual is that the specialisation of the function within the enterprise may be quite incomplete. That is, it is no longer true that men are necessarily unwilling to entrust productive services, of person or property, to an outsider without an effective material guarantee of the fixed payment agreed upon. If they have confidence in the manager's ability and integrity they may gladly work with only a partial or imperfect security for their remunerations. To the extent that this is the case such owners of productive services manifestly share in bearing the uncertainty or "taking the risk" involved in the undertaking. That they also share in the effective control will appear in the course of a more careful examination of the entrepreneur function under the complicated, vague, and shifting conditions of real life (except that progress is still abstracted), which is the next stage in our inquiry.

Chapter 6

Dual Pricing

Definition of 'Dual Pricing'

The practice of setting prices at different levels depending on the currency used to make the purchase. Dual pricing may be used to accomplish a variety of goals, such as to gain entry into a foreign market by offering unusually low prices to buyers using the foreign currency, or as a method of price discrimination.

In the context of investment and foreign exchange, dual pricing is the existence of two different price quotations. These are offered by a unit trust manager who quotes a lower price as the selling price and a higher price as buying price.

Transacting with bonds may involve dual pricing schemes. Setting two different price quotations is also particularly common in foreign exchange; where both buying and selling of currency occur. These may also be applied when, for example, a person wants to send money to another person in a different country via wire transfer. In such a situation, the bank uses the differences in price to compute the amount of money that the recipient should get, depending on the currency in that country. Of course, this also means that the amount that was originally sent is not necessarily the exact amount that will be received, because of the differences brought about by the pricing.

Investors who wish to buy and sell currency have to pay close attention to the differences in price. By doing so, an investor will be able to ascertain whether it is time to purchase a particular currency or not. In many cases, the exchange may come out to be very disadvantageous, so it might be wiser to choose an alternative investment or to wait for further pricing adjustments.

In the context of commerce, however, dual pricing refers to the sale of the same product at different prices, depending on the market. This is also known as two-tier pricing and is common in many developing nations with a strong emphasis on the tourist industry.

Under this arrangement, locals are offered lower prices while foreigners are required to pay more, in many cases without their knowledge, for the same item or service. Careful research, establishment of contacts, and negotiation skills can all help minimize the effects of such pricing schemes, at least to a certain extent.

Difference between Worldwide Pricing and Dual Pricing?

Companies that compete in the global marketplace must make use of and be accustomed to various types of pricing strategies. Two of these include dual pricing policy and worldwide pricing policy. Companies often use these types of pricing policies to differentiate the sources of their income. Dual and worldwide pricing differ in purpose and effectiveness.

Step 1

Place both dual pricing and worldwide pricing policy within the larger context of the global marketplace. Doing so will help you understand and define the differences between both. Dual pricing policy is designed for companies involved in extensive trade both home and abroad. This pricing strategy involves setting one price for the goods sold on the domestic market while setting a completely different price for goods sold in international market. It avoids standardizing a price on a global scale and is instead sensitive to local market conditions wherever the product is sold.

Step 2

Compare dual pricing policy to worldwide pricing policy. Worldwide pricing policy is also designed for companies using international markets, but it differs from dual pricing policy because it's not necessarily sensitive to local market conditions in the same way as dual pricing policy. Instead, worldwide pricing policy uses one price for goods sold internationally.

Step 3

Recognise the overall purpose of both dual pricing and worldwide pricing. These strategies are designed to help companies price their products so there will be significant demand for the goods as they're sold abroad. Both policies attempt to use pricing as a strategic weapon on the international market. Both are designed to optimize and customize price at the same time, to attract the maximum amount of business.

Step 4

Assess the overall effectiveness of each type of pricing. The problem with worldwide pricing policy is the difficulty of implementation. The lack of sensitivity to local market conditions makes it difficult to set a uniform price across an entire global market that consists of multiple submarkets, each with its own supply and demand. Dual pricing policy has the advantage of being sensitive to these markets and takes into account factors such as local currency rates, local competition and market distance.

Pricing Products

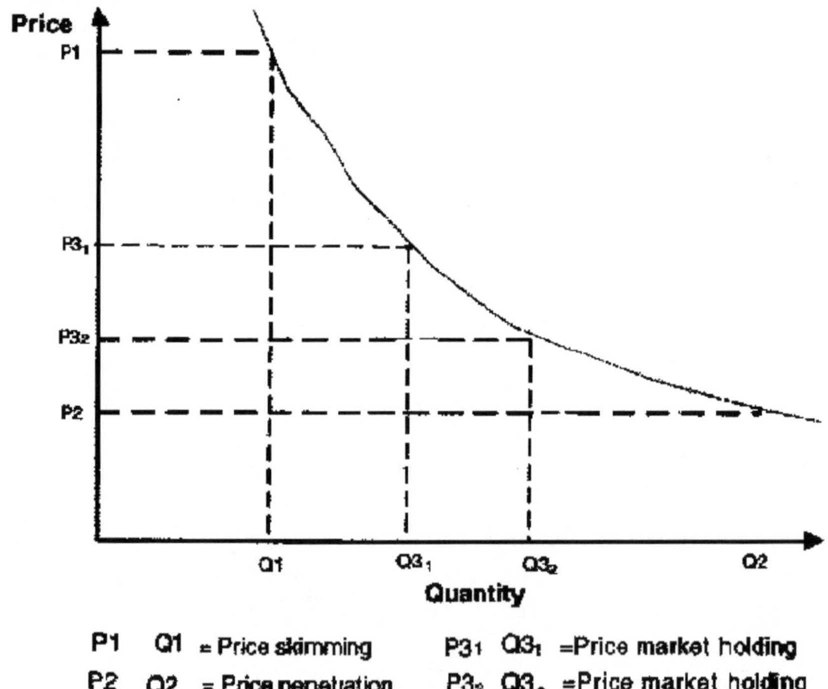

Figure: *Pricing policies*

Three basic factors determine the boundaries of the pricing decision - the price floor, or minimum price, bounded by product cost, the price ceiling or maximum price, bounded by competition and the market and the optimum price, a function of demand and the cost of supplying the product. In addition, in price setting cognisance must be, taken of government tax policies, resale prices, dumping problems, transportation costs, middlemen and so on. Whilst many agricultural products are at the mercy of the market (price takers) others are not. These include high value added products like ostrich, crocodile products and hardwoods, where demand outstrips supply at present.

In setting prices, it must be made clear what the objectives and policy are. Few organisations can now be pure profit maximisers - there is hardly a sector of industry where competition, or potential competition is not prevalent. Three frequently encountered price polices are market penetration, skimming and holding. A low price (penetration) is a volume policy. A high price (skimming) is used if the product is fairly unique, development costs are high and demand is relatively inelastic. Market holding is a strategy intended to hold share. Here products are not based on straight exchange rates at current rates but on what the market can bear.

The assumption behind all three pricing policies is that the underlying conditions governing supply and demand apply. In reality, these do not always do so, if indeed ever.

Export Pricing

Actual pricing methods are usually cost, market, or competition oriented. However, in the international arena, other factors come into play.

Cost plus pricing: There are basically two types under this heading, the historical accounting cost method and the estimated future cost method. The former includes direct and indirect costs and has the disadvantage of ignoring demand and competitive position in the target market. Estimated cost approaches are based on assumptions of production volume (depending on process) which will be a principal factor determining costs. Again difficulties may lie in trying to estimate production levels. In reality, costs may be a useful starting point but should never be used as a final arbiter.

Competitive pricing: Whilst costs are important they should be looked at alongside the prices of competitive products in the target markets. Once these price levels have been established the base price, or price that the buyer will pay for the product, can be determined. This involves four steps:

i) estimation of demand schedules

ii) estimation of incremental and full manufacturing and marketing costs to achieve projected sales volumes

iii) selection of price which offers the highest contribution

iv) inclusion of other elements of the marketing mix. These steps are by no means easy. Costs are difficult to assess properly as are demand conditions.

In products of a raw commodity nature or those traded on the international market subject to world prices, often the producer has no alternative but to take the going price - a price governed by competition, especially on the supply side. In Malawi, for example, although tobacco prices internationally may be encouraging, if too many farmers grow it, the price will be suppressed for all.

Market pricing: In certain products one can charge "what the market can bear". If the supplier is one of a few, despite all the problems associated with price fixing, the market may be able to bear a high price. If, as in Africa, an export crop fails, then other suppliers can take advantage of this to charge higher prices for a similar export crop. This was the case, a few years ago, with the Kenyan avocado market. An Israeli crop failure gave an unprecedented boost to Kenya's price and production.

In other cases the product may be so unique that the company should capitalise on its rarity by charging a high price. At one time exotic produce like Malaysian starfruit and rambutans could command a high price due to their scarcity. The problem is, encouraged by the profit margins, more entrants are drawn into the market.

Price Escalation

One major feature of international pricing is the increase on the price due to the application of duties and so on.

***Table:** Price escalation*

Target price in foreign markets	25.00
Less 40% retail margin on selling price	10.00
Retailer cost	15.00
Less 75% importer/distributor marking up cost	1.96
Distributor cost	13.04
Less 12% value added tax on landed value and duty	1.40
CIF value plus duty	11.64
Less 9% duty on CIF value	0.96
Landed CIF value	10.68
Less ocean freight and insurance	1.40
Required FOB price to achieve target price	9.26

The domestic price, the firm has alternatives:

i) forget about exporting
ii) consider marginal pricing
iii) shorten the distribution channel
iv) modify or simplify product if possible
v) find an alternative source of supply with lower cost.

Dumping

Dumping, as defined by GATT, is the difference between the normal domestic price and the price at which the product leaves the exporting country.

Devaluation and Revaluation

Devaluation is the reduction and revaluation an increase in the value of one currency vis à vis other currencies. Under the floating exchange rate system devaluation and revaluation occur when currency values adjust in the exchange rate system in response to supply and demand. The idea behind devaluation is to make the domestic price more competitive and so more of the product can be bought for the same foreign currency. However, it can be negated by the higher price and costs induced by inboard goods and services which make up the export product. If the product is inelastic in demand, prices can be maintained if the competitive position is strong.

In revaluation, the revaluing country's prices are more expensive. These price increases may be passed on to the customers, absorbed or the domestic price may be reduced.

Inflation

Inflation is a world wide phenomenon, and requires periodic price adjustments. Inflation accounting methods attempt to deal with the phenomenon. It is essential to retain gross and operating profit margins. Actions to maintain margins are subject to government controls (a typical African situation is where governments use price or selective price controls rather than rooting out the underlying causes of inflation or foreign exchange shortages), competitive behaviour and the market itself. Price adjustments may affect the demand for products, and this is the ultimate arbiter of price alterations.

Transfer Pricing

Transfer pricing is more appropriate to those organisations with decentralised profit centres. Transfer pricing is used to motivate profit centre managers, provide divisional flexibility and also further corporate profit goals. Across national boundaries the system gets complicated by taxes, joint ventures, attitudes of governments and so on. There are four basic approaches to transfer pricing.

- Transfer at cost: few practise this, which recognises foreign affiliates contribute to profitability by operating domestic scale economies. Prices may be unrealistic so this method is seldom used.
- Transfer at direct cost plus overheads and margin. Similar to that in transfer at cost.
- Transfer at a price derived from end market prices: very useful strategy in which market based transfer prices and foreign sourcing are used as devices to enter markets too small for supporting local manufacturers. This gives a valuable foothold.
- Transfer at an "arm's length": this is the price that would have been reached by unrelated parties in a similar transaction. The problem is identifying a point "arm's length" price for all products other than commodities. Pricing at "arm's length" for differentiated products results not in a specific price but prices which fall in a predeterminable range.

Many governments see transfer pricing as a tax evasion policy and have, in recent years, looked more closely at company returns. Rates of duty encourage the size of the transfer price: the higher the duty rate the more desirable a lower transfer price. A low income tax creates a pressure to raise the transfer price to locate income in the low tax setting. Harmonisation of tax rates worldwide may make the intricacies of transfer pricing obsolete.

Government controls, like cash deposits on importers, give an incentive to minimise the price of the imported item. Profit transfer rules may apply which restrict the amount of profit transferred out of the country. Other controls look at monopoly pricing like the case of the British Government against Hoffman-La Roche, forcing the price of its tranquilisers downwards.

Joint Ventures

These present an incentive to transfer price goods at a higher rate than one that would have been used in transfer pricing goods to their own wholly owned affiliates because the company's share of the joint venture earnings is less than 100 percent. It is important, therefore, to work out an agreement in advance. The tax authorities' criteria of "arm's length" prices is probably the most appropriate for joint ventures.

Global Pricing

There are three possible global pricing policies - extension (ethnocentric), adaptation (polycentric) and invention (geocentric).

Extension

The same global price. A very simple method but does not respond to market sensitivity.

Adaptation

Different prices in different markets. The only control is setting transfer prices within the corporate system. It prevents problems of arbitrage when the disparities in local market prices exceed the transportation and duty costs separating markets.

Innovation

A mix of a) and b). This takes cognisance of any unique market factor (s) like costs, competition, income levels and local marketing strategy. In addition it recognises the fact that headquarters price coordination is necessary in dealing with international accounts and arbitrage and it systematically seeks to embrace national experience.

Financing of Exports

Financing exports is a major decision area and one of some considerable complexity. Sources of funds can be both internal and external to the organisation. Internal sources include subsidiaries and transfer within groups. External sources include the international money markets, factoring, leasing, hire purchase export credit guarantee schemes etc. A discussion on sources of funds is appropriate in a chapter on pricing as it is a "cost" which affects the end price and must be accounted for in selling prices.

Internal Sources

The subsidiary: Self-funding obviates the need for currency transfers and avoids exchange rate fluctuations. It also lessens the burden on the parent company. The major problem may be the lack of sufficient funding which requires parent contribution.

Transfers within group: May take the form of loans, investment capital, material and/or licences. Remittances back in interest, dividends, etc. will depend on tax liability operating in the host country. Whilst transfers are a greater risk than internal subsidiary funding they are more flexible in dates of payment, direction (one subsidiary to another) and type and scale.

External Sources

Host country borrowing: Offers two advantages. Firstly it reduces the loss if expropriation occurs and secondly, interest payments raised locally can be paid out of revenues, leaving only excesses for exposure to transfer risk.

Export credit schemes and pre and post-shipment support facility: Zimbabwe does not have guarantee facility. Malawi is in the process of setting one up, so the schemes available are described in the following sections.

Export credit guarantee facility: The export credit guarantee (ECG) facility contributes to the growth and diversification of an export base by providing collateral support through guarantees to the banks extending pre- or post-shipment financing to enterprises for non-traditional export production and sales. The facility will help such exporters to secure financing and the facility will increase confidence among foreign buyers that exporters can fulfill their contractual commitments as reliable suppliers.

The facility is expected to be financially self-supporting in the long run, which means that the guarantee fee income will have to cover administration costs and claim payments. In order to fulfill its export development function, however, certain risks and guarantee losses will be inevitable and will have to be accepted. Malawi's facility serves as an example of an ECG scheme.

Going Private Transactions and Leveraged Buyouts

Definition of 'Going Private'

A transaction or a series of transactions that convert a publicly traded company into a private entity. Once a company goes private, its shareholders are no longer able to trade their stocks in the open market. Private equity firms will typically purchase a struggling company, make it into a private entity, reorganise its capital structure, and issue stocks once a profit can be realised.

Definition of Leveraged Buyout

A leveraged buyout (LBO) is an acquisition (usually of a company, but it can also be single assets like a real estate) where the purchase price is financed through a combination of equity and debt, and in which the cash flows or assets of the target are used to secure and repay the debt . As the debt usually has a lower cost of capital than the equity, the returns on the equity increase with the increasing debt. The debt thus effectively serves as a lever to increase returns, which explains the origin of the term leveraged buyout (LBO).

LBOs are a very common occurrence in today's Mergers and Aquisitions environment. The term LBO is usually employed when a financial sponsor acquires a company. However, many corporate transactions are part-funded by bank debt, and thus also effectively representing an LBO. LBOs can have many different forms, such as Management Buyout (MBO), Management Buy-in (MBI), and secondary buyout and tertiary buyout, among others. They can occur in growth situations, restructuring situations, and insolvencies just like in companies with stable performance. LBOs mostly occur in private companies, but can also be employed with public companies (in a so-called PtP transaction, Public to Private).

Common Cause of LBOs

As financial sponsors increase their returns by employing a very high leverage (i.e., a high ratio of debt to equity), they have an incentive to employ as much debt as possible to finance an acquisition. This has, in many cases, led to situations in which companies were "overleveraged", meaning that they did not generate sufficient cash flows to service their debt. In turn, this then led to insolvency or to debt-to-equity swaps, in which the equity owners lose control over the business and the debt providers assume the equity.

Characteristics

LBOs have become attractive, as they usually represent a win-win situation for the financial sponsor and the banks: The financial sponsor can increase the returns on his equity by employing the leverage; banks can make substantially higher margins when supporting the financing of LBOs as compared to usual corporate lending. The amount of debt banks which are willing to provide and support an LBO varies greatly and depends on the quality of the asset to be acquired—stability of cash flows, history, growth prospects, and hard assets; the amount of equity supplied by the financial sponsor; and the history and experience of the financial sponsor.

Debt Ratio

For companies with very stable and secured cash flows, debt volumes of up to 100% of the purchase price have been provided. In situations of "normal" companies with normal business risks, debt of 40–60% of the purchase price are normal figures. The debt ratios that are possible also vary significantly between the regions and industries of the target. Depending on the size and purchase price of the acquisition, the debt is provided in different tranches:

- Senior debt: This debt is secured with the assets of the target company and has the lowest interest margin
- Junior debt: This debt usually has no securities and bears a higher interest margin

Going Private and Leveraged Buyouts

Going-private transactions and leveraged buyouts have much in common with mergers, and it is worthwhile to discuss them in this chapter. A publicly traded firm *goes private* when a private group, usually composed of existing management, purchases its stock. As a consequence, the firm's stock is taken off the market (if it is an exchange-traded stock, it is delisted) and is no longer traded. Thus, in going-private transactions, shareholders of publicly held firms are forced to accept cash for their shares.

Going-private transactions are frequently *leveraged buyouts* (LBOs). In a leveraged buyout the cash offer price is financed with large amounts of debt. Part of the appeal of LBOs is that the arrangement calls for little equity capital. This equity capital is generally supplied by a small group of investors, some of whom are likely to be managers of the firm being purchased.

The selling stockholders are invariably paid a premium above market price in an LBO, just as in a merger. As with a merger, the acquirer profits only if the synergy created is greater than the premium. Synergy is quite plausible in a merger of *two* firms, and we delineated a number of types of synergy earlier in the chapter. However, it is more difficult to explain synergy in an LBO because only *one* firm is involved.

Two reasons are generally given for value creation in an LBO. First, the extra debt provides a tax deduction, which, as earlier chapters suggested, leads to an increase in firm value. Most LBOs centre around firms with stable earnings and with low to moderate debt. The LBO may simply increase the firm's debt to its optimum level.

The second source of value comes from increased efficiency and is often explained in terms of "the carrot and the stick." Managers become owners under an LBO, giving them an incentive to work hard. This incentive is commonly referred to as the carrot, and the carrots in some LBOs have been huge. For example, consider the LBO of Gibson Greeting Cards (GGC), previously a division of RCA, for which the management buyout group paid about $80 million. Because of the leveraged nature of the transaction, the group invested only about $1 million of its own capital. The division was taken private in 1982, but only for a brief period; GGC went public as its own company in 1984. The value of the initial public offering (IPO) was almost $300 million. One of the principals in the buyout group, William Simon, who was a former secretary of the U.S. Treasury, received $66 million from the IPO on an investment of somewhat under $350,000.

Interest payments from the high level of debt constitute the stick. Large interest payments can easily turn a profitable firm before an LBO into an unprofitable one after the LBO. Management must make changes, either through revenue increases or cost reductions, to keep the firm in the black. Agency theory, a topic mentioned earlier in this chapter, suggests that managers can be wasteful with a large free cash flow. Interest payments reduce this cash flow, forcing managers to curb the waste.

Though it is easy to measure the additional tax shields from an LBO, it is difficult to measure the gains from increased efficiency. Nevertheless, this increased efficiency is considered at least as important as the tax shield in explaining the LBO phenomenon.

Academic research suggests that LBOs have, on average, created value. First, premiums are positive, as they are with mergers, implying that selling stockholders benefit. Second, studies indicate that LBOs that eventually go public generate high returns for the management group. Finally, other studies show that operating performance increases after the LBO. However, we cannot be completely confident of value creation because researchers have difficulty obtaining data about LBOs that do not go public. If these LBOs generally destroy value, the sample of firms going public would be a biased one. Regardless of the average performance of firms undertaking an LBO, we can be sure of one thing: Because of the great leverage involved, the risk is huge.

Going Private and Leveraged Buyouts

Going-private transactions and leveraged buyouts have much in common with mergers, and it is worth while to discuss them in this chapter. A publicly traded firm *goes private* when a private group, usually composed of existing management, purchases its equity. As a consequence, the firm's equity is taken off the market (if it is an exchange-traded equity, it is delisted) and is no longer traded. Thus, in going-private transactions, shareholders of publicly held firms are forced to accept cash for their shares.

Going-private transactions are frequently *leveraged buyouts* (LBOs). In a leveraged buyout the cash offer price is financed with large amounts of debt. Part of the appeal of LBOs is that the arrangement calls for little equity capital. This equity capital is generally supplied by a small group of investors, some of whom are likely to be managers of the firm being purchased.

The selling shareholders are invariably paid a premium above market price in an LBO, just as in a merger. As with a merger, the acquirer profits only if the synergy created is greater than the premium. Synergy is quite plausible in a merger of *two* firms, and we delineated a number of types of synergy earlier in the chapter. However, it is more difficult to explain synergy in an LBO because only *one* firm is involved.

Two reasons are generally given for value creation in an LBO. First, the extra debt provides a tax deduction, which, as earlier chapters suggested, leads to an increase in firm value. Most LBOs are on firms with stable earnings and with low to moderate debt. The LBO may simply increase the firm's debt to its optimum level.

The second source of value comes from increased efficiency, and is often explained in terms of 'the carrot and the stick'. Managers become owners under an LBO, giving them an incentive to work hard. This incentive is commonly referred to as the carrot. Interest payments from the high level of debt constitute the stick. Large interest payments can easily turn a profitable firm before an LBO into an unprofitable one after the LBO. Management must make changes, either through revenue increases or through cost reductions, to keep the firm in the black. Agency theory, a topic mentioned earlier in this chapter, suggests that managers can be wasteful with a large free cash flow. Interest payments reduce this cash flow, forcing managers to curb the waste.

Though it is easy to measure the additional tax shields from an LBO, it is difficult to measure the gains from increased efficiency. Nevertheless, this increased efficiency is considered at least as important as the tax shield in explaining the LBO phenomenon.

Academic research suggests that LBOs have, on average, created value. First, premiums are positive, as they are with mergers, implying that selling shareholders benefit. Second, studies indicate that LBOs that eventually go public generate high returns for the management group. Finally, other studies show that operating performance increases after the LBO. However, we cannot be completely confident of value creation, because researchers have difficulty obtaining data about LBOs that do not go public. If these LBOs generally destroy value, the sample of firms going public would be a biased one.

Regardless of the average performance of firms undertaking an LBO, we can be sure of one thing: because of the great leverage involved, the risk is huge. On the one hand, LBOs have created many large fortunes. On the other hand, a number of bankruptcies and near-bankruptcies have occurred as well.

Takeovers and Leveraged Buyouts

Corporate takeovers became a prominent feature of the American business landscape during the seventies and eighties. A hostile takeover usually involves a public tender offer—a public offer of a specific price, usually at a substantial premium over the prevailing market price, good for a limited period, for a substantial percentage of the target firm's stock. Unlike a merger, which requires the approval of the target firm's board of directors as well as voting approval of the stockholders, a tender offer can provide voting control to the bidding firm without the approval of the target's management and directors.

Because it allows bidders to seek control directly from shareholders—by going "over the heads" of target management—the tender offer is the most powerful weapon available to the hostile bidder. Indeed, just the threat of a hostile tender offer can often bring a recalcitrant target management to the bargaining table, especially if the bidder already owns a substantial block of the target's stock (called a foothold block) and can demonstrably afford to finance a hostile offer for control. Although hostile bidders still need a formal merger to gain total control of the target's assets, this is easily accomplished once the bidder has purchased a majority of voting stock.

Hostile tender offers have been around for decades, but they were rare and generally involved small target firms until the mid-seventies. Then came the highly controversial multibillion dollar hostile takeovers of very recognisable public companies. By the late eighties there were dozens of multi-billion-dollar takeovers and their cousins, leveraged buyouts (LBOs). The largest acquisition ever was the $25 billion buyout of RJR Nabisco by Kolberg Kravis and Roberts in 1989.

Leveraged buyouts of small companies had also been common for decades, but in the eighties LBOs of large public companies became common. An LBO is a going-private transaction involving a tender offer for all of a firm's common stock, financed mostly by debt, made by a group usually involving some members of incumbent management. LBOs and leveraged cash-outs (first cousins of LBOs in which the target firm remains public because a small part of the compensation to selling shareholders is stock in the new, highly leveraged enterprise) rose to popularity for large public firms in the late eighties as a reaction to the hostile takeover activity. In essence the LBO was a way for management of a vulnerable public company to beat the hostile bidder to the punch, allowing management to buy out public shareholders at a premium and engage in the value-enhancing asset redeployments that otherwise would attract takeover entrepreneurs.

The vulnerability arises from a large "value gap"—which is the difference between a company's value as a going concern under the policies of incumbent management and the expected higher value of the stock, factoring in the value of redeploying the target's assets. Incumbent managements learned to tap the vast financial muscle of Wall Street in the late eighties and to engage in these control transactions to avoid being the victims of hostile attack. Indeed, many of the large leveraged restructurings were taken in direct defence after a hostile bid had been made.

Both economic and regulatory factors combined to spur the explosion in large takeovers and, in turn, large LBOs. The three regulatory factors were the Reagan administration's relatively laissez-faire policies on antitrust and securities laws, which allowed mergers the government would have challenged in earlier years; the 1982 Supreme Court decision striking down state antitakeover laws (which were resurrected with great effectiveness in the late eighties); and deregulation of many industries, which prompted restructurings and mergers. The main economic factor was the development of the original-issue high-yield debt instrument. The so-called "junk bond" innovation, pioneered by Michael Milken of Drexel Burnham, provided many hostile bidders and LBO firms with the enormous amounts of capital needed to finance multi-billion-dollar deals.

Managers of target companies in takeover battles have access to a variety of defencive tactics, many invented during the turbulent eighties. These defencive measures have always been controversial because they necessarily pose a conflict of interest for management. A top manager's own narrow interest is to save his job, which he often loses after a takeover. His legal obligation is to get a good deal for shareholders, which often means allowing the takeover. Not surprisingly, some managers go with self-interest.

The array of takeover defences includes charter amendments that require supermajorities (i.e., votes of 70 percent or even 80 percent of shareholders) to approve a merger; dual-class restructurings that, by creating two classes of stock, concentrate voting control with management; litigation against the hostile suitor (usually alleging violations of antitrust and securities laws); and purchasing the hostile bidder's foothold stock at a premium to end the takeover threat (so-called green-mail payments). Although these particular defences often are effective at delaying the hostile bidder, they rarely are enough to keep a target company independent. The two modern-day defencive weapons that can be "show-stoppers" are the poison pill and the state takeover laws.

The term "poison pill" describes a family of "shareholder rights" that are triggered by an event such as a hostile tender offer or the accumulation of voting stock above a designated threshold (usually 15 percent of outstanding stock) by an unfriendly buyer. When triggered, poison pills provide target shareholders (other than the hostile bidder) with rights to purchase additional shares or to sell shares to the target on very attractive terms. These rights impose severe economic penalties on the hostile acquirer and usually also dilute the voting power of the acquirer's existing stake in the firm.

Although poison pills are considered to be absolute deterrents to a hostile takeover, they can almost always be cheaply and quickly altered or removed by target management if they have not been irrevocably triggered. Therefore, they almost always are the subject of strenuous state-court litigation in takeover battles, and their practical effectiveness as an absolute deterrent has been decided in court more often than not. Today, the majority of large public companies are armed with poison pills of one type or another. State courts have allowed target managers to use pills to buy time (up to several months) to search for better third-party offers or develop value-creating corporate restructurings.

In the late eighties the Supreme Court upheld the constitutionality of state takeover laws, the most important being Delaware's merger moratorium law. This law prohibits a hostile acquirer from formally merging with the target for at least three years after buying a controlling interest. Widely regarded as a major deterrent, the Delaware law has an exception if the hostile bidder can acquire more than 85 percent of the target's stock, excluding shares held by inside managers and by certain kinds of employee stock-ownership plans. Since the law passed, Delaware-incorporated companies (which account for the majority of medium-size and large public companies in the United States) have engaged in various kinds of transactions to "lock up" more than 15 percent of stock in friendly hands, rendering these companies "bullet-proof" under Delaware law.

State antitakeover laws and the poison pill have dramatically reduced the scope for hostile tender offers in the U.S. market. Both defencive barriers can be overcome only by getting the target board of directors to approve the takeover. Therefore, hostile takeover activity has been moved directly into the boardroom, through the increasing use of proxy fights in conjunction with tender offers that are conditional on the bidder gaining control of the board or approval from the incumbent board. This hybrid proxy/tender offer approach is considerably more expensive, time-consuming, and risky than the hostile tender offer of the eighties. Consequently, hostile takeover activity has declined sharply, and the campaigns that have been waged were long, drawn-out proxy battles.

Was all this takeover and LBO activity good for the economy? The issue stirs strong emotions on both sides, but I believe the evidence shows that takeovers and buyouts are a good thing. Many published studies have documented the effects of tender offers and mergers on stock prices. The consensus is that these transactions confer large stock-price gains on target shareholders, averaging about 30 to 50 percent over preoffer prices during the eighties. The evidence on returns to bidders, however, is mixed. During the period from 1960 to 1980, the average stock-price gain to bidding firms was 3 to 5 percent. But during the eighties the returns to bidders began to erode, and some studies conclude that bidder firms suffered modest stock-price declines, on average, during the late eighties.

The principal reason for this erosion is the increased competition for targets. This increase in competition resulted from the target's greater effectiveness at dealing with the initial suitor and at getting rival bids, including bids from the targets' own management. The winning bidders in these auction contests of the late eighties frequently paid top dollar and saw their stock prices decline when the market learned that they had "won."

Nonetheless, the huge gains to target shareholders mean that takeovers and socalled highly leveraged transactions (HLTs) have created large net economic gains. Indeed, Harvard's Michael Jensen estimates that over the fourteen-year period from 1976 to 1990, the $1.8 trillion of tender offers, mergers, divestitures, and LBOs created over $650 billion in value for selling-firm shareholders. Moreover, this estimate does not include the additional large gains made by companies that restructured out of fear of being taken over.

Although this estimate excludes the gains and losses to shareholders of bidding firms, the empirical studies that find net losses for bidders also show that these losses—at 1 to 3 percent of the stock price—are minuscule compared with the enormous gains to target shareholders. These academic studies show clearly, on the basis of share prices, that hostile takeovers and highly leveraged transactions created huge increases in the values of companies. Moreover, several follow-up studies have shown that these stock-price gains are generally reliable predictors of real operating improvements and of increased corporate efficiency.

Critics of takeovers often complain that these share-price gains ignore the economic losses that takeovers and LBOs impose on other groups connected with the target firms. This intense debate has centred on the potential harm to corporate "stakeholders" other than shareholders, such as bondholders, employees, customers, suppliers, local communities, and taxpayers. Many takeovers in the airline industry, for example, have involved conflict between acquiring-firm management and the unionized labour of the target firm. These conflicts contributed to the popular view, shared by some economists, that shareholder premiums from takeovers come largely at the expense of labour's wages and benefits.

But the empirical research has failed to show any reliable association between takeover activity and the income of workers. According to Joshua Rosett's recent study of over five thousand union contracts in over a thousand listed companies from 1973 to 1987, less than 2 percent of the premiums to shareholders can be attributed to wage reductions in the first six years following takeovers. In hostile takeovers the data show an *increase* in union wages in years following the control changes.

Another frequent complaint is that the constant threat of hostile takeovers forces nearly all corporate managers to stress short-term policies at the expense of more valuable long-term plans, thereby impairing the economic health and competitive vigor of their companies and the nation. Although rhetorically stirring, this theory has been studied thoroughly by economists and has received no empirical support. For example, the research shows no connection between takeover activity and public companies' expenditures on research and development. Studies also show that share prices generally respond positively to long-term investments by corporations. Also unsupported is the charge that losses to bondholders finance the shareholder gains from takeovers. Although some shareholder gains have come at the expense of bondholders, banks, and other creditors who financed these deals, Michael Jensen estimates that the aggregate amount of these losses between 1976 and 1990 is not likely to exceed $50 billion, a small fraction of the $650 billion gain to target shareholders.

There is some empirical basis for the idea that reducing taxes was at least a partial motive for takeovers, and especially LBOs. Some researchers estimate that for the typical leveraged buyout, tax savings (from deducting higher interest payments) accounted for about 15 percent of the premiums paid to sellers. Still, most mergers and tender offers were not motivated by tax savings. Also, Jensen has found that, contrary to popular assertion, LBOs have actually increased total tax payments to the U.S. Treasury. That is because selling shareholders pay taxes on their gains. All in all, the evidence shows that tax savings account for only a small fraction, at most, of the huge gains to target shareholders and other selling firms.

In sum, although some individuals (incumbent management, for example) and some other groups obviously lose in any takeover, the empirical studies offer little or no support for the notion that the huge gains to shareholders reflect similarly large losses to other related parties. These zero-sum theories cannot begin to explain the large shareholder returns. The bottom line is that, on average, takeovers reflect wealth-enhancing and socially valuable redeployments of corporate resources.

Although several of these late-eighties LBOs and leveraged cash-outs ran into financial difficulties when the U.S. economy suffered a recession in the early eighties, there is much evidence that the LBO phenomenon also has been beneficial for our economy. Economists have found that the "free cash-flow" theory (developed by Michael Jensen) helps them to understand much of this activity. This theory postulates that high leverage can be a powerful disciplining device because it forces top management to undertake value-enhancing strategic changes. Companies with ample cash flow but few potentially profitable investment projects should pay out the excess cash to shareholders to maximize shareholder value.

According to this theory managements that fail to pay out excess cash, instead investing it in diversifying acquisitions or in low pay-off projects, will cause the stock price of their companies to be below their optimal value, creating a value gap. LBOs and other leveraged recapitalizations force managements to sell unprofitable divisions, avoid low pay-off investments, eliminate wasteful corporate expenses and diversifying acquisitions, and boost operating efficiency in order to meet the interest charges on the high level of debt. These forced efficiencies eliminate the value gap and create net economic gains for shareholders. Although this is a severe solution that exposes the firm to financial distress in the few years after the LBO, the evidence is that the LBOs and leveraged restructurings of the eighties created large net gains for shareholders.

In short, the U.S. market for corporate control witnessed unprecedented activity and change during the eighties as the largest public companies became frequent targets of hostile takeovers. Corporate managers reacted to this activity by lobbying hard for legal restrictions on the so-called raiders, and by restructuring and refocusing their companies while increasing debt levels and shareholder payouts.

Leveraged Buyouts and Private Equity Law - Overview

Unlike public equity securities, which are traded on a stock exchange, private equity (PE) consists of investments made directly into companies by private retail or institutional investors. There are many different types of investors, which employ different strategies depending upon their goals.

For example, one type of investor, the specialised PE firm or fund, might invest in a company by initiating a leveraged buyout, thereby obtaining majority control of the company for purposes of a turnaround, bringing in new management and possibly an eventual sale. This type of investment is usually made into more established companies, either private or public—although a buyout of a public company, usually accomplished by several PE firms pooling their funds together, will result in a delisting.

Another type of investor, the venture capitalist or angel investor, tends to focus more on smaller, emerging companies. These investors provide money to help the company grow and operate, or fund technological research or development, for a certain return, but they rarely take over majority control. Distressed investments, in which PE funds purchase debt that is trading at only a percentage of its real value with the goal of reselling those securities for a profit, and mezzanine capital, which is a more expensive source of financing due to its unsecured and more junior status in terms of repayment rights, are two other common strategies also commonly employed in PE.

Private Equity is usually a subset of the a law firm's Corporate Department. Representative clients might include PE funds, PE divisions of financial institutions, and venture capital investors or portfolio companies. PE attorneys may assist these clients with initiatives such as start-up ventures (venture capital), early stage venture capital investments, acquisitions of public as well as private companies, asset acquisitions, growth capital transactions, management buyouts, recapitalizations, going-private transactions, leveraged acquisitions, "turnaround" or "vulture" investments, and purchases and sales of companies and divisions in Chapter 11 bankruptcy proceedings.

A well-rounded PE group can assist clients with all phases of their investments, including formulating bids in auction situations and in their initial investment and financing, as well as refinancings, restructurings, recapitalizations and add-on acquisitions, and in designing exit strategies and liquidity events (including initial public offerings and business sales). PE lawyers can also assist their corporate clients with structuring and negotiating the various layers of senior and subordinated debt and equity financing typically utilised in connection with leveraged acquisitions, including registered and Rule 144A high-yield debt offerings, private placements of senior and subordinated debt, secured and unsecured bank financing and various forms of seller financing.

A History of Leveraged Buyouts

Leveraged buyout (LBO) funds arose as an investment vehicle in the 1980's as a result of several market condition factors. First, there was a high level of accessible capital in the markets. In addition, there were a large number of investors who were beginning to seek various alternative investments in the early stages of growth of various companies. At the same time, financial professionals were beginning to recognise that management was becoming haphazard in the operation of large companies and that in some cases, firms had been engaging in gross excess – wasting corporate assets for their own personal entertainment or benefit.

In such an environment, it was inevitable that the markets would react to help put companies back on track. At the same time, of course, these market participants hoped to put some money into their own pockets. However, what was unexpected was that in certain instances, the cure, that came in the form of LBO (then known as private equity) investors, was worse than the disease.

Given the then existing market conditions, small groups of investors began organising pools of capital in much the same manner that was discussed previously in the section on venture capital funds. Pension funds, state benefits plans, insurance companies, high-net worth individuals, etc., began to invest in these first LBO funds that promised extremely high returns.

Initially, as funds began making investments – purchasing companies and taking them private – the results were strong. In several instances, LBO funds were able to take positions at such low valuations, and turn the companies around quickly for resale. In such cases, huge profits were made on investments that lasted for mere months. Throughout the 1980's, as competition in the field began to increase, profits for the LBO industry began to decrease as more players entered the field and bid up prices for companies to levels that could not support a profitable model.

Ultimately, the 1990's saw a decline in LBO activity, though many funds remain very active. In the modern economic climate, LBO funds have adjusted their operations, often entering into transactions that look more like venture capital investments or more standard corporate acquisitions. Whether the model will continue to operate into the future is a question that remains unanswered.

Operation of an LBO Fund

Like venture capital funds, LBO funds operate as Limited Liability Partnerships. The reasons for this are identical to the reasons why LLP's were created in the first place. Namely, the LLP provides a vehicle whereby the LBO fund's management may achieve their objectives without exposing their investors to heightened liability. Moreover, the management may operate the fund with the knowledge that the investors are not going to become overly involved in the operation of the fund because acting in such a manner would expose them to liability as "presumed" general partners.

Process of an LBO Transaction

LBO transactions are typically very complicated affairs. The method of the transaction – typically a purchase of a controlling share of the company's stock, or on occasion, a proxy contest – is straight forward. However, it is the size of the transaction that an LBO fund undertakes that makes such deals exceedingly complicated.

Essentially, the process of an LBO investment is as follows. First, the investment fund identifies a target for acquisition. Typically, LBO funds look for companies that have weak management or management that has allowed the company's assets to dwindle at the shareholders' expense. Additionally, LBO managers look for situations where a company has a large cash account, readily saleable assets, and a large public float.

After identifying a target company, the LBO fund will typically begin acquiring the company's stock up to near the level requiring a 13-D disclosure or up to near the level that would trigger the company's poison pill (if there is one). Once that point is reached, it is inevitable that the fund's goal to acquire the company will become public knowledge. As such, the fund typically will want to be in a situation where it can approach management (if it has not already done so – most funds usually try negotiations first) and discuss the nature of the transaction.

If management is not amenable to the transaction, then the standard rules of engagement for a hostile takeover, which were discussed previously, are triggered, and the firm will begin maneuvering to avoid being taken over. However, if management is agreeable, and many LBO funds will only work with a firm where management agrees to go along with the takeover, then the fund and the firm will begin structuring a deal.

An alternative name for a textbook LBO transaction is a "going private" transaction. This name may help to clarify the actual LBO process. The LBO fund will acquire shares of the company by borrowing extensively against the company's assets. With those borrowed funds, the fund and the company begin purchasing the company's shares from other shareholders. Ultimately, the goal of the transaction is to acquire a controlling stake in the company and then make a distribution to the shareholders of the LBO fund that allows the fund to purchase all remaining outstanding shares and give the fund complete control over the firm.

Once the fund has control over the firm, two things happen. First, the remaining shareholders are bought out of the company; turning the once public company into a private, closely held firm. Finally, the firm, now controlled by elements of the management and members of the LBO fund, begins to reorganise. The reorganisation is accomplished by the new management team's selling off corporate assets to pay down the debt – the leverage money – as quickly as possible. In addition, the team will also begin streamlining the company's operating procedures and overhead by reducing the number of employees and/or making other alterations to the company by redeploying personnel and by generally improving the firm's operations.

However, the ultimate goal of an LBO transaction is not to keep the company in a private, stand alone condition. While such a situation may produce strong operating cash flows, the return would not be great enough to justify the risk that the fund took in making the investment.

In the end, what the fund will attempt to do is to get the firm to a point where it is either able to sell the firm at a rate much higher than its original investment, or to retake the firm public at a raised valuation after it has improved the firm's economic state.

Leveraged Buyouts

The term leveraged buyout (LBO) describes an acquisition or purchase of a company financed through substantial use of borrowed funds or debt. In fact, in a typical LBO, up to 90 percent of the purchase price may be funded with debt. During the 1980s, LBOs became very common and increased substantially in size, so that they normally occurred in large companies with more than $100 million in annual revenues. But many of these deals subsequently failed due to the low quality of debt used, and thus the movement in the 1990s was toward smaller deals (featuring small- to medium-sized companies, with about $20 million in annual revenues) using less leverage. Thanks to low stock prices, looser regulatory restrictions, and a rally in high-yield bonds, *Barron's* predicted that 2001 would be the biggest year since the 1980s for LBOs.

The most common leveraged buyout arrangement among small businesses is for management to buy up all the outstanding shares of the company's stock, using company assets as collateral for a loan to fund the purchase. The loan is later repaid through the company's future cash flow or the sale of company assets. A management-led LBO is sometimes referred to as "going private," because in contrast to "going public"—or selling shares of stock to the public—LBOs involve gathering all the outstanding shares into private hands. Subsequently, once the debt is paid down, the organisers of the buyout may attempt to take the firm public again. Many management-led, small business LBOs also include employees of the company in the purchase, which may help increase productivity and increase employee commitment to the company's goals. In other cases, LBOs are orchestrated by individual or institutional investors, or by another company.

According to Jennifer Lindsey in her book *The Entrepreneur's Guide to Capital,* the best candidate for a successful LBO will be in growing industry, have hard assets to act as collateral for large loans, and feature top-quality, entrepreneurial management talent. It is also vital that the LBO candidate post a strong historical cash flow and have low capital requirements, because the debt resulting from the LBO must be retired as quickly as possible. Ideally, the company should have at least twice as much cash flow as will be required for payments on the proposed debt. The LBO debt should be reduced to 50 percent of overall capitalization within one year, and should be completely repaid within five to seven years. Other factors improving the chances for a successful LBO include a strong market position and an established, unconcentrated customer base.

In order to improve the chances of success for an LBO, Lindsey noted that the deal should be undertaken when interest rates are low and the inflation rate is high (which will make assets more valuable). It is also vital that a management, employee, or outside investment group wants to own and control the company. Many LBOs involving small businesses take place because the owner wants to cash out or retire and does not want to sell to a larger company. LBOs can be very costly for the acquiring parties, with expenses including attorney fees, accounting evaluations, the printing of prospectus and proxy statements, and interest payments.

In addition, if either the buyer or the seller is a public company, an LBO will involve strict disclosure and reporting requirements with both federal and state government agencies. Possible alternatives to an LBO include purchase of the company by employees through an Employee Stock Ownership Plan (ESOP), or a merger with a compatible company.

Advantages and Disadvantages

A successful LBO can provide a small business with a number of advantages. For one thing, it can increase management commitment and effort because they have greater equity stake in the company. In a publicly traded company, managers typically own only a small percentage of the common shares, and therefore can participate in only a small fraction of the gains resulting from improved managerial performance. After an LBO, however, executives can realise substantial financial gains from enhanced performance. This improvement in financial incentives for the firm's managers should result in greater effort on the part of management. Similarly, when employees are involved in an LBO, their increased stake in the company's success tends to improve their productivity and loyalty. Another potential advantage is that LBOs can often act to revitalize a mature company. In addition, by increasing the company's capitalization, an LBO may enable it to improve its market position.

Successful LBOs also tend to create value for a variety of parties. For example, empirical studies indicate that the firms' shareholders can earn large positive abnormal returns from leveraged buyouts.

Similarly, the post-buyout investors in these transactions often earn large excess returns over the period from the buyout completion date to the date of an initial public offering or resale. Some of the potential sources of value in leveraged buyout transactions include:

1) wealth transfers from old public shareholders to the buyout group;
2) wealth transfers from public bondholders to the investor group;
3) wealth creation from improved incentives for managerial decision making; and
4) wealth transfers from the government via tax advantages.

The increased levels of debt that the new company supports after the LBO decrease taxable income, leading to lower tax payments. Therefore, the interest tax shield resulting from the higher levels of debt should enhance the value of firm. Moreover, these motivations for leveraged buyout transactions are not mutually exclusive; it is possible that a combination of these may occur in a given LBO.

Not all LBOs are successful, however, so there are also some potential disadvantages to consider. If the company's cash flow and the sale of assets are insufficient to meet the interest payments arising from its high levels of debt, the LBO is likely to fail and the company may go bankrupt. Attempting an LBO can be particularly dangerous for companies that are vulnerable to industry competition or volatility in the overall economy.

If the company does fail following an LBO, this can cause significant problems for employees and suppliers, as lenders are usually in a better position to collect their money. Another disadvantage is that paying high interest rates on LBO debt can damage a company's credit rating. Finally, it is possible that management may propose an LBO only for short-term personal profit.

Criticism of LBOS

Ever since the LBO craze of the 1980s—led by high-profile corporate raiders who financed takeovers with low-quality debt and then sold off pieces of the acquired companies for their own profit—LBOs have garnered negative publicity. Critics of leveraged buyouts argue that these transactions harm the long-term competitiveness of firms involved. First, these firms are unlikely to have replaced operating assets since their cash flow must be devoted to servicing the LBO-related debt. Thus, the property, plant, and equipment of LBO firms are likely to have aged considerably during the time when the firm is privately held. In addition, expenditures for repair and maintenance may have been curtailed as well. Finally, it is possible that research and development expenditures have also been controlled. As a result, the future growth prospects of these firms may be significantly reduced.

Others argue that LBO transactions have a negative impact on the stakeholders of the firm. In many cases, LBOs lead to downsizing of operations, and employees may lose their jobs. In addition, some of the transactions have negative effects on the communities in which the firms are located.

Much of the controversy regarding LBOs has resulted from the concern that senior executives negotiating the sale of the company to themselves are engaged in self-dealing. On one hand, the managers have a fiduciary duty to their shareholders to sell the company at the highest possible price. On the other hand, they have an incentive to minimize what they pay for the shares. Accordingly, it has been suggested that management takes advantage of superior information about a firm's intrinsic value. The evidence, however, indicates that the premiums paid in leveraged buyouts compare favourably with those in inter-firm mergers that are characterized by arm's-length negotiations between the buyer and seller.

Chapter 7

Global Deal Making

Deals are getting done differently as economies connect and bring the world closer together.

Global Deal-Making Scene

The increasing clout of state-owned oil companies, fuelled by their willingness to venture beyond their borders, has increased competition in the global energy deal-making space while adding in geopolitical variables that can make it harder to get deals done, energy attorneys say.

In 2014, state-owned oil companies outnumbered investor-owned companies on Energy Intelligence's list of the top 10 oil and gas concerns in the world for the first time in a decade. Some of the names are familiar, like Saudi Arabia's Saudi Aramco, but also include relative upstarts such as China's China National Petroleum Corp. and Russia's OAO Rosneft and OAO Gazprom.

> *"It's not a passing phenomenon," said Jay Cuclis, who co-chairs Vinson & Elkins LLP's energy transactions and projects practice group and splits his time between the U.S. and Hong Kong. "You have to expect that all the national oil companies are going to remain major players."*

Energy Intelligence's rankings consider several factors, including size of oil and gas reserves and production. In that sense, it's not surprising that state-owned firms like Saudi Aramco and Rosneft, located in oil-rich countries, are among the world's most influential, according to Akin Gump Strauss Hauer & Feld LLP partner Steve Davis.

However, China isn't a major oil and gas producer, yet thanks to the country's voracious appetite for energy, companies like CNPC and China Petroleum & Chemical Corp., better known as Sinopec, have become global oil and gas forces.

"What you've seen is many of the consumer national oil companies have gone outside of their boundaries and have begun acquiring oil and gas reserves in other parts of the world, and in that part of their business, they are competing directly with international oil companies, as well as competing with other consumer national oil companies," said Davis, who's worked extensively in Asia and has represented state-owned GAIL (India) Ltd. in securing supplies from Dominion Resources Inc.'s Cove Point liquefied natural gas export project in the U.S.

Even producing state-owned companies like Saudi Aramco are starting to venture outside their borders in order to diversify their operations, attorneys say:

> *"Some are seeking out new resources, some of them are seeking markets, and some of them are seeking technology," said Baker Botts LLP partner Jason Bennett, who works on global oil and gas project development. "Aramco is constantly hunting for markets and trying to go downstream."*

The shift abroad has been accompanied by a shift in behaviour, with state-owned companies increasingly looking to operate like their investor-owned competitors rather than an arm of their backing governments, attorneys say.

"You're beginning to see a recognition in some national oil companies that in order to be competitive, they can't simply be a revenue source, they have to be able to make logical and market-driven investment decisions, and that has not only led to national oil companies making large investments outside their host countries, but also a change in philosophy," said Mayer Brown LLP partner Thomas Moore, who's represented both state-owned and investor-owned companies.

That adds up to a more heated pursuit of oil and gas assets around the globe, and more competition for oil and gas supermajors long used to being the biggest kids on the block.

"They're not the only game in town anymore, because you have a group of state-owned oil companies that are not only technologically sophisticated and have the capital to invest, they have intangibles that investor-owned companies don't," Moore said.

Those intangibles including having extremely deep pockets and no public shareholders to satisfy, as well as a different set of priorities than investor-owned companies.

> *"The state-owned companies are probably willing to take more legal and political risk, particularly in the emerging markets," Cuclis said. "They may have higher priorities on securing significant reserves of oil and gas."*

Chinese state-owned oil companies, for example, have sunk billions into securing oil and gas reserves in all corners of the world, stable and unstable. Meanwhile, many investor-owned companies, especially U.S.-based independents, have scaled back their foreign operations to focus more on domestic development that may be just as lucrative, but more stable.

But the global clout of state-owned oil companies extends beyond simply an ability to write big checks. It's the ability to leverage the power of a sovereign government, whether through the formation of export credit agencies to finance international acquisitions or projects, or inking broad trade and development deals with countries that hold significant oil and gas reserves.

Moore says that's been especially apparent in Africa, where Chinese state-owned firms have grabbed a significant piece of oil and gas interests in countries like Angola in part due to the billions the Chinese government has sunk into overall economic development.

> *"It's been able to link government-to-government support in a way that's simply impossible for a supermajor," Moore said. "Where that leaves the classic investor-owned oil company: It still has an advantage in making technology available and ... significant capital resources to make available, but it has to compete with someone on what is becoming an increasingly unlevel playing field."*

Still, investor-owned oil companies, especially the supermajors, have decades-long head starts on many state-owned firms when it comes to devising ways to effectively and profitably pull oil and gas out of the ground.

> *"The international oil companies have a long track record of developing large, complicated oil and gas projects and that is an area where many consumer national oil companies are still catching up," Davis said. "That skill set is a very valuable skill set and one the international oil companies justifiably play up."*

That's one reason why you're increasingly seeing joint venture agreements between investor-owned and nationally owned oil companies, both abroad and in their home countries, attorneys say. One example is Rosneft, which inked a deal with ExxonMobil Corp. to jointly drill for oil in the Russian Arctic, hoping to tap the offshore, deepwater expertise of the world's largest supermajor.

> *"The national oil companies now control a vast percentage of the oil and gas reserves in the world. The international oil companies are increasingly going to have to demonstrate how they give the national oil companies something they don't have," Cuclis said. "More and more, the international oil companies are going to have to find ways to distinguish themselves in areas that the national oil companies can't just go out and buy using an oilfield service company."*

But making a deal with a state-owned company, whether it's selling assets or forming a JV, carries its own set of complexities rarely seen in arm's length negotiations between private companies, attorneys say.

No matter how much a state-owned company asserts its independence in its operations, it's still part of a sovereign government, which adds potential political obstacles to getting a deal done in the form of a stricter approval process by countries affected by the deal.

> *"They're quasi-governmental entities that have to consider how this deal puts them in the jurisdiction of the country and the impact of those laws," Bennett said. "It's not just tax planning and the like."*

For example, state-owned companies eager to tap the shale-rich U.S. may have to first get through the Committee on Foreign Investment in the U.S. And if a company wants to make a deal with Rosneft and Gazprom, it has to work around increasingly restrictive sanctions imposed on the Russian energy sector in the wake of the crisis in the Ukraine — ExxonMobil has already hit the pause button on its Arctic work with Rosneft.

And there's this simple fact: Governments change, and a new government could decide to steer its oil company in a completely new direction.

State-owned companies "aren't driven by shareholders' demands and capital budgets," Bennett said. "They can be affected by changes in strategic policies of their home country."

Global Dealmaking Shows Return to Vigour

High quality global journalism requires investment. Please share this article with others using the link below, do not cut & paste the article. It was with qualified optimism that Ian Read, Pfizer's chief executive, boarded his private jet to London on the penultimate day of April, just 48 hours after launching a $102bn bid for UK rival AstraZeneca.

The deal would be the largest foreign takeover of a UK company, but the conditions were ripe: the risk aversion besetting corporate ideology since the financial crisis had started to evaporate, particularly in healthcare, and investors were seemingly welcoming any deal put before them – the bigger the better.

Political Players

Some of the second quarter's most high-profile deals saw dealmakers square off not only with each other but also with politicians and governments who found themselves intervening beyond regulatory matters. Governments, especially in Europe, showed their sensitivity to the potential impact that large cross-border deals can have by voicing their concerns where interests such as employment or scientific research were also at stake.

Arnaud Montebourg, minister of economy and industry, declared victory for France after entering the battle between General Electric and Siemens for Alstom, the French energy and rail group. GE prevailed over its rival industrial conglomerate only after revising the terms of a $17bn bid for large parts of the previously rescued French national champion.

The final deal included conditions that allow the French government to impose penalties if GE does not add 1,000 new jobs in France over the next three years. With the government also taking a 20 per cent stake in what remains of Alstom, Mr Montebourg, who has also been a central figure in consolidation discussions around the country's telecom industry, has perhaps been the most prominent politician getting involved in large transactions.

> *"The shift whereby governments have gone from indirect stakeholders to direct protagonists in deals is, in part at least, a consequence of the financial crisis," says Antonio Weiss, global head of investment banking at Lazard. "Governments became active investors in the crisis, and to an extent remain so today, and therefore have a seat at the table in more transactions."*

Mr Weiss added: "Even when they have no direct involvement, or few tools with which to intervene, governments are increasingly looking at employment as a national interest, and need to be treated as partners, not opponents, in the discussion."

Pfizer chief executive Ian Read and AstraZeneca head Pascal Soriot testified for two days in May in front of select committees of Parliament after the US pharmaceutical company's approach stirred heated debate about the future of UK scientific research if a deal were to be reached. Meanwhile, Scottish engineering group Weir dropped a €4.6bn for Finnish rival Metso after the revised offer faced continued opposition from Solidium, the country's state investment fund and a large shareholder.

Charlie Jacobs, M&A partner at Linklaters, says: "It is not uncommon in large takeovers involving certain sectors of the economy, such as previously privatised companies or strategically important businesses, for governments or politicians to express their views."

"The UK has generally been more light touch, perhaps an issue can become political, but in other countries it can show up in the form of more regulatory or direct government intervention," he says.

Yet a month later Pfizer's deal was dead; flattened by a tide of political pressure and adverse publicity about the job cuts and harm to British industry such a takeover would effect. That such a sizeable transaction could fail and global M&A still enjoy its best six months since 2007 is testament to a deal market that is recovering not in fits and bursts but with confident thrust.

The value of global M&A hit $1.75tn during the six months to July, an increase of 75 per cent over 2013 and the strongest year-on-year increase since the late 1990s, according to data from Thomson Reuters. Such has been the strength of the recovery that dealmakers, long starved of activity, have found themselves overwhelmed by the number of companies wanting to transact and are running large backlogs of prospective deals. Also, and in contrast to other recent spikes, the increase in activity levels, while not divided equally, has not been limited to a few sectors undergoing structural changes disconnected from the wider economy.

> *"People are now prepared to look at opportunities to transform their businesses through M&A," says Rick Leaman, managing partner at Moelis & Co, the investment bank. "Even as recently as last year, there was just no appetite for doing things that risked the company".*

He eschews comparisons with the last sustained period of M&A activity, however. "The big difference between now and 2007 is that there has been a lot of deleveraging in the banking system. It is a different ball game in terms of credit market regulation, so you won't see the same level of risk going into the financial system".

Piero Novelli, chairman global M&A at UBS, adds that the market is entering the last phase of an M&A cycle, "where you see several quarters of real, transformational transactions. But the deals, while large, are well thought out and have often been long in the works – waiting for the right market conditions".

One of the hallmarks of the recent run of dealmaking has been the size of transactions. While the overall value of deals has soared globally, the number of transactions is the lowest it has been for a decade. The average size of deals of more than $50m so far this year is $695m, compared with $491m last year. The swing toward scale is a function of the two busiest sectors for deals having been healthcare and telecoms, respectively.

Both industries are already highly consolidated, meaning the deals being undertaken typically involve targets – and acquirers – worth many billions of dollars. This is particularly true in healthcare, where a flurry of deals worth in excess of $10bn helped M&A in the sector hit $317.4bn year to date, nearly triple the levels seen in 2013.

Drew Burch, head of healthcare M&A at Barclays, identifies a confluence of factors driving the activity.

"We are in a period of very active portfolio repositioning, where the big healthcare companies are all trying to become more dominant in whatever areas they want to specialise. On top of that, there is the tax inversion dynamic.

> *"The ideas aren't new, but they are now being supported by a general shift in shareholder sentiment towards M&A. The combination of those factors has created a 100-year storm in healthcare M&A"*

Rakesh Patel, co-head of EMEA healthcare coverage at JPMorgan, says management and boards are feeling emboldened to pursue deals "against a backdrop of search for growth because of healthy share price gains, a more benign regulatory approval environment and a surplus of cash on balance sheets."

The trend of tax inversions – where US companies look to use acquisitions of foreign rivals as a way to re-domicile, or invert their headquarters, thus lowering their corporate tax bill – has informed many of the largest deals attempted this year. Both Medtronic's $48bn bid for Covidien and Abbvie's $47.5bn bid for Shire are underpinned by a desire on the part of the acquirers to relocate. Indeed, Pfizer's pursuit of AstraZeneca was motivated, in part at least, by the impact such a deal would have had on the US group's tax rate.

In spite of the abrupt acceleration in M&A, and the inevitable questions that provokes about bubbles, many advisers and industry experts believe the deals being done now mark the start of a long-awaited return to normal market conditions.

> *"I see no signs of collapse in M&A," says Scott Barshay, a mergers and acquisitions lawyer at Cravath. "Everything to under pin an upward cycle exists; as long as debt stays cheap and the market keeps rewarding smart deals, we will continue to see a strong activity."*

Financial sponsor dealmaking is one segment of the market dealmakers are hopeful will heat up in the next quarter after a period in which buyout groups have favoured IPOs over sales when exiting portfolio companies. Many have raised big, new funds to finance the next wave of acquisitions.

> *"The exit rate for private equity has been low over recent years," says Johannes Groeller, co-head of M&A for EMEA at Morgan Stanley. "But, with the environment for M&A transactions improving and strong valuations achievable we expect there to be a significant pick up in sponsor exit activity over the coming months."*

What is Due Diligence?

Transactional due diligence is the investigation by an investor or its advisers of the accurate and complete character of the target company's business. The target may be an acquisition candidate, a joint venture or strategic alliance partner, a prospective public offering registrant, or a company the investor is considering for minority interest private placement purposes. Due diligence must be linked to the investor's corporate strategy; in fact, the goal of much of the legal, financial, and operational due diligence is to determine whether a transaction with a given target is in the service of that strategy. Due diligence also includes investigating the target's legal status, from its proper legal authorization to do business to its actual or contingent liabilities and all points between. In addition, it includes analyzing the target's historical, current, and projected financial statements. It involves scrutinizing the target as a whole and its corporate, divisional, or subsidiary affiliates. When the investor and the target are in the same industry, transactional due diligence explores financial, operational, or managerial synergies between the investor and the target.

Transactional due diligence is not the exclusive province of the investor. Target companies should perform transactional due diligence on the investor, especially if the investor is offering consideration other than cash. Even in an all-cash transaction, a thoughtful target investigates the extent to which an alliance with the investor will assist it in growing its business, not to mention the critical question of whether, in an M&A or joint venture situation, corporate cultures can mesh. History's lesson is that transactions resulting in personality clashes or dramatically different styles of doing business (entrepreneurial versus highly structured companies, centralized versus decentralized, or the special culture wars that sometimes arise in cross-border deals) seldom produce attractive post-transaction outcomes.

No two due diligence efforts are alike, and for the practitioner each transaction presents novel issues. Due diligence may reveal that a Native American tribe claims title to the land under the target's principal facility, disclose questionable transfer payments between the target and its corporate affiliates, or unearth unfavourable information on the target's CEO. However, no solution can be provided unless the fundamental facts are discovered in due diligence.

Types of Due Diligence

Although due diligence practices are far from uniform around the world, they can be categorized roughly in two forms. What has been characterized as the "Anglo-Saxon" practice involves comprehensive legal and financial due diligence and significant disclosure before the signing of an agreement. The deal is embodied entirely in the documents, which set out in detail the rules governing the parties' rights and obligations. Contrast this with the practice in much of the rest of the world, which involves more modest preliminary legal and financial due diligence with correspondingly limited disclosure.

The goal among many non-Western transactors, for example, is to build trust between the parties, leading to provisional agreements. These provisional agreements are followed by more intensive due diligence, culminating in a final agreement embodying a business relationship in which the contractual documents form one of the constituent parts. Thus, U.S. parties involved in outbound transactions with companies in countries in which Anglo-Saxon-style due diligence is not practiced often must obtain the necessary information and assurances by means other than the highly documented, full-disclosure process to which they are accustomed in their home market. International deal makers must be flexible and sensitive to the differences between what is acceptable in a domestic deal and what is acceptable in certain cross-border deals.

Constitutes Operational Due Diligence

Operational due diligence may involve consulting environmental experts on toxic tort exposure, actuaries on pension and profit-sharing matters, or insurance experts on risk management concerns. Because operational due diligence varies dramatically from target to target, meaningful generalizations are difficult to make, but operational due diligence concerns likely to surface in most transactions include the following:

New product or new service creation. Due diligence requires understanding how the target firm creates the new products or services it sells. Is the process organised or random? Is there one "genius," the loss of whom will be materially adverse to the business, or is there a staff? Has the target skimped on R&D to inflate earnings? Is R&D responsive to customer needs? How good is the target's intellectual property: Is there real, defencible know-how? Does the target own the rights to the intellectual property it uses?

Markets. Is demand basic or created? Who buys the target's products or services (individuals, companies, governments)? Is the market growing or mature, and what is the target's market share? What factors affect demand (general business conditions, population changes, new products or services, energy availability, ecological considerations)? Is the market expandable? How is it segmented (for example, by customer type, product, geography, distribution channels, or pricing)? To what extent is the market seasonal or cyclic? One need look no further than the collapse of many dot-com companies to recognise the mistakes that even savvy financial investors can make if they skimp on market analysis.

In cross-border deals it is easy to overestimate market demand. The 90 percent market share of an Eastern European company before privatization may be sharply eroded in the post-privatization period, when it must compete against new and tough rivals, many of them from outside the country. Although hindsight is 20/20, one wonders about the assumptions the Daimler-Benz economic gurus made in 1998 about projected U.S. auto sales when they were negotiating the Chrysler deal.

Thoughtful due diligence allows companies to avoid costly mistakes in what may prove to be misguided notions of globalization. Thus, an employee benefits consulting firm catering to multinational corporations might think twice about expending time, money, and effort on a globalized acquisition, joint venture, or cross-marketing strategy if it turns out there is no consistency in the legal, tax, and accounting rules of the countries whose companies offer pension, profit sharing, or stock option plans, or if local affiliates of those multinational clients couldn't care less whether their employee benefits consulting firm was global. In such a situation it might be wisest simply to have offices of the consulting firm share leads, perhaps with a financial incentive to the referring office (and perhaps to the individual referrer) providing the lead, payable out of the fees generated by the office to whom the lead was referred.

Competition

Due diligence must ferret out the competition. Who are the competitors, and what market share do they have? On what basis is competition waged: price, service, quality, or something else? What is the market size now and prospectively? To what extent is the market subject to significant federal, state, and local regulation?

Sales. Who sells the company's products or services: Employees? Independent agents? The principals themselves? How is the sales force organised: Centrally? Regionally? How are salespeople compensated: salary, commission, or both?

People/organisational matters. How many employees are there, and what are their functions? Is there an adequate labour pool in the geo-graphic areas in which the company operates? Are these areas likely to attract a trained workforce?

Over the years, human resources professionals have developed techniques to determine what sort of workforce an investor is acquiring in a target. They ask, are there unfilled positions in key slots? What's the morale like? They check for data on Friday/Monday absences, frequency and length of sick leave, worker turnover, poor safety reports, and strikes.

Due diligence must also address the nuts and bolts of pay. What are the terms of existing collective bargaining agreements? What are the benefit programs (vacation, sick leave, insurance, stock options)?

Examine the organisation chart. Who are the senior managers, and who are the successors? Is there merit in considering the use of private investigators to uncover what may be embarrassing and costly disclosures concerning one or more of the company's senior managers? What are the career paths, and what is the retention outlook? What is the nature and size of management's compensation package, and, as in the case of the workforce, how does it compare within the region and with-in the industry?

People and organisational matters often are highly sensitive issues in cross-border deals. The cost of laying off redundant workers should be calculated as a component of the purchase price in those countries where terminated employees typically receive large settlements. When acquiring targets in former Soviet bloc countries, for example, investors have typically bid a modest purchase price to accommodate the extraordinarily high termination costs. In the final analysis, for both investors and targets, the bedeviling, sleep-depriving questions may be "Can we live with the managers on the other side of the bargaining table?" "Can we trust them?" "Is their corporate culture sufficiently similar to ours so that we can deal with the difficult issues that will necessarily attend our joining forces?" Double the importance of these issues in cross-border transactions.

Bibliography

Ackoff, R. L.: *The Democratic Corporation: A Radical Prescription for Recreating Corporate America and Rediscovering Success*, Oxford University Press, USA., 1994.

Ashkanas, R., D. Ulrich, T. Jick and S. Kerr: *The Boundaryless Organization: Breaking the Chains of Organization Structure*, Jossey-Bass, New York, 2002.

Amram, Martha; Kulatilaka, Nalin: *Real Options: Managing Strategic Investment in an Uncertain World*, Harvard Business School Press, Boston, 1999.

Baligh, H. H.: *Organization Structures: Theory and Design, Analysis and Prescription*, Springer, New York, 2011.

Binder, Kurt: *The Monte Carlo Method in Condensed Matter Physics*, Springer, New York, 1995.

Caflisch, R. E.: *Monte Carlo and quasi-Monte Carlo methods*, Cambridge University Press, London, 1998.

Close, John Weir: *A Giant Cow-tipping by Savages: The Boom, Bust, and Boom Culture of M&A*, Palgrave Macmilla, New York, 2007.

Denison, Daniel, Hooijberg, Robert, Lane, Nancy, Lief, Colleen: *Leading Culture Change in Global Organizations*, Jossey-Bass, San Francisco, 2012.

DePamphilis, Donald: *Mergers, Acquisitions, and Other Restructuring Activities*, Elsevier, Academic Press, New York, 2008.

Douma, Sytse & Hein Schreuder: *Economic Approaches to Organizations*, Pearson, London, 2013.

Fishman, G. S.: *Monte Carlo: Concepts, Algorithms, and Applications*, Springer, New York, 1995.

Fleuriet, Michel: *Investment Banking explained: An insider's guide to the industry*, McGraw Hill, New York, NY, 2008.

Galbraith, J. R.: *Designing Matrix Organizations that Actually Work: How IBM, Procter & Gamble and Others Design for Success*, Jossey Bass, New York, 2008.

Garud, R. A. Kumaraswamy and R. Langlois: *Managing in the Modular Age: Architectures, Networks, and Organizations*, Blackwell Publishing, New York, 2002.

Gilson, S. C.: *Creating Value Through Corporate Restructuring: Case Studies in Bankruptcies, Buyouts, and Breakups,* John Wiley & Sons, 2001.

Hubbard, Douglas: *How to Measure Anything: Finding the Value of Intangibles in Business,* John Wiley & Sons, New York, 2007.

Hubbard, Douglas: *The Failure of Risk Management: Why It's Broken and How to Fix It,* John Wiley & Sons, New York, 2009.

Lodge, G. C.: *Perestroika for America: Restructuring U.S. Business-Government Relations for Competitiveness in the World Economy,* Harvard Business School Press, Boston, 1991.

Miles, R. E. and C. C. Snow: *Organizational Strategy, Structure and Process,* McGraw Hill, New York, 1978.

Müller, Jürgen: *Real Option Valuation in Service Industries*, Deutscher Universitäts-Verlag, Wiesbaden, 2000.

Nohria, N. and R. Eccles: *Networks and Organizations: Structure, Form, and Action,* Harvard Business School Press, Boston, 2000.

Popp, Karl Michael: *Mergers and Acquisitions in the Software Industry - foundations of due diligence*, Books on demand, Norderstedt, 2013.

Roberts, J.: *The Modern Firm: Organizational Design for Performance and Growth,* Oxford University Press, 2004.

Rosenbaum, Joshua; Joshua Pearl: *Investment Banking: Valuation, Leveraged Buyouts, and Mergers & Acquisitions*, John Wiley & Sons, Hoboken, NJ, 2009.

Smit, T.J.; Trigeorgis, Lenos: *Strategic Investment: Real Options and Games,* Princeton University Press, Princeton, 2004.

Straub, Thomas: *Reasons for frequent failure in Mergers and Acquisitions: A comprehensive analysis*, Deutscher Universitäts-Verlag, Wiesbaden, 2007.

Trigeorgis, Lenos: *Real Options: Managerial Flexibility and Strategy in Resource Allocation*, The MIT Press, Cambridge, 1996.

William, T. Moore : *Real Options and Option-embedded Securities*, John Wiley & Sons, New York, 2001.

Index

I

J

L

M

O

P

R

S

T

U

V

W

❑❑❑